STRANGE SECTS AND CURIOUS CULTS

STRANGE SECTS
AND
CURIOUS CULTS

By Marcus Bach

BARNES
&NOBLE
B O O K S
N E W Y O R K

This edition published by Barnes & Noble, Inc.,
by arrangement with Marcus Bach.

1993 Barnes & Noble Books

ISBN 0-88029-743-3

Printed and bound in the United States of America
M 10 9 8 7 6 5 4 3 2

To Vivian

CONTENTS

viii § CONTENTS

INTRODUCTION

THE

LURE

OF THE

QUEST

§ *THE LURE OF THE QUEST*

Religion is my beat. For twenty years I have been reporting on the things men live by, the faiths they follow, and the creeds they hold as truth; not reporting only, but sharing with others the experiences inherent in their worship.

In the intensive rounds of my research, I have been continually impressed with the fact that there are surprisingly few heretics among those we call heretical. In fact, *our* beliefs may seem heretical to them. Heterodoxy, as has been said, is the other fellow's orthodoxy, and heresy may simply be the other person's living faith.

This was impressed upon me in one of my earliest ventures, an "investigation" of a group known as The Brothers Penitent in the American southwest. All I had ever heard about these religious enthusiasts was that they whipped themselves during certain days in Lent and that on Good Friday they crucified one of their young devotees on some shadowy *Calvario*. Condemned even by the church whose austerities had brought them into being, labeled as extremely strange and curious, they were driven into the darkness of the New Mexico hills where only the night wind and the stars could share their ecstatic liturgies.

Only after three attempts during three successive Easter seasons was I finally permitted to attend their services, not as a reporter, but as one who wished sincerely and sympathetically to enter into the spirit of their quest. For I was becoming more and more persuaded that the quest for meaning in religion was the very heart and soul of not only the Penitentes, but of every group which we had thoughtlessly lumped into the ominous category of "strange sects and curious cults."

What were these groups really like, I wondered, if looked at from the inside? If a person could, in spirit at least, project himself into these "off-beat" religions, what would he find? What truth would be revealed if we could identify ourselves with certain religions of the past—religions commonly despised and rejected, like Baalism and Osirism—the so-called "sex sects" which, it was claimed, still persisted in such contemporary expressions as Shivism in India and Voodoo in Africa and Haiti?

Fate was cooperative. A Rockefeller fellowship made additional research among little-known American groups possible, after which, on my own, I extended the field to Mexico and Central America. Later, a Department of State assignment provided me with an opportunity to exchange religious ideas with worshipers in India and Pakistan. Encouraged by the phenomenal interest in this experiment, I traveled at my own expense to Baalbek in Lebanon and then on to Syria and Palestine, following the thinly camouflaged route of the "Great God Baal." From there I went to Egypt to discover what footprints of Osiris might remain among the sand-swept dunes or in the fertile valleys of the Nile.

Then, lured by the call of Voodoo, I visited Haiti where the haunting rhythm of the drums got into my blood, along with malaria. Haitian physicians were skilled in controlling the latter, but not even a witch doctor has a cure for the fever induced by the tantalizing spell of the native's magical faith. I went back three times. Always there was the unanswered question, "Just how strange and curious is this impassioned ritual of the enchanted *loa*?"

That was the magnet: "Just how strange and curious—?" I was also beginning to wonder by what standard the bizarrerie of any group is to be measured? By what instrumentality of a man's mind are the depths of another man's conviction to be appraised?

The field of faith, so vast, so subtle, so sacred to so many, was always near at hand, and the harvest was always ripe. There was, for example, the sensationalized work of the Negro leader, Father Divine, and there was the phenomenal commonwealth of religions forged by the intrepid Frank N. Buchman into the auspiciously titled Oxford Group. There were the rapidly expanding ranks of Jehovah's Witnesses, which the churches had relegated to the lunatic fringe, but whose apocalyptic viewpoint had mesmerized its followers into becoming tireless servants for Jehovah God.

There was Psychiana, a mail-order religion whose founder, Frank B. Robinson, had been condemned by institutionalized religion as a heretic *sui generis,* a modern Montanus or a Simon Magus in a category all his own. I visited this man of Moscow (Idaho) several times, hoping to be able to brush aside the web of preconceptions that religious gossip had spun into my mind. When I met him and came to know him, I caught the inner moving of his faith. Then, as I spoke with many of his students throughout the country, men and women whose lives he had changed, I determined that someday I would tell his story as I saw it—come what might.

There were other stories which my collaborator, Destiny, shoved into my hands. Interviewing conscientious objectors during World War II started my many trips into Doukhobor country in British Columbia. These stubborn Russian Tolstoyans had the "incredible" belief that man is a God in ruins, but that he can find his true identity if given half a chance. Organized religion did not know this. All it knew about the Doukhoborski was that its members staged nude parades. How was I to find out anything more? In searching for a way, I told myself, "Imagine for a little while that you are a Doukhobor! And if his life still seems strange and curious to you, then it is strange indeed!"

My work was no longer mere reporting. It had become an adventure in understanding. It led me not only among the "mad Douks" but into the company of the "good Douks" as well; it also guided me to other communal attempts, to what is left of the Shakers and what is still to be found in the rapidly dissolving Amana Colonies. It took me time and time again into the colonies of the bearded Hutterites whose way of life I was permitted to share, whose songs I sang, and whose prayers I prayed even when church and state in South Dakota and in Manitoba, declared that it was time these "clannish pseudo-spiritual cooperatives" were broken up.

And there was Mormonism. Accepted and rejected, acclaimed and condemned, blessed and cursed depending upon what its critics had seen or imagined they had seen, or on what they had heard or thought they had heard, Mormonism was no stranger to ridicule or cries of heresy.

The Mormons permitted me, as the only non-Mormon, to accompany them when their seventy-two car caravan set out from Nauvoo, Illinois, to re-enact the historic trek across the plains and mountains into Salt Lake City. For seven days our simulated Conestoga wagons retraced the route of the pioneers of a hundred years ago. For seven days I lived with these Latter-day Saints and learned more about them than I ever had in my earlier research among the farms and hillsides in upstate New York where their church had been born.

They belonged in my anthology, I was sure, when the time came for such a book to be written. In fact, that is the way I felt about all the groups I have mentioned. And as they fell into a pattern which I came to classify as *The Sex Sects, The Conscience Cults,* and *The Search For Utopia,* the book took form.

How strange and curious are these groups really? There is but one way to answer that. Let us go and see.

PART

ONE

 ——————————————————————

THE

SEX

SECTS

1 § THE SEX SECTS

WHEREVER MAN LIVES man worships. The search for a satisfying religion has ever been his greatest adventure and his boldest quest. As far back as we can go in history, even before there were altars or churches or prophets or priests, man was trying to come to terms with the mystery and magic of the universe.

Primitive man asked himself the same questions that modern man asks himself today. "How can I understand the hidden forces that play upon my life? How can I deal with the mysterious power which is sometimes so near I can control it with a prayer, and at other times, so far away it defies my prayers and my faith?"

As early man set about to solve the enigma of his personal relationship with the Unseen, he often used methods that seem curious and strange to us. But he was beginning his quest for truth, and seeking as best he could to unravel the mysteries of existence.

It was only logical that every stick and stone and plant and tree appeared to be impregnated with life. Sticks were the

7

source of both fire and fuel; stones provided both weapons and places of protection. Certain branches when stuck into the earth began to grow; certain plants contained magical powers to heal. Certain trees seemed never to die; certain herbs when eaten gave exotic visions of a life to come. Man learned all this as he moved upon the bosom of the earth, having been placed here by whom or what, he did not know; he only knew that he must make his peace with a strange, unmeasured, and, at times, a lonely and a frightening land.

The animals around him gave him his first clue to his own inherited instincts. In beasts and reptiles he dimly discerned what he believed were his own progenitors and, in interpreting them, he arrived at a better knowledge of himself. Each creature had the ability to reproduce its kind and, through its sexual functions, overcame the awesome power of death, gaining, it seemed, a small, sure step toward some sort of immortality.

Man's first religious symbol was a totem, a pole in the shape of a phallus on which he crudely carved an image of his ancestral animal god. His first ceremonies were mimetic, in which he imitated the animal which his clan or tribe had chosen. His dances, chants, and earliest prayers mimicked the movements, utterances, and habits of this deity. His most intimate ritual was patterned after the copulative act as he observed it in the brute creation which was his totem guardian and his god.

As man began to recognize the reproductive urge, not only in animals but in all growing things, his relationship with his world deepened and enlarged. Birds were reverenced because they flew upward toward the source of light. Fish became symbols of life, because ancient man somehow knew the modern truth that they resembled spermatozoon. The virile animals, particularly the bull, the ram, the lion, were honored for their creative power and the hint of conquest over fear. These were the gods and demigods etched upon the totem and reverenced in ritual and song, unfolding the qualities man hoped to find within himself.

From the worship of the totem, man turned to the adoration

of nature itself; nature in whose arms he was cradled and by whose mercy he was sustained. Nature, the creator, was, of course, more powerful than its creatures. At times it was cruel and formidable, but it was also loving and kind. Always it was an unpredictable force with which man had to reckon. The wind was a spirit, the rain a messenger, the night a spectre, the moon an eye, and the sun, a god.

There was no god greater than the sun. It blessed and cursed, brought joy and grief, filled man with fear when it dropped from sight and aroused in him a hymn of praise at its reappearing. Most of all, the sun stimulated and energized man's creative powers. Light and life were its attributes and there was nothing in man's vast world more worthy of worship and awe. Surely the sun was a king and the earth a queen; a queen endowed with never-ending life by her royal consort. Man reasoned that the rising and setting of the sun was a sexual act which fertilized the earth. As a mother begets her children, so mother earth begot her fruit. Out of this thought came the first hint of the cosmic father-mother relationship—the uroboros or sexual union of the universe—of which man and woman were themselves a part. Here was an answer to the mystery of creation; here was light upon the puzzle of birth and death.

For man reasoned that the earth had its springtime of impregnation, its summer of fruitful productivity, its autumn waning and its wintery death, and he saw himself as a part of this cosmic drama. He, too, was born, grew fruitful and productive; he, too, aged and died. As the earth received from the sun the impulse to create and bear fruit, so man reasoned, he, too, was dependent upon the sun god for his creative powers. From such early deduction man related the magic of procreation to the creative function of the universe. In a very real sense he considered himself a solar being, an offspring of the solar deity, the sun.

From this attempt to understand his relationship with the universe, pre-historic man developed the rudimentary concepts of religion. In our modern time many will find it unreasonable to believe that worship, as we know it, evolved from such naive beginnings. On the contrary, the origins were quite profound. They have, in fact, left their influence upon worship all through the ages. The meaning behind the sacrifices, the chants and litanies, the rituals and rites, the ceremonies and ceremonials, together with the sexual symbolism, have persisted until our present day even though, with malice of forethought, we have sought to destroy their ancient meaning.

The earliest elements of divine services had to do with the sun and sex and these have persisted all the way from the lingam and yoni in the temples of Hinduism to the towering minarets of Islam; from the star of David in Judaism to the phallic *crux ansata* in the Christian faith.

If we reject the evidence pointing to some form of uroboric union and the evolution of thought it inspired, the entire history of world religions becomes unintelligible and grotesque. If, however, this key to religion is grasped, it will unlock the past and show us that all that has happened is meaningful and profound. We may even find a link between faiths no longer existent and that living faith which bases much of its hope upon Christ's miraculous conception and mysterious birth.

So let us now turn the key and open the first strange and curious door. Let us venture into one of the earliest sects of recorded time, whose sorcery was spun around man's most primitive passion and beliefs.

2 § BAALISM

In the spring of 1928 an Arab peasant working in his field on the Syrian coast of the Mediterranean struck his plow against a slab of solid rock. After he had loosened the ground from around it and lifted it out, he discovered that the rock concealed a partially-broken stairway leading deep into the earth. He dug away the molded dirt, took a lantern and followed the stairs some fifty feet into a vaulted tomb. Here, hidden in the dust of time but miraculously preserved, were a number of artifacts, metal vessels, and potsherds, and beyond, in the wavering shadows of his light, lay a veritable city of the ancient dead.

Within a few months after a report of this discovery had reached the Director of Antiquities of the French Mandatory Government over Syria, a team of French archeologists started excavations nine miles north of Ladhiqiyah at a spot now known as Ras-ash Shamrah. Here they unearthed many cuneiform tablets which they restored and deciphered. The peasant's plow had cut a furrow so deep into time it took men back nearly 4000 years. It did something more. It resurrected for a brief and thought-provoking moment an ancient deity, the great god

Baal who, some thirty centuries before the time of Christ, was worshiped throughout the entire Middle Eastern world.

The excavation became a kind of requiem. The clank of shovels, the careful sifting of the earth, the silent, patient brushing of the artifacts was like a litany dedicated to the memory of this half-forgotten god who was Baal to the Babylonians, Mercury or Hermes to the Greeks, Jupiter to the Romans, and Adonis to the Phoenicians. But to the Canaanites, he was Baal, god of the sun and sex.

His influence was so great in Canaan that many minor deities were known as Baalim as if to prove that the god was everywhere at once. Even the places of worship, where his symbol of the phallus stood, were spoken of as "Baal" as though the god himself were there. The Semitic word, *baal*, meant husband, possessor, or lord and prince, so that everywhere in Canaanitic life, from home to temple, Baal was a living word. Mothers named their children after him; names like Hannibal (the grace of Baal), Baal-Sham (the power of Baal), and Asdrubal (Baal is my helper.) Cities, dedicated in his honor, were given the names of Baal-Gad, Baal-Parazin, and Baal-Hana.

The priests of Baal declared that the great god first appeared when a primal universal force called El, the elemental god, and Athirate, the goddess of the earth, who holds the ocean in her womb, became the parents of the gods. Baal was their firstborn and was given the sun for his throne. Soon the priests decreed that Baal and El were one and the same, and that Baal's consort was Astarte or Ashtoreth. She was known as Aphrodite to the Greeks, Ishtar to the Babylonians, Nana to the Sumerians, and Venus to her devotees in Rome, but regardless of her name or place, she was the wife of Baal, the virgin queen of heaven who bore fruit although she never conceived.

Marble temples and altars honoring Baal and Astarte glistened on sacred hills throughout the land of Canaan, magnificent structures with towering colonnades, intricate bas-reliefs of nature symbols, and spacious outer courts. Occasionally a moat surrounded the temple and its grounds, and there was beauty everywhere. Here, when the evening fires burned on Canaan's hills, when the wind was still and the ground was breaking with spring, the worshipers of Baal wended their way.

Responding to the stimulant of impassioned ceremonies, they came to involve their lives intimately with the life of the god. To the Canaanite, the reproductive force was the most powerful and mysterious of all manifestations. It was the cause of all life. By it, all things came into existence; his flocks, his harvest, his children. Beyond his comprehension but intimately associated with his own reproductive urge, the power of generation was the object of his devotion. Baal was its personification.

All the land was Baal's, and the location of smaller temples and shrines was determined by the phallic character or proved fertility of some natural object; a tree, an obelisk, a stone, a stream which suggested it was here that Baal particularly dwelled. Here the god's shrines were built and fruit trees were planted. Here walls were constructed to sanctify them and to keep out the beggars and the lepers and the itinerant vendors who loved money even more than sex. The worshipers, too, were restricted in how far they might intrude, and only the priests advanced into the inner sanctum where the young and muscular figure of Baal, hewn out of granite, sat upon a throne bathed in the light that filtered through a lattice open to the sky. Adjoining the temple were courts and chambers for the temple prostitutes, women chosen for special duties to gain the favor of a god who was best worshiped in the union of the sexes.

When a man approached a woman in the court, he tossed a coin to her and said, "I beseech the goddess Astarte to favor thee, and Baal to favor me." The money became a part of the temple treasury, and the art of prostitution a sacred obligation to be fulfilled.

In groves and fields throughout the land, the presence of Baal was marked by naked pillars or tree stems stuck upright into the ground. Because Baal impregnated the land by copulation, the ceremonies in his honor were often imitative sexual acts, the people devoutly believing that there was secret power waiting to be unleashed through the mimetic rite. Worship to the Canaanites was sympathetic magic, which meant that there was a special virtue in mimicking the god, and, through endless years, this sorcery had been proved effective and fixed into ceremonial forms. As there were periods when Baal demanded sexual union, there were also times when he demanded chastity. The priests dictated the acts. How did they know what the acts should be? They observed nature and the seasons. Nature reflected the moods of Baal, and the priests reflected nature. During certain winter periods when Baal lost his generative power, the people were instructed to practice continence, and in the spring, when Baal freely fertilized the earth, the worshipers responded to his will.

The influence of the great god Baal was slowly reconstructed in our time as the archeological requiem at Ras-ash Shamrah revived the histories of ancient lands: Ugarit, Mesopotamia, Mycenae, Persia, Laodicea, and Canaan.

Were they a sex-infested, barbaric people? On the contrary, the records showed that the semitic Canaanites were an industrious, freedom-loving people. Their houses were large with spacious open yards between. They were great admirers of horses and loved games in which horses played a major part. They were thorough agriculturalists and expert artisans who worked with clay and metal, creating impressive sculptured pieces in bronze, copper, gold, and silver, always reserving their ablest talent for creating statues of Baal. Sometimes the god was shown astride a bull, an animal symbolic of procreative power. Sometimes the sun was a nimbus which enclosed him; at other times he was a phallus with the head of a god. Images of Astarte depicted her in the nude with her legs apart, holding two white doves in her hands, while at her feet a lion and a coiled serpent lay stretched out submissively.

Baal's earthly home, where he lived with Astarte, was on Mount Casius, north of Ras-ash Shamrah. From here the god could observe his people as they made their way to his altars, carrying banners by day and torches by night. Days sacred to Baal, days when the earth sprang to life, the spring equinox, the time of planting, found the populace going to the temples and the groves en masse. As far as eye could see, the faithful dotted the land. Above the sound of laughter and song, the clangor of gongs could be heard calling the populace, summoning rich and poor to share in a common dependence upon the only god they knew.

The fields were being prepared for planting, the intoxicating incense of burning grass hung over the land; fires lighted the nights and hallowed the warming days. The witchcraft of nature spun a web of passion into which the worshipers were lured by chanting priests, while the vendors vied with one another in selling effigies of the god and phallic charms. At the head of the processions an image of Baal seated in an alabaster chair was borne on the shoulders of his devotees. Priests in white robes and wearing golden mitres preceded these acolytes carrying wands with which they blessed the land and the people. Lesser clerics who flanked the marchers were dressed in women's garments, their faces painted red. As they walked, they chanted the great god's name and swung urns of smoking incense, pausing to drink love philtres from their silver chalices.

The spring festivals reached their climaxes in sexual acts performed on housetops, where the participants felt they were nearer the sun god's power, and in groves where, it was believed, Baal himself would join them in their worship. There were those who spawned their human seed upon the ground sincerely trusting that this invoked a special heavenly blessing. At the temple feasts, proxies for the invisible god and goddess gorged themselves and, in wanton dances, called upon the "bull god" to appear. Women, intoxicated by concoctions of herbs and wine, lay naked upon the newly-planted fields in adulation of Astarte. These were the occasions when fathers gave their daughters to their own sons for harlotry or took their own daughters to play the role of wife.

For seven days and nights, the demonstrations continued

while chanting worshipers ceaselessly wound their way across the land, pausing to kiss the phallic symbols in the fields. Priests, impersonating pregnant women, walked among the people, but in the fields the serious business of the planting of the grain by the Canaanitic farmer was begun. It was a ritual, solemnly enacted within the sound of the festivities and within sight of the fertility rites. And, to the planter in the field, there was nothing strange or curious in the acts. He knew that the god was pleased. He believed that the seed, through some mysterious alchemy, was able to respond. He was confident that Baal would lend his magic assistance and make this a fruitful year.

At the edges of the field, dancers punctuated their rhythmic choreography by rolling on the ground to imitate the mothering of seeds and by leaping in the air in the belief that the higher they leapt, the taller the grain would grow. If the land was dry or if a drought ensued, the priests enacted other mimetic rites, simulating rain by slashing their bodies with knives until the blood gushed out. This was to show Baal how he should pour rain upon the fields. Meanwhile, they chanted,

> Where is the victor Baal,
> Where is the prince lord of the earth?
> The virgin earth is awaiting him!

If a drought persisted, the priests mourned as though the god had died. In whirling, frenzied dances, holding aloft a first-born lamb impaled on the point of a spear, they offered this sacrifice to Mot, the god of death, confident that Mot would resurrect and free the imprisoned Baal and let him send rain upon the parched earth once more.

How these performances were enacted and how the spectators vicariously shared Baal's experiences were secrets that the excavations at Ras-ash Shamrah dramatically revealed. As the tablets were deciphered, it was seen that Baalism was by no means all sexual ritual and orgies in a modern sense. The Canaanite loved beauty and truth and sought as best he could to come to terms with them. Perhaps he never saw the indecent meaning behind the symbols which we have come to see, nor did he have the moral sense of right or wrong which we profess; nature was his god, and his god was Baal.

In the temple dramas, couched in many metaphoric truths, he was shown the struggles of his god. One such spectacle told of a contest between Baal, depicted as the controller of rain; Athter, god of springs; and Yam-Nahar, god of the seas and rivers. This trio, symbolic of the three types of irrigation, vied for the favor of El, who was characterized as a white-haired, long-bearded super-god of the heavens. Yam-Nahar built a palace from which he could direct the watering of the earth by controlling the rivers and lakes. Ashter, confident that only springs could ever properly supply the earth's needs, challenged him. Baal, enraged over their presumptions that artificial irrigation of any kind could be the answer, enfolded himself in a storm cloud and, with thunder and lightning as his weapons, destroyed both Athter and Yam-Nahar. He then built his own mansion in the sky, a mansion with windows to let down the rain, thereby proving to the people their inevitable dependence upon him as well as his love for them.

As ritual dramas of this kind were enacted 4000 years ago and as mimetic magic worked its miracles to produce a prosperous nation, the popularity of the god of sun and sex attracted other Semitic tribes from far beyond its borders. The lush fields and the abundant earth of Canaanland were continually enticing people to "bend the knee" to Baal. Among these worshipers were the Israelites, who had long been aware of the great white temples, the symbolic worship, and the impressive teraphim of Baal. Abraham had sojourned here and for many centuries the tribes of the Israelites had continued to seek the land. There were elements in some of the poetic Canaanitic dramas which reminded the Biblical Hebrews of their own traditions, like the story of the man sorely tempted of God who, upon the death of his wife and children, pondered, as did Job, the riddle of suffering. Baal's holy mountain, Mount Casius, was reminiscent of Mount Zion, and the Josephites brought their God Jehovah with them when they came.

But the Semitic monarch of Samaria, King Omri, built a temple for Baal and ordered his people to worship the sun god and his bull. Jezebel, wife of King Ahab, built an even greater temple and placed in it three altars; one for Baal, one for Astarte, and one for Molock, the god of fire. Around these three altars, five hundred priests, conducted the worship to Baal, and carried his gospel to Jerusalem where Jezebel's daughter, Athaliah, also erected a temple in his name.

A thousand years of struggle were to take place between Baal, god of the sun, and Jehovah, God of destiny; between a god of the flesh and a God of the spirit. During these years, the Canaanites and the Israelites intermingled, each often worshiping the other's god. For a thousand years, the god of sex consistently triumphed and his followers increased. For a thousand years the cult of Baal worked its magic, rewarding its followers with the joy of life in a productive land. The temples of Omri, Jezebel, and Athaliah flourished. It was as though the god of fertility lavished his abundant harvests upon the people to convince them that he was mightier than Jehovah, that worship to him was honorable, and that a spiritual power was inherent in the orgiastic rites. So successful was he that there were Israelites who said, "If the worship of the sun god is an offense to Jehovah, why does not Jehovah rise up and defeat the great god Baal?" But there were also those who, condemning the idolatry and turning from the immoral spectacles to the rituals of their holy faith watched and waited to see what the God of Israel would do.

So, throughout the years, while hymns were sung to Baal, the psalms of the Israelites were chanted to Jehovah; and even while the history of Canaan's god was being dramatized, the history of the God of Israel was taking form. Many times the services of Baal, like the services of Jehovah, were rites of purification and rituals involving burnt offerings, for rooted deeply in both religions was the need for ceremonials which would assure good fortune, good crops, good health, and the favor of the gods.

These things, too, the requiem portrayed as the cuneiform tablets yielded their long-kept secret strophes. More than 200 references of similarity between the Christian Bible and the records of Baal were discovered. There was a Canaanitic legend about a certain Daniel and a reference to Leviathan, and texts of love which sounded like Solomon's *Song of Songs*. The hymns and rituals of the land of Canaan were to leave their imprint upon the worship of Jew and Gentile alike. From the records it could now be seen that Baalism's festival of the first fruits had been perpetuated in Judaism as well as in Christianity; that Baal as the god of the harvest prepared the way for Jehovah; that the first sheaves which were placed upon Baal's altars and burned as holy incense, that the juice of grapes, which was once consumed by the sun god's priests, were to be sanctified in a new God's name and transposed into His communion; and that the oil of olives, which had been used for the Canaanitic ceremonials, was to become a part of the worship among the Israelites.

But though these and other rites and rituals found their way into the Judeao-Christian faith, the worship of the phallic-symboled, sex-infested god was doomed. Jehovah would have none of it. In a series of Biblically-recorded events, filled with sexual metaphors, the story of Baal's defeat is chronicled. It describes how the prophets of Israel, aroused by the abominations of worship, led the attack among their own people, warning them to "come out from the worshipers of Baal," lest they be destroyed. It tells of Jeremiah who accusingly cried, "How can you say, 'I am not polluted, I have not gone after Baalim?' Thou art a wild ass used to the wilderness, that snuffeth up the wind at her pleasure and in her occasion who can turn her away?"

The story captures the wrath of Ezekiel, who flayed his people with an anguished plea, "Thou hast multiplied thy fornication in the land of Canaan . . . How weak is thine heart, saith the Lord God, seeing thou doest all these things, the work of an imperious whorish woman!" It records the words of the prophets who said, "As the thief is ashamed when he is found, so is the house of Israel ashamed; they, their kings, their princes, and their priests. For they said to a stick, (phallus), 'Thou art my father!' and to a stone, 'Thou hast brought me forth!' "

Then on Mount Carmel, on the holy hill of Jehovah, the prophet Elijah confronted the priests of Baal, four hundred and fifty of them, to determine which God was the greater, and whose would first send down fire from the skies. Baal's priests shouted aloud to the god of the sun and sex who had never failed them, while Elijah taunted, "Your god is sleeping and must be awakened!" The cries of the pagan priests increased. They lashed themselves with knives until the blood gushed out upon the ground, but Baal was silent. Then Elijah built an altar with twelve stones. He put the wood in order, dug a trench, filled it three times with water, and called upon the Lord of Abraham, Isaac, and Jacob. Within a moment the lightning flashed, the altar burst into flames, the sacrifice was consumed and so were the stones and the water and the dust as well. (I Kings 18.)

Now that the lustful appeal to the senses had been put to shame in this Olympian struggle; now that the forces of evil had been destroyed on Mount Carmel, Canaan became the battlefield. Jehoiada, a mighty man of the God Jehovah, entered the temples of Baal and slew the priests. In Jerusalem, King Josiah seized the vessels and statues on Baal's elaborate altars and burned them on Kidron's banks. As for Jezebel, when she heard that the destroyers of Baal had come for her, she appeared at her palace window, high above the street, adorned with precious jewels, holding a sceptre in her hand. She looked down and, catching sight of King Jehu advancing with his men, called out, "What will you have, you regicide?" Jehu answered by ordering the eunuchs of the palace to throw her into the street, and they obeyed by casting their once-honored queen over the palace walls. The horsemen of Jehovah, followed by packs of yelping dogs, trampled her body so fiercely that when men came to bury her they found only her skull, her feet, and the palms of her hands. The three altars she had built were desecrated, stone by stone. Her priests were slain. Her mighty pagan deity was dead; and the Israelites re-named him Baalzebub, the prince of devils.

The requiem has ended. Yet ever and again, as at Ras-ash Shamrah, the altars of the sun god are unearthed among their ruins; and, as at Baalbek in Lebanon, men still walk in awe beneath the overpowering pillars where once Baal's temples stood. Throughout the years there are always those who catch a fleeting glimpse of Baal's shadow. Sometimes they cry out to the people as did Jeremiah of old, "Will ye burn incense unto Baal . . . and then come and stand before me in my house and say, 'We cannot help all these abominations?'"

Penitent beneath such words, the faithful build new altars to honor the God Jehovah, but in a little while a hymn to Baal echoes again from somewhere deep within the throbbing earth and steals once more into the minds and acts of men.

The great god Baal is dead.

Or did he ever die?

3 § OSIRISM

Osiris was a god of many names and many faces. Worshiped first in Egypt, he was destined to be idolized by the Greeks and, later, by the Romans.

When the Egyptian farmer planted his corn, the grain upon which his life depended, he gathered his family around him in the center of the field. Out of the moist earth he made a fetish, an image of the corn god Osiris, modeling it as artistically as he could and studding the figure with seeds. When he had fashioned this to the delight and admiration of his wife and children, he reverently dug a hole and inserted the effigy into the earth. It was a holy act. He was committing the seed of the god into the womb of the goddess Isis, impregnating her with life.

Assured by this act that the earth would yield its fruit, the family began the planting. Often they feigned a few tears over the seed, mourning because the good god Osiris would have to die before he could rise again. Little, if anything, did they know of the orgies connected with fertility rites in other lands. Nor would they have been interested had they known. Here in Egypt where, it was believed, human life began, here along the fertile deltas of the sacred Nile, the farmer was confident that this ritual, tried and tested since the beginning of time, was one which would always produce a bountiful harvest.

If Osiris was worshiped as the lord of the living by the people, to the priests he was the judge of the dead. In the elaborately lamp-lighted rooms of the temples, the religious leaders of Egypt conducted their secret rituals in which the cosmic symbolism of Osiris was enacted. The temples were the castles of the gods, marble shrines of exquisite beauty along the walled-in banks of the holy stream. Here, within the sacerdotal walls, unheard by any save the members of the sacred sect, unseen by anyone excepting the priests and, occasionally by the Pharaoh himself, was dramatized the death and the resurrection, not of the corn, but of the soul of man which was, to them, the soul of god. For it was believed that Osiris ruled over Amenti, the cavernous realm of infinite blackness where the soul of the departed had to make its way by whatever light it had within itself. Here Osiris, seated on a lotus blossom, waited with the jackel-headed god Anubis, ready to weigh the wayfarer's deeds on his delicate horizontal scale.

Judge of the dead, lord of the living, god of the corn, Osiris was also king of the immortal Nile. Several times in the course of a year, worshipers formed a huge procession and carried his statue from the temple to the banks of the river. Here they ceremoniously placed the image in a ship so that Osiris might inspect this longest river of the world, a river that rose, so it was said, from the fertile heart of the god himself and flowed four thousand miles to the sea. A flotilla of worshipers rattling castanets, piping on flutes, and chanting hymns, accompanied the floating temple on its journey. All along the shore great throngs waited to pay homage to the mighty river deity. Whenever a temple site was approached, the god-ship was steered close to the shore so that all who had patiently awaited its arrival could crowd about the god they loved.

Because Osiris was also the sun god, the men and women on the boats were permitted to disrobe, if they wished, and fling their arms upward to the sun so that it could bathe their naked bodies with life-giving rays. Often the devotees gave vent to their wickedness by shouting words of abuse and making suggestive remarks to one another. All the pent-up frustrations and suppressed desires which had been stored up against this day were now released, washed clean, for Osiris was also a god who purged men's souls in strange and wondrous ways.

When the worshipers arrived at cities sacred to the god who ruled the Nile, such places as Memphis, Busiris, and Abydus, they honored Osiris by partaking of much wine, for was he not also god of the vineyard? He was a god of many names and many faces, and in these days of the early dynasties, more than 3400 years before the Christian Era, there were few indications that sexual orgies of any kind accompanied the rituals or holy rites conducted in his name.

There was a legend, however, built upon a sexual symbol. Where and how it began no one knew. Like the great pyramids which stood on the Gizeh sands, it seemed always to have been a part of Egyptian life. Like the Sphinx, the legend was an enigma, permitting everyone to read into it his own interpretation, finding guidance for a new life or justification for an old, whatever he might wish.

It was the legend of Osiris-Isis, and it told the story of the great god's immaculate birth, how he was conceived by ancient Mother Earth, whose name was Geb, and by the still older Father of Heaven, whose proper name was Nut. It explained how the child Osiris found himself entwined in the cosmic womb with his female counterpart, Isis. This holy virgin was divinely destined to be both sister and wife to him, and after their birth, they journeyed as husband and wife to Egypt where the people were eagerly waiting to receive them. Here Osiris was anointed king and by this act all future Pharaohs became his successors. According to the priestcraft which grew up around him, he was the Lord of Lords and Lovely Isis was the Queen of Heaven.

Osiris taught the people agriculture, familiarized them with the arts and language, and gave them a code of civil laws. Then he traveled for a time over the world, civilizing people everywhere, becoming many gods in many lands, known by many names and having many faces. His only force was reason; his only weapon love; his greatest power was germination of the spiritual body in order to prove that men are indeed immortal. He had only one unconquerable enemy, so the legend said, his brother Set who, during the god-king's absence from Egypt, would have usurped the throne had not the ever-faithful Isis kept close watch.

Set, however, hatched a plot, aided, the legend continued, by the Queen of Ethiopia. Secretly they measured the body of Osiris, constructed a priceless, gold-covered ark, a kind of casket, made to fit the young god in every detail. When the Lord of Lords returned from his travels—his age now being twenty-eight —Set honored him with a festival and announced that whoever among his guests would fit the ark would become its owner. Everyone failing, Osiris was persuaded to get in. As he settled himself inside, Set's henchmen clamped down the lid, spiked it fast, sealed it with molten metal, and cast it into the Nile.

Desperate and in mourning, the beloved Isis, after many days of searching and many adventures, located the ark. It had floated to the coast of Byblos where it had lodged in a tree whose branches affectionately enfolded it in their embrace. Gratefully the sister-wife Isis prepared to bury the body, but was accosted by Set who, fearing that the people would make the grave a shrine, dismembered the corpse of Osiris into fourteen pieces and scattered them over the land. Undeterred, the indomitable Isis began to reassemble the dismembered parts. Wherever she found one, she built a shrine.

In time she recovered thirteen portions of the body and enshrined them in thirteen temples, the greatest being at Abydos where, it was said, the head of Osiris was reclaimed. However, the fourteenth part of the body of the god was never found. This was the genital organ. According to the legend, it had been thrown into the Nile and swallowed by a fish. In its stead, Isis made a golden phallus and consecrated it with great festivals in temples throughout the kingdom.

The legend ended with an account of the battle between Horus, the son of Isis and Osiris, and Set. Having vowed to avenge his father's death, Horus overpowered the bestial murderer and brought him captive to his mother. "But," concluded the story, "when the gentle Isis saw Set in chains, she compassionately set him free out of mercy for his soul. After which Set was subdued, and Isis, copulating with Osiris after his resurrection, conceived and brought forth the prematurely-born and weak in his lower limbs, Harpocrates."

Such was the myth, passed on from generation to generation, and finally finding its way into the recorded narratives of the Egyptian gods. Like the names and faces of Osiris, it had many meanings. One that persisted was based upon the analogy that the Nile was actually the god Osiris himself and the earth it irrigated was the goddess Isis. Horus, their first-born, was the new-born day. Set personified the sea which, as everyone knew, continually warred against Osiris, the Nile. The treasured ark or casket made to fit the good god's measurements was in reality the river bed. The twenty-eight years of Osiris represented the twenty-eight cubits to which the river rose at its greatest height. The Queen of Ethiopia was the south wind.

The fourteen dismembered parts of the great god's body symbolized the fourteen channels of the river which, at flood stage, became the tombs or shrines for portions of the overflowing Nile. The genital organ which could not be recovered was a symbol of the hidden current of the stream, the life-giving, procreative principle by which it lived. Harpocrates, born of Isis after Osiris' death, was the personification of the prematurely-born corn, a weak and scrawny after-growth which appeared when the flooding of the river had subsided.

The people had other interpretations. To some the legend was more than a mere nature myth; it was an insight into the everlastingness of life as embodied in the sexual principle. Just as the impulse of sex remains in the mind of man even after he is no longer biologically able to procreate, so the impulse of life persists after death. They believed that not only the impulse, but the life-giving act itself was sustained when one learned the secret hidden in the legend. That secret, evidently, was never easy or clear, but it was rumored that in the sombre chambers of the great pyramid and in the funerary temple rites, the death and resurrection of the Osiris phallus were enacted. In the ceremonies a make-believe phallus died, was mummified, and interred as though it were a human being, and in its tomb it not only retained the power of life, but had the mysterious power of reassembling the dismembered parts of the mind and body of man.

The conquest of death through the everlastingness of the "sexual spirit" assumed an increasingly dominant role in the symbolic rituals of Osirism, but it meant different things to different people. The peasants who worked the land clung to Osiris as the god of corn; to the river people and the townsmen, he remained the god of the Nile; to others, he was a vague deity to be enjoyed on his holy days in whatever way best fit their needs, and to the priests he continued to be the god of hidden truths.

The priests had their occult interpretation of many rites. For example, circumcision was widely practiced by the Egyptians as a blood offering to Osiris, but the priests who performed it claimed it had a meaning which they alone knew and which none would divulge upon penalty of death. When an Egyptian died and was mummified, the brain and the entrails were extracted from the corpse. To the people it was part of the ritual, but the priests implied that the thoughts inherent in the brain never died. The people sought understanding of these and other practices in the festival dramas which the Pharaoh often sponsored. They struggled to find answers to the symbolical ceremonies which they were permitted to witness but, since Osirian religionists never gave them any clear-cut explanation, they went away perplexed and confused.

They were never allowed inside the inner sanctum of the temples, the holy of holies; they were not permitted to pass through the sealed doors or glimpse the god secreted in that sacred room. They only knew that every morning, at a moment astrologically determined, a high priest led his vested celebrants into the temple chambers. From the outer courtyard or the colonnaded halls, the people watched the procession of clean-shaven, white-clad clerics who, wearing papyrus sandals on their feet and bearing jeweled mitres on their heads, filed solemnly by, deigning to raise a hand in blessing.

The people were told that these beardless men shaved not only their faces but their entire bodies every day in preparation for this sacred ritual. They ate bread which had been baked from sacred corn, corn made holy by having been blessed in the temple; they feasted on meat and fowl which had been sanctified by elaborate ceremonies; they drank consecrated wine from lavishly-decorated cups. They wore the finest of linen; no wool ever touched their bodies. They carried golden staffs which were believed to possess the power of magic wands. The golden rings they wore were encrusted with emerald scarabs, symbols of everlasting life. Often they donned headgear representing certain objects of nature in which the mystical power of Osiris and Isis was thought to dwell: a jeweled lotus blossom; a coiled silver serpent; a delicately-molded ibis wrought from strands of spun gold; an alabaster dove; or a miniature empty chair carved from sacred wood which symbolized the empty place left by Osiris when he had been murdered.

So the people watched as the seal on the door leading into the holy of holies was broken. They gazed in wonder while the awesome priests entered the sanctuary to pay homage to the god who occupied a throne hewn from a massive granite block. As the doors swung shut behind these privileged few, the masses turned and left, each carrying with him his own thoughts of Osiris, calling him by whatever name he knew him best and seeing him in his mind's eye by whatever face pleased him most.

Inside the sacred hall, in a room perfumed with incense, the priesthood indulged in intimate relations with the youthful god.

They washed him in scented water, clothed him in soft linen, and crowned him with a sacred tiara. Then they ceremoniously supplied him with food, the spiritual content of which he would consume and thereby be sustained until the next morning when the priests would return to repeat the entire ritual.

Statues of Osiris varied. One showed him wearing an elaborate headgear of lotus blossoms, symbolic of the vortices of sexual energy. Another revealed the god's creative power by depicting the dead Osiris lying in his golden ark with a phallus fully animated. Gradually the sexual aspect of the great god persuaded the people to include the phalli in their public ceremonies, and to emphasize the symbols ever more frequently in their festivals. Soon, on the eve of the Osirian feasts, when pigs —which no Egyptian would eat—were offered as sacrifices, processions of women worshipers roamed the streets carrying small images of the god constructed in such a way that the phallus could be operated by strings. A piper preceded these women and behind them came worshipers reciting the names of the many gods of Egypt who, in their minds, shared with Osiris the same procreative powers.

Another vital object of worship was Apis, the bull. It was said that the mighty animal was engendered by a moonbeam and born beneath a star-studded sky on the eve of an Osirian holy day. One morning Apis wandered into the temple in Memphis on the Nile, arriving just as the nimbus-headed priests were chanting their orisons. No one had ever seen Apis before and no one had an inkling of where he had come from or why, but the masters of mysteries knew at once who and what he was. There was a square blaze of white on his forehead; the outline of a phoenix on his back, a scarab on his tongue, and two perfect strands in his carefully parted tail. Everything that was needed to symbolically relate the bull to the god was here: the square of white represented the earth mother; the phoenix, the resurrection; the scarab, immortality; and the parted tail, the roads to heaven and hell. The jubilant priests declared that Apis was the vehicle for the transmigration of the soul of Osiris, lord of the living and judge of the dead.

They built a stable for Apis adjoining the temple and watched over him with paternal care, proudly leading him out on holy days as the main attraction in the processions. Powerful and virile, symbolizing the substance of life, Apis was soon an inseparable part of the worship. Whomever he breathed upon became inspired and whatever he touched became illustrious. Revered and pampered, Apis lived as the reincarnation of Osiris for twenty-seven years. Then, on his twenty-eighth birthday, robed like a monarch, decked with chaplets of flowers, he was led to the banks of the Nile. Here, surrounded by the disconsolate masses of faithful worshipers, Apis was ceremoniously drowned.

Because it was believed that every twenty-eight days, a lunar month, Osiris died, what was more natural than that his death be symbolized by the drowning of Apis? Following this sacrifice, mourning covered the land until a new Apis was found, which somehow did not prove to be too difficult. Thus, this re-enactment of Osiris' death and resurrection became an integral part of the ceremonies. The twenty-eight days of a lunar month were symbolical of the twenty-eight years that Osiris had lived, and just as the moon waned and died every twenty-eight days, only to return to its place in the sky as a full and brilliant power, so Osiris died and was raised from the dead every twenty-eight days. Thus the god became interwoven with the cosmic forces on the one hand and with the earth on the other. But as this occultism increased, the people began to look upon Osiris as the god of sex.

In this role he was understood. For this they did not need the exclusive priestcraft. And because the gap between people and priests increased, Osiris became more and more a deity of the phallus.

Nor was the holy mother Isis spared. The lovely virgin of the world, whose symbolism had been rich in the mystery of motherhood and conjugal love, became, for many, a most unholy prostitute. Oddly enough the works of art—and none in all the world could compare with those of ancient Egypt—took on a double meaning, one for the religious masters of the secret mysteries and another for the masses. For the first Isis, was the "Veiled One," the concealer of hidden truth. Her naked form was draped with scarlet cloth. Her right breast was a cluster of purple grapes, a hint of the lust of man's eternal passion; her left breast was a sheaf of wheat, symbolizing that in the grain is hidden the sperm of life. The priests said all this was high and noble in meaning, but the disenfranchized multitudes made her a courtesan.

They saw her depicted as a goddess holding an ankh, a cross with a loop at the top, and they knew this meant the male and female elements united as the principles of generation. The masters of the mysteries used the ankh as a talisman. They laid it upon the bodies of the dead in the assurance that eternal life would be theirs through the sexual forces which the cross symbolized. Destined to come down through the ages as the *crux ansata*, or the cross of life, it also represented the triad: Osiris, the father; Isis, the mother; and Horus, the son. But to the people, the ankh, decorated with a coiled serpent or the crescent moon, or the phallic pillar of Osiris, clearly meant that sexual union has ever been the highest gift of nature and the gods.

Sometimes the statues of Isis depicted her as cow-headed, or orbit-headed, or as a madonna with Horus suckling at her breast. Often she was shown with serpents entwined about her feet or snakes interlaced within the olive leaves that wreathed her brow. Her musical instrument was the sistrum, an avowed sexual symbol consisting of an oval metal frame pierced by loose metal rods and furnished with a handle so that when it was shaken it produced an enchanting sound. It was ornamented with the figure of a cat, symbolic of the magnetic forces of nature. Did not everyone know that a cat needed only to be stroked to transmit the mysterious energy of creative cosmic force? The people did not know. All they knew about cats was that they were sacred in Egypt, that they had their special burial places, and that they were symbols of the powerful urge of sex, for it was in Egypt that it was first discovered that the male cat kills the kittens so that the female will want to be mated again. Which, when so explained, was more easily understood than esoteric mysteries propounded by the priests.

Meanwhile the people who toiled on the land saw the corn god fulfill his promises to them and observed how the goddess of the good earth rewarded them with the fruit of her womb. At harvest time, when the corn was ripe, families again went into the field. For a little while the wife of the farmer became something of a priestess, a privilege which was never granted to women in the Egyptian temples. Here among the ripened grain, briefly elevated to this high and worthy position, the woman assumed a leading role. For a moment, she was an earth goddess. Surrounded by her children in the midst of the field, she identified herself with Isis. Reverently breaking off the first ear of corn from the stalk, she peeled back the outer layers to reveal the milk-filled kernels inside. Then handing this to her husband, she watched him take several of the fine silks, representative of the female element, and stroke them tenderly. Handing some of the leaves from the stalk to her children, she aided them in forming images of the corn-god Osiris, after which a suitable image of the earth goddess was also fashioned and stuffed with corn.

Thus, the male and female symbols of Osiris and Isis were symbolically embodied in the corn itself. Holding aloft these effigies, the family offered a prayer from the Book of the Dead: "I have gained the mastery over the river and the land; I have gained the mastery over the furrows; I have gained the mastery over the things which were ordered to be done for me upon the earth. I shall live upon the cakes of white grain, and my ale shall be made of the red grain. I shall sit down, and I shall stand up, and I shall place myself in the path of the wind like a guide who is well prepared."

Then the husbandman, surrounded by his family and his bountiful harvest, pulled the first stalk of corn from the ground.

In that moment no priest in any temple ever held a more consecrated staff.

So seasons passed, and ages passed, and dynasty followed dynasty in the recorded history of Egypt. The scribes recorded the accounts of the good Pharaohs and the wicked ones; the loyal priests and the corrupt ones; the faithful people and the sinful ones. Always the kingdom deteriorated with the deterioration of the gods. Gradually, through the slowly moving years, Osiris became a confused and divided figure. Sex was his emphasis and sexual orgies were introduced until he was once more dismembered, not by the cruel god Set, but by the priests and the people. The priests clamored for his mind and his soul; the peasants wanted the procreative elements which, exemplifying conjugal affection between male and female, produced abundant crops; while the masses, seeking justification for their lust and passion, demanded the symbols of sex. As for the Pharaohs, they wanted a god who would serve their needs, little caring what name he had or what face he bore. As a result, the gentle, all-loving, creative god Osiris became Ra, Ptah, Thoth, Amon, Set, Horus, Seropis, and even the Unknown God of King Amenhotep IV. Torn into fragments by the changing times and the fortunes of a changing people, Osiris was once again scattered over the land and, this time, Isis, reduced to harlotry, was powerless to perform her earlier miracle of restoring her ill-starred consort to his throne.

At about this time, during the period of the 18th Dynasty (1788-1580 B.C.), a son of the tribe of Levi named Moses, a blood brother of the captive Israelites and an initiate into the mysteries of the Egyptian wisdom, met a God more powerful than the god of the Nile or the god of the corn; a God more mighty than Osiris, lord of the living and judge of the dead. The God of Moses was a lonely, long-suffering God, a God more compassionate than gods had even been, but He had reached the end of His patience with the corrupt Egyptian kings. He summoned Moses into His presence by setting a burning bush before him and speaking to him from the flames. "I will send you to Pharaoh," He said, "that thou mayst bring forth my people, the children of Israel, out of Egypt."

Moses, a strange man, a member of the Illuminati, had almost as mysterious an origin as Osiris. Had he not been found in a basket cradled in the bulrushes much as Osiris had been lodged in the golden ark cradled in the branches of a tree beside the Nile? He, like Osiris himself, had been adopted by the family of the Pharaoh and had been raised as a beloved son in the royal court. He, too, destined to "civilize the world" as Osiris had done, was to carry many traditions and customs of Egypt into other lands. But here, the similarity between them abruptly ended. Moses was the first to write upon his altars the solemn warning, "Let there be Holiness unto the Lord!"

The God of Moses sent His voice thundering like a roaring wind along the Nile. The echoes of His wrath resounded throughout Egypt, demanding that Pharaoh let His people go. Once the power of Osiris might have withstood this voice, but now, reduced to a god of sex, he heard the cries of the priests of Pharaoh in vain. Even as God's chosen people moved out of bondage, the foreign gods of Syria, Ethiopia, and the Hittites infiltered and invaded the land, and Osiris was powerless to resist. Like Baal, sex was his undoing.

Disenchanted, the people turned to anything or anyone who would bring them good fortune, whether it was an ankh, an Apis, or any ordinary animal. The priesthood, as well, began to doubt the heretofore unquestioned power of their god. Then strange things happened. The man in the field realized that his grain grew just as well without the corn god's aid; the masses, convinced that Osirism was but an excuse for licentiousness, turned their rituals into unabashed sexual orgies. The priests, degraded by the rumors that they, too, held indecent sexual ceremonies in the secret chambers of the temples, found themselves shorn of any holy illusion so far as their once awed worshipers were concerned.

The pyramids, the people now declared, had not been miraculously built, but were instead only massive monuments erected at the cost of innumerable lives and indescribable suffering by the selfish Pharaohs who had sought to outdo one another. The secret chambers became targets for invaders, and the treasures which they contained became the coveted prize of vandals and conquerors. The temples, themselves, were gradually being closed as the great god's hallowed shrines were desecrated.

Often, to save themselves, the gods must flee. To flee, they must frequently be disguised. So it was with Osiris. Masquerading now under the title of Dionysus, lord of the Eleusinian mysteries, Osiris fled to Greece. He was already well known in that land, for he had visited it in his youth during the years he was striving to "civilize the world." He had not been forgotten in Greece during the many thousands of years of his deification in Egypt, for tradesmen, plying the seas between Greece and Egypt, had taken his symbols back with them. Philosophers, traveling the earth in search of eternal truth, had already interpreted his story for their countrymen, so Osiris was assured not only protection but devotion and reverence from the Greeks.

Gods and goddesses were a familiar part of the Greek culture. Though these deities claimed to have been born on Mount Olympus, most of them had come from other lands, particularly Egypt. The goddess Demeter was in reality the Egyptian Isis; Typhon was analogous to Set; and Hermes bore a singular likeness to the jackel-headed Anubis. It was not too difficult, therefore, for Osiris to mount the Olympian pantheon and declare himself the Greek god of vegetation and the vine, claiming that he was actually Dionysus, the son of Zeus and Semele. He took an honored place with the twelve Olympian deities, but no longer did he have the lofty position which had once been his as god of the corn and lord of the dead. As the god Dionysus, he was the god of sex, commissioned to satisfy man's deepest passions and desires. Only a god could have understood how he felt in his newly-acquired role.

His attendants in the evanescent mists of Mt. Olympus were the satyrs. In human form they were actually old roués whose course of sexual merriment was running out, but under the enchanted spell of Dionysus they saw themselves as sylvan deities with the tail and ears of a horse, trotting through Elysian fields like young colts in search of a mate. When they became older and more senile, their imagery only increased. They now imagined themselves to be woodland nymphs with the legs and virility of young goats. Actually they were lecherous old men, baldheaded and barely able to stand on their spindly legs, but when the wine of Dionysus flowed and the hymns of Dionysus filled the groves, they were immortal sileni.

Their female counterparts were also victims of the Olympian illusion. Their charm and prowess in the art of making love had long been spent, but under Dionysus they saw themselves as irresistible *femmes fatales*. They also had a righteous resentment against the gods for having been penalized with the annoying consequences of old age, but Dionysus rejuvenated them with all the lust of virgin maids. There had been occasions in the past when they had sublimated temptation in piety, but now, since it was growing late, they inverted the process. With the help of wine, song, and aphrodisiacs, they imagined themselves to be nymphs, maenads, portraying their role in frenzied promiscuity under the spell of the great god of sex.

If Dionysus sat on his Olympian throne and laughed or if he held these masquerading worshipers in derision, he never let it be known. He remembered all too well from his Egyptian experiences that religion and worship are fully as much a way of escape as a way of life. Furthermore, did he not have other neophytes who were neither old nor senile? His proselytizing had won for him many young barbarians who had never been able to satisfy their energies, as other Greeks had, in art and beauty. These youthful anarchists demanded more than the wine of grapes or the hymns of love. They wanted blood and sex and, even more, intimate communion with the gods.

So Dionysus, as if remembering the power of Apis, took to himself the universal figure of the bull. When the young barbarians worshiped, they were first compelled to lose themselves in the Olympian fog of ecstasy. Whatever was needed to induce this desired state was allowable; whatever they did when they were once god-possessed was justified. In a fanatical effort to become one with their god, these young worshipers drove a bull into an arena and with crude spears or, better yet, with their bare hands, tore him into shreds, and, in a gory sacrament, drank his blood, and ate his flesh. How else does a mortal become like a god unless he eats the flesh of his deity and drinks his blood?

After the bull had been dismembered and consumed, the blood-stained, sex-crazed worshipers formed a procession. To the blare of flutes and the crash of cymbals, they added their bull-like bellowing and stampeded into groves to indulge their orgiastic lust. Who could oppose them? Who could condemn them? Had not the god himself set the wheels of passion into motion?

So it seemed. It was as though the coming of Osiris to Greece had thoroughly defiled the original worship of Dionysus. The earliest Dionysiac feasts were festivals of gratitude to the gods of the vineyard. They had developed into initiatory ceremonies of an extremely high order and finally into fraternities which included men who were to become immortal: a Plato, a Plutarch, a Euripides, and an Aeschylus. But the great god sex whom the people had lifted to a pinnacle surpassing that of the lesser gods had by his very popularity defiled those whom he had once hoped to inspire.

It was time for the God Jehovah to come to Greece as He had come to Canaan and to Egypt. This time He brought His Son, another God, a Saviour who was to challenge the immortal, ageless gods of the Greeks, to question religious practices, to reexamine religion as the deification of reason and philosophy. Most of all, he came to destroy the gods who had corrupted the purity of motive by encouraging impurity of acts. Chief among these corrupted deities was the god of many faces and many names: it was toward him that Jehovah directed his relentless wrath.

Dionysus had heard Him coming. Could he save himself once more behind another mask and hide his identity behind another myth? He decided to try and fled into another land which, in his youth, he had also helped to "civilize." He went to Rome, wearing a new mask and bearing a new name. This time he was known as Bacchus, but he was actually Osiris-Dionysus. Isis, who had left Greece as the goddess Demeter and who now bore the name Ceres, was waiting for him. To her Osiris came, having grown more callous, more offensive, and more cruel, but he was still a god. Usurping Bacchnalian ceremonies, which had been initiated to lift men to their highest level, Osiris claimed them for his own. Heralded by the people as a god risen from the dead, Bacchus was thought to have been born of a virgin, to have performed miracles, to have died and risen again. But now, degraded and debauched, he—as Osiris—sanctioned orgies more vile and corrupt than those which he had condoned in Greece. No wilder worship could be found than the Bacchanalia over which he ruled. No more sadistic rites had ever been held than these. Whatever Bacchus may once have been, he now became the vilest of the pornographic gods.

Then once again were heard the voices of the new faith; the ominous sound of Jehovah, who had first assailed Osiris in Egypt and then in Greece, was moving into Rome. Christianity, carrying a cross much like the ankh which Osiris had known in Egypt, came marching through a path of broken pagan shrines, pledged to destroy the pagan deities. The Man-God Christ was moving inexorably across the land. The voice of the great God Jehovah and His disciples rang in the ears of Osiris-Dionysus-Bacchus: "We will find you, Osiris, no matter where you hide. We will search you out no matter where you go. Destroy you we must."

And destroy him they did.

It will never be known exactly what happened to the aging, vine-crowned, debauched god of lust and sex who had corrupted the many who worshiped him in his time, but the decrees of the Roman state and the divine command of the priests of the new order put an end to him early in the Christian era.

Isis remained as a goddess in the Roman Empire until the 6th century, continuing to be a symbol of virginity and honored as the patroness of motherhood. Navigators looked to her for guidance on the wide seas; they pictured her holding a ship with a distaff for a mast, a sign that it was she who spun the threads of life and guided the ship of fate safely to its homeland. Sailors declared that they saw her in the sky on moonlit nights traversing the heavens in her ethereal bark, but with the passing of the years, she sailed off into space never to return and never to be seen again.

Osiris had run his course, a path which led from his role as king of kings in Egypt to the orgies of a wine god in Rome. Legends still speak of his symbolical death and his impressive resurrection, but, even so, he truly died. Myths relate the wisdom with which he judged the dead, but, in the ultimate judgment, the dead as well as the living came to judge him. His statues, once so reverently worshiped, have become today mere curious works of art; his Book of the Dead, a record of an ancient people's quest. Occasionally, beneath the sands in some musty ruin, archeologists find the broken fragments of his once-honored symbols: a staff, an obelisk, a phallic stone. Or perhaps their spades uncover a portion of a head-piece much like the Pharaoh's crown. Nothing else remains. Were there an epitaph upon his unknown tomb, it would probably read, "This is how a false god dies."

There are those, of course, even today who cling to their belief that Osirism still lives on. They have no basis for this point of view and no proof for this stubborn opinion unless it is their mystic sight to gaze into the hearts of men or their surmise that human nature never changes and that human passions never die. As if to prove that they are right, they occasionally walk among the pyramids of Gizeh or stroll again along the restless Nile. They say that they can see the spirits of Egyptian priests shuffling across the sands to enter the holy of holies; that they can hear the voices of Osiris and Isis still whispering in the waves of the great river. Who was he, this god of many faces and many names? Does no one know? Or are those who know, pledged by some secret order not to tell?

4 § SHIVISM

Slowly, imperceptibly, so quietly that one can hardly sense the change, the symbols of sex are disappearing from the temples of the Hindu faith. Once they were found in great profusion everywhere in India, objects of veneration and worship, calling the devotee to prayer and praise. The most revered symbol was the round, polished, upright stone, known as a lingam, which was sacred to Shiva, the destroyer; one of the three gods in the Hindu trinity which included Brahma, the creator, and Vishnu, the preserver.

The statues of many other amorous Hindu gods are also disappearing. The frescos delineating goddesses cavorting with their lovers, the medallions portraying Bacchanalian scenes, and the bas-reliefs depicting the art of conjugal love will soon be found in museums, if found at all. A changing world, a changing attitude, a changing India are conspiring to reconstruct and redefine the historic past in an effort to adapt the once-accepted concepts to an era which has made sex in religion literally taboo.

The story of this gradual transition spans a period of at least 4000 years. It began in the days when sex was considered a natural, basic impulse of life, in the period when the mysterious force worshiped by the aboriginal tribes of northern India were challenged by the nature forces of the conquering Aryans. Thus it developed that the early Hindus, like the early people of any land, came to personify and to worship both the passions they felt within themselves and the powers they saw in nature. They deified abstractions as well as cosmic elements and gave them the names of gods and goddesses. Thus, they symbolized wisdom by the goddess Saraswati; wealth by the goddess Lakshmi; and love by the god Kama or Cupid; they anthropomorphized the moon as Soma; the sun as Surya; the sky as Indra; and the fire as Agni.

Hinduism, the religion of some 360,000,000 people in India today, has always had many sects because it has always had many gods. In fact, it has been said that there is an individual god for every Hindu worshiper, and this may well be true, for with its customary candor, this ancient faith concedes that gods are usually made in the image of man. Long before the androgynous deities were discovered by other religions, or before there was ever developed the theories of virgin queens or mothers of heaven, the sages of India had been relating their religious philosophy to these concepts.

Certain gods, however, gained popularity because in the minds of the people some were related more closely with their own experiences than others. Such a god was—and is—Krishna, the ever-passionate, ever-tender lord who was, and is even yet, idolized as the Hindu Apollo. The embodiment of bliss and the fulfillment of desire, he is the paradoxical symbol of both absolute love and absolute temptation. Thought to be the incarnation of Vishnu, it is believed that Krishna actually lived as a mortal. He is portrayed as a youthful, effeminate young man with flowing hair who seduces his devotee with lilting music of his flute. When Krishna's physical beauty and provocative music have stirred the deep springs of physical desire, the moment has come for the emotionally-aroused devotee to determine whether he will succumb to lust or transcend to the heights of spiritual love. He is also a god who sanctifies what others might condemn as a sin. "To the pure in heart, there is no sin," says Krishna. "When I look upon the chaste women of respectable families, I see in them the Mother Divine arrayed in the garments of a pure woman. When I look upon the public women of the city displaying themselves in their robes of immorality and shamelessness, I see in them also the Mother Divine, but now conducting herself in a different way."

Every Hindu is acquainted with the erotic romances of Krishna recorded in the *Bhagavata Purana,* one of the Hindu scriptures. Every devotee knows the legend of Krishna and the Gopis or cowgirls, which relates what took place one moonlit autumn night when these impetuous women began to crave for something which is ordinarily unobtainable: physical union with a god. Burning with desire and stirred by the nectarian rays of the moon, they heightened one another's excitement by the whispered confessions of their mounting passion. When they had been stimulated and tantalized to a feverish intensity, they heard the seductive tones of Krishna's flute. "When this love-exciting melody entered the Gopis," said the sage Sukadeya, "their minds became full of lust. Neither walls, nor trees, nor bowers could stop them. Each, forgetting everything but her overwhelming desire, ran and threw herself at Krishna's feet."

Lord Krishna said, "Look, maidens, it is improper for you to tarry here. Surely your husbands will be looking for you." When they refused to answer, when they merely gazed up into his face and smiled, he disrobed to "show them the beauty of his form," and to determine whether or not they were simply charmed by his physical being, or whether they recognized him as the "sinless god." "If you have come to me because of affection and attachment," said Krishna, "there is nothing wrong in this, for all beings are gratified when they see me. But if you have come to satisfy your lust, your infamy will be exposed to the world."

The impassioned Gopis defended themselves by saying that since Lord Krishna was the incarnation of all life and that without him nothing would exist, must he not then be the true husband of each of them? Impressed by this reasoning, Krishna probed their faith by asking them many philosophical questions related to love and lust. Satisfied at last by their answers, "he robbed them of their clothes" and the Gopis stood naked before him. Realizing that "the veil between the individual soul and the soul of God" had been removed, they bowed their heads in adoration. Charmed by this reverence and convinced that the Gopis were expressing pure love for him, Krishna "granted them the boon for which they sought. The Divine Lord consorted with the Gopis."

The gurus—the enlightened teachers and philosophers of Hinduism—endeavored to explain this provocative legend for the people. 'True love," they said, "kills the lustful propensity. The all-beautiful Lord gave satisfaction to the Gopis as a sign that he accepted their physical service because it had been disassociated from the stain of desire. It was no longer lust, it was love."

The people listened and thought they understood. They heard the gurus say that religion is an ever-lasting test of strength and an eternal challenge of choice, that the mission of the gods is to keep the mind alive and the soul alert. But even as they heard the words, the listeners beheld the sculptured gods of Hinduism playing their amorous games, deliberately arousing passion and then demanding sublimation, showing them their nakedness while directing their minds to purity of thought. Poised upon the narrow ledge between lust and love, the worshipers sought their uncertain way. "If the heart is pure," the gurus said, "then the erotic behavior of the gods are lofty lessons in piety; if the heart is carnal, you will see only debauchery and become defiled by the grimy world of sex."

Thoughtfully the worshipers moved among the temples and the shrines, wondering why one must renounce physical passion to find purity of soul, or why life had to be burdened with the challenge of continual choice. The gurus, claiming to be celibates, turned their backs upon the world, inviting others to emulate them in their ascetic life. "Transform the sexual impulse into transcendent devotion," they urged, "or you will never experience the true presence of God." Yet even as the words were driven deeply into the mind of every Hindu, ever around him loomed the images of the ambivalent gods who never seemed to set a specific example for man—unless man could keep in mind the difference between lust and love. But where did the one end and the other begin? The gurus, seeking to explain this paradox, said, "Lust gives place to pain; love to heavenly bliss. In lust, there is satisfaction and gratification of the senses; in love, there is absorption of Self. Lust is honey mixed with poison; love is the divine, celestial nectar."

How could the people understand? How were they to distinguish between the gratification of the senses and the absorption of self? They were as confused as the gods themselves seemed to be. What did Krishna have in mind when he accepted the advances of the Gopis, or what did Kama, also called Cupid, desire from his worshipers when he tempted them with his arrows of love? Sometimes Cupid was pictured as a golden-haired youth astride a parrot and attended by nymphs. He carried a bow of sugar cane strung with a bowstring of bees, from which he released his lotus-tipped arrows; sometimes, pictured as a black beast, he symbolized animal passion.

And who was the great god Shiva? What did he represent? Why was he called the destroyer? The gurus said that he destroyed matter by proving that matter was but the energy of spirit. He destroyed desire by satisfying it, lust by sanctifying it, and passion by transforming it into spiritual love. Shiva, they contended, was also the destroyer of bondage, for he released souls from the slavery of illusion by removing the veil of ignorance and revealed to them the power and the glory which lay behind the misty facade of earthly life. Destruction in Hinduism implied reproduction, so Shiva is he who reproduces power which is perpetually restoring that which has been dissolved. Under the character of restorer he is represented by the lingam or phallus, typical of reproduction. He is also the Maha-yogi, the great ascetic in whom the highest perfection and the most unlimited powers are attained through meditation and the sublimation of sexual energy. In this role he is the naked ascetic whose body is smeared with ashes.

So spoke the gurus, but the eighty million followers of Shiva, like the many millions who worshiped Krishna, were more interested in what the gods represented to them than what the gurus said they should represent. The Shivites, divided into many sects and sub-sects, were bound together by the *Puranas* and other Hindu holy books. But most of all, they were united by what Shiva meant to them as they groped their way through their often aimless lives. To his devotees, Shiva continued to be the god of sex, although philosophers insisted that he was the "generative cause, the supreme reality, the eternal, formless, beginningless, taintless One-without-a-second."

His beloved consort, Shakti, also known as Parvati, Kali, Durga, Chaudi, Chamindi, Tripurasundari, or Rajeswari, was the symbol of passive power. She was the female counterpart of Shiva's cosmic self and together they comprised the primeval creator, the melding of male and female in the universe. "They are one body," the gurus explained, "half male and half female. They are twin aspects, static and kinetic. Shiva is unlimited cause, the principle of change. Shakti is that which, in itself unchangeable, produces forms out of itself. Shakti is Shiva; Shiva is Shakti. There cannot be one without the other."

But to the people, the poor, the illiterate, the struggling masses, who chanted their mantras before the Shiva lingam, to those who molded lingams out of sand or crudely fashioned them out of wood or stone, to those who responded more to inner feelings than to philosophies, the words of the gurus and sages conveyed little meaning. Even the priests in the temples, like the people, apparently wanted worship, not the philosophy of the gurus. They, too, understood the great god Shiva best when they bathed the Shiva lingam in milk and murmured their adoration to him and felt his presence pulsating through their bodies in waves of passion and praise.

The priests and the people were convinced that Shiva was pleased with them when they made their pilgrimages to his holy city, Benares, where the sacred Ganges flowed. Here they sat in the water, chanting prayers to the lingam, surrounded by the music which floated from the temples in constant praise of their lord. Bathing in the murky waters, they knew without doubt that their god was pleased. Here, they were close to the burning ghats whose fires seemed never to go out, for it was here that the bodies of the dead were being cremated by the holy flames, and here the ashes and bones were tossed into the sacred waters. Every worshiper was comforted by the knowledge that whoever died in Benares would be blessed, and that whoever bathed in the holy stream would have his sins forgiven.

In Benares, the numerous lingams of Shiva dotted the banks of the holy Ganges, and it was toward these gross phallic denizens of stone and wood set into their circular bases, hallowed and dedicated to the great god of sex, that the pilgrim to the city made his way. Walking reverently around and around the lingam, he never forgot to keep his right hand toward the shrine. Were not those who worshiped with the left hand crude and cruel and given only to orgies and lust? Every devout worshiper knew that much. He knew, too, how to go into the shrine and how to strike the gong with his hand or with a mallet to arrest the attention of the god. He knew that the priest would then blow through a conch shell and would wait for him to advance to the lingam and make his offerings of fruit or flowers. After these amenities were observed, the worshiper was free to remain and pray. Often, he would pour water on the lingam and kiss it reverently. Occasionally, he would fashion a lingam out of clay and leave it in the shrine with a prayer that it would become animated and would thereby animate his life. Frequently, these rituals were ceremoniously performed to the rhythmic accompaniment of temple drums and clanging metal gongs. It was at such times that the Lord Shiva seemed very near.

It was not strange, therefore, that Benares became the chosen center for festivals and pilgrimages, the most famous of which honored Shiva. One such celebration, known as the Kumbh Mela, occurred whenever Jupiter, Aquarius, Aries, and the Sun were in juxtaposition. So momentous was this occasion that people prepared for it months in advance by eating only fruits and drinking only milk and devoting most of their time to meditation. The gurus explained that the Kumbh Mela had a deep and mystical zodiacal significance for it related the four heavenly bodies to the four great aims of Hinduism: Artha (material possession); Kama (love or lust); Dharma (religion); Moksha (spiritual release). Just as the zodiacal signs are in balanced agreement, so, too, should one's life be in balanced harmony, counseled the gurus. The people, however, unable to grasp this philosophical explanation, came to worship their own special gods, their hearts and minds centered on Krishna or Cupid or Shakti, or whoever their favorite deity might be. Usually, however, it was Shiva, Shiva the god of the lingam and of love.

Often the city was so crowded that the people could find no room to kneel or to reach a shrine or even to catch sight of the symbols which they had journeyed so far to worship. Sadhus and sannyasins (holy men) in saffron robes, fakirs, and beggars jostled their way through the throngs. Quarrels and fights often flared up amid the dust and the dirt of the outlying encampments. Finally the gurus, growing ever more fearful of losing control over the intensity of such situations, declared that the spirit of the festival was being corrupted, the meaning was being lost, and the gods were being forgotten. Their misgivings were not without basis in fact, for, on one such morning of a Kumbh Mela, in 1956, the rising crescendo of religious frenzy reached an unprecedented climax.

Inspired and over-stimulated by twelve days and nights of constant prayer, a thousand so-called holy men, stripping off their clothes and throwing ashes over their naked bodies, seized the symbols of Shiva and raised them high above their heads. Others, hysterical, lifted the sacred trident of the Hindu trinity; Brahma (fundamental creative force), Vishnu (female principle), and Shiva (the lingam) and followed the holy men, marching toward the Ganges, as the millions of awe-struck worshipers crowded around them. To the sound of cymbals and bells, the rattle of conch shells, and the beating of drums, the thousand nude fanatical holy men waded into the sacred stream. Close behind them, the hordes of enchanted worshipers broke into a frenzied forward rush. In a moment, they became a wildly screaming mob, each shoving and struggling to be the first to enter the holy river. Some fell, never to rise again, for, as the multitudes stomped over them, they trampled their cries of anguish and terror into silence and pressed on until they stood immersed in the water, crowding as close to the holy men as they possibly could. Some plunged under the water, scooped up a handful of clay and shaped it into a lingam, and then raised it to the skies, shouting, "Shiva, I have made thy image! Fill it with thy spirit and bless it with thy life!"

The helpless gurus, standing afar off, cried out in vain, "You are turning the festival into an orgy and a place of death. Pure consciousness is not a matter of ceremonies and enormous crowds. It is, rather, the unperturbed substrata in Shiva. Pure awareness is as the reality substrata in Shakti!"

Wandering through such a wilderness of words, the gurus continued to coin their ambiguous phrases. Their expressions of "root-substance energy, self-and-not-self, eternal-being-consciousness, and static-kinetic force" continued to bewilder and confuse the people. The gap between their philosophizing and the uncritical, impassioned worship of the masses widened. Their intellectualizing conflicted with the emotional reactions of the people. Still from the lofty heights of their inspired reasoning, the gurus declared, "The Absolute is a word, a logos! It is Shiva-Shakti; Man-Woman; Spirit-Soul! It evolves into the world of finite existence and yet never ceases to be exactly what it is!"

The people despaired of ever being able to understand. All they knew was that they idolized their gods and found their desires satisfied in them. Did they not love Lord Shiva and did he not love them? Was this not more of a reality than the words which they were being taught? Why should they care for wisdom or admonitions? The insistent gurus, however, declared that *they* cared. Condemning the priests and the people, they continued their plea for an intellectual faith. They advocated a classical Brahmanical approach; they appealed for a religion of respect, a theological religion. "True sexual union," they cried, "is the union of the supreme Shakti (energy) with the Atmen (spirit); all other unions are merely carnal acts."

They conducted ashrams and retreats to pursue their studies in a determined effort to build a linguistic faith. "Maya (illusion)," they sought to explain, "evolves into the subtle principle and then into the gross. The individual soul experiences pleasure and pain through Vidya or knowledge. Shiva is the basis of all consciousness and action. The Shakti of Shiva starts her activities. Then Shiva becomes the experiencer and is called Sadasiva, known also by the name of Sadakhya, who is in reality not different from Shiva."

Thus on and on, they tried to interpret the gods, until the people finally ceased asking what it was all supposed to mean. Even though the gurus seemed to understand, the eighty million Shivites and the millions more among other Hindu sects cared only that the symbols be related to themselves, to their passions, and to their needs. To them, Shiva and Shakti were their own desires expressed and sometimes purified. Shiva was sexual power in the male; Shakti was submissive passion in the female. The notion that either the impulse or the symbols were wrong never occurred to the simple-hearted people. Why should the gods be offended with what the gods had made?

It was not long before the gurus began looking with pity and contempt upon the masses. True religion and absolute holiness, they insisted, could come only through their teaching. The myths and the legends, they explained, were not what they appeared to be. They were narratives clothed in the deepest of subtle meanings, meaning so mystical that only a selected few could grasp their truths. The people, however, unable to read the holy books, could only wonder whether these claims were true or false. They only knew that there was no separation in feeling, so why should the gods dominate the mind with knowledge or logic and thereby breed separation?

There were a few, however, who sat at the feet of the gurus and sought to learn the deeper truths. Occasionally, some became adepts and dedicated their lives to study. Now and then, one became a sadhu or a sannyasin. But the milling masses, to whom the gods were their greatest and most cherished possessions, refused to contemplate on the obscurities of the gurus' philosophies. Unable to intellectualize sex and eager to perpetuate the love they had for Krishna, Shiva, Shakti, and all the others, they continued to identify themselves with the gods and to put them on a humanized level. To them, Shiva and Shakti remained the supreme gods, for they were divine husband and wife. Most of all, they were lingam and yoni, male and female symbols, which could be found in the temples and worshiped and adored.

Righteously aroused, the gurus warned, "The world looks upon Hinduism as a religion of sex and evil. It is a mistake for you to believe that the Shiva lingam represents the phallus. It is a serious blunder to look upon the yoni as a symbol of regenerative force. These images are merely signs of the presence of a power. The whole world is the form of Lord Shiva; the whole world is a lingam. Shiva-Shakti cannot be grasped as you grasp reality, for reality itself is the illusion."

Finally they attempted to clarify the confusion in the minds of the people by explaining that although the gods were like men, they were not men, and that, although they were many and seemingly different from one another, they were, in reality, all alike. By way of parables, they sought to rectify the misconceptions and control the emotions of the masses. To be pure in heart, they said, one must banish all base thoughts and sublimate all sexual desire. Always, as they extended their philosophical structure to relate the lingam and the yoni to cosmic and physical forces, they reminded the people that only the educated could ever hope to understand the deeply hidden meanings.

Perhaps they were right. But behind the popular temple worship lay the kind of ritualistic understanding that gave the Shivites a sense of nearness to their god. They kept a Shiva lingam in a box and set it on a shrine in the homes or hovels where they lived. Each devotee cherished the lingam which he wore as an amulet around his neck, believing that failure to wear this fetish was bound to bring misfortune, and that the loss of it would result in tragedy. Women sat upon the lingam believing that it would help them conceive and make them fruitful; in the temples, they prayed to the lingam asking for assistance and protection during childbirth. Who was to judge their acts? Who was to say that they were wrong and the gurus were right?

One of their greatest joys came from repeating the stories of the gods as they heard them from the temple priests, the very priests whom the gurus condemned. They recited the many legends of Shakti, one of which told the story of Lord Ganesha, a child with the face of an elephant who had been created by Shiva's consort for her own pleasure. To him, she had assigned the work of clearing the forest paths so the gods would have an open and easy path to travel. When Lord Shiva, in a playful mood one day, offered an apple as a prize to the god who would race around the world in record time, all the gods hurried forth, dashing across the sky as fast as they could. Lord Ganesha, however, simply walked around the Shiva lingam and won the award.

They repeated another legend which portrayed Shakti as a provocative and flirtatious wife who rushed up to her lord and covered his eyes with her hands, asking him to guess whom it might be. Instantly, the whole world was plunged into total darkness. Thoroughly angered by this, Lord Shiva commanded her to do penance and while she knelt in prayer before the lingam, he created a flood which threatened to engulf her and the whole world. Shakti, however, quickly embraced the lingam and it became a rock upon which she and all the people were saved.

There was another legend which told of the day a devil

drove all the gods from heaven and Brahma said, "The only god who can save us is Lord Shiva. Tempt him to have intercourse with Shakti. A powerful son will then be born and he will destroy the devil." So Cupid was assigned to the task of tempting Shiva and Shakti. Quickly mounting his parrot, Cupid winged his way to the mystical abode of Shiva and concealed himself behind a tree to wait for an opportune moment. Soon Shakti and Shiva strolled into the garden and Shakti, wishing to show her adoration for her lord, knelt before him with an offering of flowers. Taking careful aim, Cupid released a lotus-tipped arrow from his bowstring of bees and sent the shaft into the heart of the unsuspecting Shiva. When the arrow penetrated Shiva's body, he was suddenly consumed with such a wave of passion that he spilled his seed upon the ground. Angered and betrayed, Shiva, catching sight of Cupid, opened his third eye, a fire flashed and Cupid was burned to ashes. Quickly Shiva cast his seed into the fire, but the fire god, Agni, unable to bear it, threw the seed into the Ganges. The Ganges, equally unwilling to receive this, hurled it into a cluster of reeds from which Shiva's son, Kartikeya, was later born and cradled in an ark of bulrushes. Destined to destroy the devil, he later rid the heavens of the imposter just as Brahma had predicted.

As these tales were told and retold by the Shivites, their love for Shiva and Shakti grew. The devotees painted three white chalk marks across their foreheads to indiciate their faith and to acknowledge their belief that the power of Lord Shiva could destroy the three impurities of a man's soul: egotism, selfishness, and illusion.

When they were told that Lord Shiva had introduced the practice of yoga, which would develop complete mastery over self and nature, some became adepts and devoted their entire lives to the study of yogic art. When the true yogi sat lotus-fashion, he believed that through posture and meditations, he could transmute the mystical current of sexual passion into spiritual energy. Sex glands, said the yogis, are linked with the power of the mind, and sex discipline is directly connected with the growth of the soul. Through intricate exercises, the yogi could arouse the coiled up spiral of energy, known as the *kundalin shakti,* and direct it into various parts of his body, into his brain, and even into space.

Although the practice of yoga gained popularity among the masses, very few became adepts, and seldom was its deepest meaning understood: complete discipline over body, mind, and spirit. Shivites did not realize that, to the true yogi, renunciation of sexual desire was more thrilling than realization of that desire. Nor did the masses understand that Shiva, the destroyer, never destroyed a passion without restoring a virtue, or robbed men of an illusion without rewarding them with reality.

Many fanatics, imagining yoga to be a form of magic, sat on the banks of the holy stream, gazing into the sun until they became blind. Some, even more ardent, refused to move at all and chanted mantras until their bodies became emaciated and their minds deranged.

Still on every hand, symbols of sex confronted the people. Sometimes the gods tempted individuals to go the sinful way, as Krishna had done with the Gopis, so that they might be shown the virtue of a more worthy choice. Lust was the illusion; love was the reality, but in the minds of millions of Hindus, the distinction between the two was never clearly defined. Through thousands of years, the gurus developed a philosophical approach which satisfied them, but which never met the needs of the masses. The average Hindu knew nothing about Moksha (salvation), or about Dharma (true religion and its duties), or Arcismatci (the striving for perfection).

These concepts had never been explained in terms the people could understand and apply to their personal lives. Even the statues of the gods had different meanings for the gurus than they had for the people. For example, the statue of Shiva astride a milk-white bull, Nandi, holding the nubile Shakti on his lap, was intended to represent the union of procreative power in a zodiacal sense, but it was a symbol that had meaning only for those who had a knowledge of the occult. Other statues portrayed Shiva with a deer in his hand to signify that he ruled the Vedas, the Hindu holy books. In others, he brandished a sword to indicate that he was the destroyer of birth and death. Pictures depicted him entwined with a serpent to illustrate how the individual soul was linked to the over-soul of the cosmic world. But, regardless of what the symbols were intended to mean, the eighty million Shivites still saw them only as objects of sex.

The holy men revered images of the dancing Shiva which, they insisted, symbolized the graceful movement of the ego stepping from the magic circle of primeval birth. This was to signify that all movements in the universe were but the shadows of Shiva (cosmic power) dancing. He touched primeval matter and it sprang into life; he embraced Shakti and she became fruitful; when he stimulated the sounds and the spaces of the heavens and the planets, the stars began to sing. He taught his dance to mortals and, for a little while, they became gods. So because of his talent for the dance, the gurus gave him yet another name, Nataraja, the dancer divine; Nataraja, the graceful god of four hands, who wore the holy Ganges and the crescent moon upon his head.

The worshipers, the pilgrims, the masses, however, who knew the gods only as supermen, gazed upon the images of the dancing Shiva and formed their own impressions. He dances quietly, they whispered, for if he danced with violence, the earth would sink away. He dances with eyes closed because the brilliant light from his blazing sight would consume the world. He dances with Shakti and his spirit is merged with hers. Without her, he is a motionless snake. With her he is a snake in motion. Without her, he is a waveless sea; with her, he is a sea alive with power, moved by her as the tides are moved by the moon. If there were those who saw only the symbolism of sex, might there not have been those who saw pure spirituality? And who was there to discern the difference between the two?

Throughout these many slow-paced centuries of Hinduism, various treaties on the meaning and art of love had been developed by scholars. As early as the 4th century, a pharmacopaeia had been prepared to describe the minutest details of eroticism. A literature of love and lust became part of the Hindu canon, but whether it was inspired by saints or sinners remains a question even today. Such a book was the *Kama-Sutra*, a breviary which discussed the art of prostitution, offered various prescriptions for the making of aphrodisiacs and revealed secret instructions on the art of making love designed to please the most discriminating paramours and wives. There was a chapter on "The Art of Erotic Biting," another on "The Categories of Passion," a third on "The Technique of Approaching Another Man's Wife." The scholarly author, the guru Vetsyayana, writing in the 6th century, created a book so outsopken and frank that it is still banned today in the United States, and is said actually to have shocked those versed in erotic practices. When it appeared for the first time in 1943, as an English translation from the original Sanskrit, the gurus said that only the pure in heart should ever read it, only the holy could ever appreciate it, and only the medical scientist could ever understand it.

When the Hindus who could not read heard about this book, it merely reinforced their belief that there is no sin unless thinking makes it so; that the gods, like men, have their own ideas as to where lust ends and love begins, and that every living mortal must eventually admit that among his most cherished images stands the great god sex.

But gradually and quietly, the symbols are disappearing from the temples of the Hindu faith. An era is ending. A more sophisticated attitude toward sex, a shifting standard of values, and a more educated people are causing the amorous gods to disappear from their once-sacred walls. In the gopurras—the temple gates—the niches are bare, and in many a temple court there is no longer any object suggesting sex to which even an innocent reverence may be paid. They were said to have been revolting to Christians and to Hindus of culture and to have given the religion of India an undeservedly bad name.

Today, even the festivals have lost their original meaning.

Now, a stilted dignity or a crude burlesque of former ceremonies has transformed and redirected the homage once paid
to the creative principles, Shiva and Shakti. Shiva, the active
force, and Shakti, the passive power, whose union made the
world, have fallen into disrepute and have been lost in shame
because the gurus sought to make them shameless. Philosophers
have usurped the altars where the deities once ruled. Even the
holy books are being "purified," and more and more the people
are losing their identity with the gods who once shared their
experiences.

The gongs still sound at the shrines; the mantras still echo in
the hollow temple halls; the barefoot sadhus in saffron robes
still shuffle through the crowded streets; the faithful still make
their ablutions in the sacred streams. But growing in the heart
and soul of worshipers who watch the changing scene is a be-
wilderment half-expressed and half-concealed which says, "They
have taken away my gods and whom shall I now worship in
their stead?"

5 § VOODOOISM

Voodoo worshipers on the island of Haiti have never forgiven outside interpreters for insinuating that their religion is a mixture of sex and superstition. They have not forgotten that author W. B. Seabrook branded them in his book, *The Magic Island,* as a "blood-maddened, sex-maddened, god-maddened" people who pay their respects to a "hermaphroditic deity." They remember that Richard Loederer in *Voodoo Fire in Haiti* described their faith as "pure sexuality," and that Faustin Wirkus in *The White King of La Gonave* identified Voodoo as a worship centered around a black pope and black queens which flourishes in a series of sexual orgies. To these accusations, a ringing reply was voiced by Voodoo's only bonafide American initiate, Stanley Reser, who lived with the Haitian peasants for over thirty years. He retorted, "There is no more emphasis on sex in Voodoo than there is in any other religion and maybe not as much."

To get at the truth of the matter it is necessary to understand how and why this primitive faith was introduced into Haiti and to see what part it played in the black man's struggle.

58

The story begins on December 6, 1492, when an explorer's ship, the *Santa Maria,* sailed into an inland bay on a Caribbean isle. The young adventurer Christopher Columbus, planted the flag of Spain near what is now Cap Haitian and named the island *La Espanola.* The inhabitants at the time were a million brown-skinned Arawak Indians, proud and unacquainted with conquest, who abandoned their fishing villages and fled to the mountains rather than submit to the conquerors.

Spain lost no time in sending settlers to this first European settlement on the "American continent." Within fifty years the forty adventurous Spaniards whom Columbus had left on the island were joined by three thousand of their countrymen, enough to rob the Indians of their gold and to begin the building of an empire. Since the Arawaks preferred death to slavery, they were totally annihilated, and the Christian colonizers turned to Africa, to the dark and brooding jungles of Dahomey. Here they found superstitious black men, suckled on animistic beliefs, beating their drums and chanting their hymns to spirits called the *loa.* The Spaniards uprooted these illiterate aborigines from the only land they knew, herded them into ships, and brought them in chains to the brackish land they hoped to tame. Here the slaves were sold, beaten into submission, and killed when no longer useful to their masters. The Spaniards' wanton cruelty set a pattern which was followed by both French and English buccaneers who for two centuries fought to claim their countries' share of the coveted island.

The black man, caught between the incredible barbarism of these opposing forces, was the pawn in both triumph and defeat. The only comfort he could eke out of the misery inflicted upon him was his faith in the *loa*: the invisible, personalized spirits of gods and men whom he had worshiped in his African homeland. The *loa* were his guardian angels, his protectors, guides and friends. The *loa* sustained him when he labored in the insufferable mines, when he dragged the mahogany timbers beneath the blows of the whip, and when he hauled the crushing cargoes to build a white man's world. The *loa* were the "little gods" who represented the one great god, the Gran Mait, in a religion called by the French: *vaudou*.

It was the staccato beat of the Voodoo drums that filled the slave with messages of hope. Voodoo dances were a therapy. Voodoo chants and Voodoo fires and Voodoo rituals aroused in his tortured body a will to live. Voodoo, the composite of all instincts and emotions, was a release from the realities of life. It still is.

Today, the worship of the bewitching *loa* and the black and white magic of Voodooism can still be found in the Haitian hinterlands. The encircling hills around the cities resound only occasionally with the hypnotic beat of the drums and most of the "Voodoo services" near Port-au-Prince are staged for tourists, but back in the mountains and on the plains where visitors seldom go, the *hounforts* (Voodoo chapels) still stand and the *houngans* (Voodoo priests) still perpetuate their ecstatical rites.

A stranger, venturing into this isolated Voodooland, may, if he is sincere, be permitted to witness a service on a Saturday evening or on the special holy days which follow rather closely the Christian liturgical year. Days like Christmas, Epiphany, Easter are sacred to the Voodoo faith, a faith which has become a strange and curious mixture of Christianity, spiritualism, and animistic beliefs. But is it strange and curious?

On the contrary, the Voodoo of Haiti is a religious hybrid as surely as the patois, the language which the more than 2,000,-000 Haitians speak, is a concoction of African, French, Spanish, English, and coined phrases.

As the Voodoo priest greets you, you realize that he is a man chosen for his position because of his supernormal, psychic talent. He wears no priestly robes or vestments and, like the worshipers, is of peasant stock, a man who lives and works with the land. A group of men and women have gathered in the peristyle, the thatched-roofed building adjoining the crudely built *hounfort*. Three drummers bend over their paint-daubed drums in the shadows, straw hats pushed back on their heads, solemnly watching as a group of white clad *hounsi* (the *houn-*

gan's female assistants) place jars and burning candles around a center pole called the *pitou-mitan*.

Some say this pole represents a phallus and that the crude shaped altar encircling it is the yoni. You are informed by the priest that the *pitou-mitan* is sacred to Damballa, a mighty *loa* whose symbol is a serpent. When the early Christian colonizers heard of Damballa, they insisted that Voodoo was snake worship. They failed to see that Damballa represents the fertilizing phallus of creation. He was double-sexed, as all creative nature gods must be, and was originally called Damballa-Wedo. In time the female attribute became personified and was named Aido-Wedo.

Her sign was the circle or diadem. She was pictured with her royal consort, Damballa, in poses of conjugal love. Their home was everywhere—on earth, in the seas, and in the air—for the creative power is everywhere. Their castle was the rainbow.

As you fix your eyes on the center pole, visualizing that the serpent, Damballa, is coiled there, you are asked to recall that Damballa is also the source of all knowledge. Coiled forever in the Tree of Life, he tempts man to know himself. As a sign of immortality, he sheds his skin and reappears in a new body; as a symbol of the endlessness of time, he is depicted as a snake eating its tail. His devotees revere him so much they become his bridegroom or bride in special Voodoo ceremonies. In Africa, where he originated, men honored him by building snake houses beneath the tallest and most beautiful trees. In these "serpent chapels" they kept a living snake which they bore on a carpet of silk in religious processions, its writhing form encircled with a golden diadem representing the female Aida-Wedo.

When the black man, coerced into Christianity, heard the remarkable account of the serpent in the Garden of Eden, he imagined that the snake was Damballa. To him the Biblical account of the temptation was just another story of the "great god sex" and if the Christian did not understand the symbolism, the Voodooist did.

Now the drums start beating and the *houngan* steps authoritatively to the circular altar. He is rattling the *asson*, a small gourd covered with beads and snake vertebra and having a small bell attached. This is the symbol of the *houngan's* office, a kind of holy cha-cha and an emblem of the magical power that starts the service in a burst of drumfire and sends the *hounsi* into a swaying dance. On the altar the candles are burning. Above the entrance to the peristyle a lamp is lighted. In the semi-shadows the worshipers begin to murmur and sway to the intoxicating rhythm of the drums.

Then, at a motion from the priest rattling the *asson*, the drums begin a muffled beat and the *houngan* intones an invocation honoring the snake god Damballa. The litany mingles Christian creeds with Voodoo charms. Chants call upon Catholic saints and Voodoo *loa*. The *hounsi* form a semi-circle around the *pitou-mitan* and respond antiphonally to the priest's chant. Then *hounsi* and *houngan* make the sign of the cross.

Everything is a mixture of Christianity and animism and the early evangelizers can be held responsible for this amazing state of things. Ever since his first exposure to the Christian gospel, even while he listened and rattled his chains, the slave of Dahomey felt he understood the white man's religion. Why could not the white man understand his? Did not the Christian know that every divine phenomenon must be a universal phenomenon, that it could not be confined to any one place or to any one person? The Voodooist was convinced that what had happened in Biblical lands had also happened in African jungles, and could also happen in Haiti by reason of the fact that men take their *loa* with them no matter where they go or whether they go as masters or as slaves. If the Christian wished to believe that it was Jesus who walked on the water, well and good; the Voodooists knew it was actually Ague, their *loa* of the sea. And if the white priests insisted that it was the Virgin Mary who miraculously conceived, let them believe it; the black *houngan* knew that the virgin was actually the *loa* called Erzilie Freda, who knew the secret of bearing children without the intercourse with men.

You realize all this as you sit in the peristlye and as your mind throbs with the pulse of the everlasting drums. You can count it neither strange nor curious that the religiously-active mind of the black men satisfied itself with similarities. The pictures he has affixed above the Voodoo altars in his home are pictures of Christian saints Voodooized. St. Patrick, since he has snakes around his feet, is but another incarnation of Damballa. Abraham entertained not angels, but *loa*. When the dead rose with Jesus at the time of His resurrection, was not this an evidence that zombies are real? For zombies in Voodoo are supposed to be the living dead, those who have died and been resurrected by the mystical power of the *houngan* who works with God. Through the years the black man intertwined his Voodoo beads with the Catholic rosary, drank Voodoo rum on Saturday night in the *hounfort,* and sipped Christian communion wine on Sunday morning in the church. This was Voodoo.

You see it now. You hear it all around you. The *houngan* and *hounsi* are dancing an impassioned ritual, inviting the *loa* to possess their swaying forms. For an hour and more the tide of emotion surges on. It is a melange of excitement and then calm, whirling dances and then sombre liturgical chants. There are times when the dimly-lighted peristyle might be a Christian revival center with the drums substituting for animated gospel songs. There are periods when it could be a calypso cabaret with the performers reeling under the bewitching rhythm.

Worshipers continue to come into the peristyle, taking their places on the improvised benches or simply standing motionless in the shadows. In many outlying groves and plantations throughout the island, similar services are being enacted, for the drumbeats and the chants, and every other form of Voodoo magic flows in the veins of most Haitians, even those who have been proselytized from their native faith. They are often lured back to the peristyle to watch entranced, as you now watch, the deepening mystery of the worship.

The *houngan* has been handed a bowl of cornmeal which he raises to the four cardinal points of the compass in blessing.

Now he moves swiftly around the *pitou-mitan*, letting the corn-meal filter in a thin stream between forefinger and thumb as he deftly traces a mystical drawing on the dark earth. With fantastic skill, body bowed to the ground, he makes his unerringly swift strokes, leaps back to view his art, then plunges again into his inspired work. The earth is his blackboard and the corn-meal his chalk.

The drawing he makes is called a *veve* and its purpose is to invoke and honor the *loa*. *Veves* are of many configurations and constitute the esoteric art of the priestcraft. The one you see resembles a huge revolving wheel with serpents weaving in and out between the spokes. There are wheels within wheels with many interlacing lines. The *veve* honors Damballa, and as the drums sound their throated drone, the white clad *hounsi* suddenly whirl like dervishes, bending their supple bodies to kiss the *veve* and stooping low as if to caress the *houngan's* feet with their lips.

The magical spell of Voodoo is being spun on the subtle cord of religious emotions. The people around you begin to weave and sway. The drums become more ominous as the *houngan* finishes the *veve* and seizes his *asson*. You rise to your feet because *houngan* and *hounsi* are now leading the worshipers into the *hounfort* to an accompanying clamor that rises like a mighty charivari.

This is what the early colonizers tried to stamp out, condemning Voodoo as witchcraft. The skilled *houngans* insist, however, that it is an inspired ritual, reaching back to the old Eleusian mysteries and having a connection with the pythoness of the Greeks. As the oracle at Delphi sat engulfed in vapor and mist, so the *houngan*, inundated by the drone of the Voodoo drums, prophesies and works his spells. Voodoo followers fully expect their *houngans* to possess magical powers. If these powers are lacking, how is a priest different from any ordinary man? The supernatural was a touchstone by which the African slave measured the spiritual prowess of the Christian friars. And that is why, when the black man was told that the Christian priest, during the Mass, was possessed by the Holy Spirit, he drew another parallel, insisting this was the same phenomenon as when his *houngan* was possessed by the spirit of Damballa.

"Possession" takes place in the *hounfort*. It resembles the baptism of the Holy Spirit in a high-powered revival service. What began hours ago as a simple litany now hovers on the edge of a spiritual stampede. The drummers have entered the *hounfort* without missing a beat in their thunderous cacaphony. The *houngan* vigorously rattles his *asson* and the *hounsi* give themselves over to paroxysms that shake the *hounfort* walls where dangling lanterns sputter out their eerie yellow light. Only rarely do the dances suggest sexual exhibitionism. For the most part, the *hounsi* seem already to be in a trance-like state. The tremors which seize their relaxed and swaying bodies indicate that the electrifying *loa* are gaining control. It is not a sexual orgy. It is, Voodooists believe, the reciprocal flow of power between the unseen spirits and their devotees.

Possession comes like an electric shock of crushing voltage. It strikes a *hounsi* and causes her to leap higher and higher until someone grabs her writhing, struggling body and another catches hold of her hair and twists it until it is a rope that holds her motionless. Another one of the possessed may roll on the floor. Occasionally, when a particularly violent *loa* engages his willing victim, the possessed may catch hold of an overhanging timber or a rope and hang suspended until the strong hands of less inspired worshipers bring her down. Then she lies quivering upon the *hounfort* floor, miraculously spared from being crushed beneath the feet of the stomping dervishes of Damballa. The *houngan*, always in control of the service no matter how confused the scene, chants and rattles his *asson*, his sweat-smeared face ecstatic in the lantern light.

The early missionaries called this the "saturnalia of sex" and referred to the worshipers as "fat, black bucks." Only these are not fat, black bucks. They are the ordinarily quiet and industrious people of a "magic island" who customarily till the land, work the cane fields, pick the mangoes, and carry the commerce of the country on their heads. The active Voodoo participants are mostly women. They are all properly dressed. They wear headscarves and some have a small crucifix dangling on a chain around their necks. Some of the *hounsi* are young girls with the silken skin and sturdy bodies of the Haitian peasant. Mothers sit in the bleak recesses of the room clasping babies in their arms. Older children crowd around, their tiny bodies vibrating to the pulsebeat of the provocative drums. Men stand in the background like mahogany figures, stoically trying to belie the fact that belief in Voodoo still courses in their blood.

What is the good of all this? For one thing, Voodoo is what it has always been: an escape; an escape from reality into unreality—or is it the other way around? It is an impulse toward participation in a world that transcends intellectualism and which depends for its effect upon intuition and a feeling for the unknown. It is close to the ecstacy of sex while bearing the approval of the gods.

Voodoo is a key that opens the hidden doors of the mind. The Voodooist understands this when he sees the Pe, the altars of noted *houngans* and *mambos* (priestesses). On these primitive shrines are objects whose powers no Haitian would deny. Nor does anyone know what force lies latent in their use. Consider the polished stones called *pierre tonner* or thunder stones. These black apports, it is believed, drop out of space during electrical storms. The *houngan* is directed to them through the guidance of the *loa*. Rubbing the stones, he can send his thoughts through space working good or ill, blessing or cursing a person as he sees fit.

The *wanga* is another object to be feared. It is a shapless black "doll" sewn with feathers or human hair and stuffed with many things: ashes, graveyard dust, magic leaves, sulphur and salt. Let the *houngan* stick a pin into a *wanga* and a victim upon whom his mind is fixed can feel it, be he ever so far away. Death or life resides in the mind, according to Voodoo, and you do not stamp out this fact by your unwillingness to believe it. Denial is no escape. The only power against a *wanga* is a stronger *wanga,* just as the only power that can neutralize a thought is a stronger thought.

These truths are recorded in the altars found in the *houngans'* private chapels. Here are lithographs of the Christian saints, votive lights consisting of a bowl of sweet oil in which a pitch pine wick is floating, calabashes containing holy water, earthern patens, amphores, mortars with spices, sacramental wafers, eggs symbolizing fertility, ears of corn representative of procreation, *paquets* which are good luck charms, *assons, pottete* or pots with nail parings and wisps of body hair of the *hounsi,* banners, bottles of rum and liqueur, swords, sacramental candles, and other religious articles which comprise a laboratory for the transmission of psychic force.

Most of all, Voodoo is faith in the *loa,* who assure a person that he is never alone and that his link to the invisible, eternal world is still secure. No Voodooist will question the power of the *loa* which, as every Haitian knows, are divided into two major families: the Rada and the Petro *loa.* The first take their name from the Arada tribe of Dahomey and include such impressive spirits as Damballa-Wedo, Aida-Wedo, Erzilie Freda, Ague, Baron la Croix (spirit of the cemetery), Guede-nibo (spirit of the tombs), Legba (god of the crossroads), Oyizan (wife of Legba and spirit of the market places), Ogo-ferraille (spirit of warriors and magicians), and many more.

The Petro *loa* are the more malevolent of the two groups. Emerging from Africa and augmented by Haitian spirits, they include such euphonious spirits as Simbi Gallone (spirit of waterfalls and fountains), Mait Kalfu (spirit of charms and sorcery), Krabinay (spirit of demons), and others who have specific functions in the invisible world, as well as in the world of men. The *loa,* as we have seen, "ride" their victims during possession as a rider mounts his horse, and the *houngan* is able to recognize who the invisible riders are. He knows them by their characteristics, by the sounds and expressions emittted by the possessed, and by the manifestations exhibited during the hypnotic states.

Ogu, a Petro *loa*, inspires his victims to stick their hands into burning oil, but protects them from being harmed. Jean Baptiste-Trace is a *loa* who, when someone dies, shows the relatives where to stake out the dead one's grave. In south Haiti a *loa* called *Taureau trois granes*, a bull with three testicles, creates great disturbances whenever he invades a victim because he urges the possessed to rudely leap upon the nearest bystander. Often when the mighty Damballa overpowers a devotee, the person hisses like a snake, writhes on the ground, and demands what the god himself would demand: a white cock or an egg. The *loa* Ogoun insists on being worshiped with a red rooster, corn, plantains, and a bottle of rum. Guede Nibo can easily be recognized because he causes his possessed to bathe his wide-open eyes in pimento peppers. He dresses in black, smokes a big cigar, sings risque songs, and makes suggestive gestures as he walks. Often he will say, "Laugh with me, but don't make a fool of me. Laugh with me, but don't laugh at me."

In Africa the *loa* Legba was a phallic god and had his concubines just as gods in other lands had their temple virgins. The lovers of Legba, usually the *hounsi*, were frequently loaned to male worshipers during the ceremonies, and this was considered a great honor by both the men and the women involved.

A more subtle encounter with Legba or any other god is the "*loa* sleep" in which, it is believed, a *loa*, able to assume either male or female form, visits the slumbering worshiper for a nocturnal rendezvous. A priest may have many wives or no wife, he may have many loves or few, but he always has the virgin *loa*, Erzilie Freda. She is wealthy and beautiful, she can be voluptuous and seductive, her heart knows sadness and sorrow, but her soul is full of joy and compassion for all men. When a Voodooist marries, he thinks of Erzilie, for she is the example of perfect womanhood. Before a child is born, it is well to bring her an offering. It is good to have Erzilie as an unseen godmother. When Erzilie calls, a man will leave those he loves, however dearly, and follow her voice. On Erzilie's days, which are Tuesday and Thursday, the *houngan* goes to a private bedroom adjoining the *hounfort,* and feels the tender embrace of Erzilie's presence. She is his highest passion and delight, and her favorite sacrifice is a pair of white hens or white pigeons. To sleep with Erzilie is to realize that during the subconscious state the energizing spirit force is more vital and vivid than in one's waking hours.

Voodoo is steeped in this sort of psychism. The spirits are as real to the worshiper as is the *houngan* who is the "medium" or intermediary in inducing spirit manifestation. There is, for example, a service called *Retrait de l'esprit de l'eau,* the Return of the Spirits from beneath the Water. It is believed that the spirits of the dead can, with proper ritual and magical ceremonial, be imprisoned and preserved in a *govi* or sacred jar. In fact, immediately after the death of an *houngan* or a *mambo,* it is customary for associate priests to perform the obligatory service of *dessounin.* In a secret ceremony the deceased is stood upright against the *pitou-mitan* and after a prescribed ritual and the making of the proper *veve,* the *maitre tete* or personal *loa,* is invoked into a *govi.* This sacred jar is then carefully sealed and, it is believed, the spirit may be consulted in time of need.

During the ceremony of the *Retreat* the spirits not only of *houngans,* but of ordinary Voodooists are consulted. A canopy of cloth about six feet high and four feet square is constructed in view of the worshipers either inside or outside of the peristyle. The canopy, called a *card,* resembles a spiritualist's cabinet in which mediums are secluded during their entranced states. Inside this cabinet is a tub of water containing a concoction of liqueurs, cakes, and eggs, leaves of *mombin* and *lal-guinin,* upon the surface of which a *veve* has been reverently sketched.

The *hounsi,* each bearing a sacred *govi* on her head, circle the *card* to the accompaniment of the inevitable drums, and finally lie face down on the ground, each clasping her *govi* in her arms. They lie with bodies touching or with feet interlaced to create the "psychic current." Then they are covered with a sheet. As the *houngan* steps inside the *card,* taking his place near the tub of "holy water," he intones a lengthy litany in which the *hounsi* antiphonally join. After the family of heaven has been implored to release the *govi* spirits, the *houngan* requests his assistant, called *la place,* to hand him a *govi.* A *hounsi* extends a sacred jar from beneath the sheet and it is passed to the *houngan.*

After somberly presenting the *govi* to the four cardinal points, the priest immerses it in the holy fount. Now there is a babbling of water like a brook rushing over stones, then a brief instant of quiet, out of which a "spirit voice," usually deep and gasping, brings a message, calling the name of the worshiper for whom it is intended. It is believed that the departed soul not only speaks, but that it is liberated for a time from its "purgatory" through the efficacy of the ritual. As each *govi* is presented to the *houngan,* the spirit voice is conjured from beneath the water.

The Voodooist sees nothing incongruous in this possibility of contacting discarnate entities, for he is convinced there is no break in continuity between this world and the next. He has been taught that he carries within himself two souls or angels, a big soul and a related soul. Like the ancient Egyptian, he believes that the big soul hovers about the old haunts with which it was acquainted while in the physical body. The related soul goes to God, the *Gran Mait,* for judgment, and becomes a good or a bad angel, whichever it has merited. It may also become a wandering soul, an invisible *zombi,* unfitted temporarily for any abiding home. The psychical connection between the big soul and the related soul in this life continues after death, and it is understandable that the big soul may be confined in a sacred *govi,* quite willing and able to communicate with the living.

Christian missionaries past and present insist that this phase of Voodoo is either deliberate deception or the work of the devil. They are convinced that the same diabolical influence which energizes such "black magic" gave rise in an earlier day to sexual orgies and Voodoo cannibalism. Typical of the legends is the one related to the author by a religionist who said a friend once concealed himself in a clump of shrubbery and watched the *mambo* do a sex-inspired dance until the people were aroused. "Then the 'goat without horns' was brought out, a blonde white child apparently only a few months old. The *houngan* took the sacrificial knife, made two cuts into the breast, pulled out the heart and drained the blood into a gem-encrusted chalice. This was the sacrament. After it came the drums and the dances, following which each person leaped upon the most convenient of the opposite sex and satisfied the demand of the moment, until nude bodies scattered in the postures of their last exessess created a vision of hell worthy of Dante." Upon questioning, it was said that this orgy took place in Cuba some fifty years ago in the mountains near the border of the province of Oriente.

So rare are cases of such subhuman acts in Voodoo, that critics even today still resort to the one authentic case of "cannibalism in Haiti" reported long ago (December 5, 1886) in the New York *World*. "A small Negro boy was blessed in the name of the sacred serpent and was asked what he most desired in all the world. The little fellow replied, 'The one object above all which I most desire is the possession of a little virgin.' Hardly had he spoken when from the encurtained apartment came two women leading a Negro girl of four or five. . . ." The account then went on to say that these two children were "cut up, cooked, and eaten."

Members of the cult insisted this was not a "Voodoo ceremony" but a drunken debacle whose participants were quickly brought to trial by the Haitian government. Many Christians, however, believe that this was by no means an isolated case. A Jesuit spokesman, Fr. Joseph J. Williams, said in 1930, "Despite the loud protests of the friends of Haiti it is hard to believe that the practice (cannabalism) is entirely extinct. It would, of course, be a grave mistake to suppose that it is a regular practice or connived at by the present authorities. Still it would be even more surprising if the sexual excitement of their various dances with the concomitant excessive use of stimulants, did not at times break down the nervous systems of individuals here and there, and induce a kind of paranoia with a recrudescence of all that is vilest and most degraded in fallen nature."

What the early evangelizers failed to see was that in the groping mind of the superstitious African slave, the Christian Eucharist was itself construed as a dimly-veiled cannibalistic ritual in which the body and blood of a victim were vicariously consumed. It was difficult for the black man to grasp the symbolical spiritual meaning even after he had embraced the Christian faith. In fact, "conversion" to any religion is quite inconceivable to the Voodooist. He belongs to his native faith by nature of birth and by the destiny which has placed him within the sound of Voodoo drums and the sight of Voodoo worshipers. That there should be more than one *Gran Mait* is beyond his conception, and that there are numerous spirits or *loa* representing the attributes of this one and only God is readily accepted.

The most strange and curious feature about this religion of Damballa and Legba and all the other *loa,* is that it is *not* steeped in sex and that it is, instead, still coexistent with the customs and traditions of a people who for four hundred years have sought to free themselves—or be freed—from slavery, poverty, illiteracy, oppression and disease. Voodoo is the spiritual avenue by which the Haitian peasant has sought this liberation, for he is by nature carefree, fatalistic, and christened of the gods. Deep in his heart he has little capacity for greed or pettiness. He is easily bewitched by the drums, quickly enchanted by any evidence of supernormal powers, and responsive to every ritual that arouses his passion.

In this connection, one of the most significant Voodoo ceremonies has to do with the glorification of motherhood, a service that can be observed in almost any Voodoo peristyle or *hounfort* on Christmas Eve. At these times Legba, the opener-of-the-gate and the shower-of-the-way is saluted and a chant is introduced invoking the Virgin and the Saints. The customary drummers, the ritualistic dances of the *hounsi,* and the mesmerism of the *houngan* are all part of the service, but the climax toward which the ritual leads is the baptism of recently born infants whose mothers have brought them to the *hounfort* to have them blessed and made immune against disease for the coming year.

Occasionally, for this ceremony, a clumsy, barrel-like object called a *pie-lon* is rolled into the room. It resembles a Voodoo drum upside down, and the *houngan* blesses it by sprinkling it with rum inside and out and gracing it with several rattles of the *asson*. Around this crude representation of the "cosmic womb" the ritual revolves and at the most climactic moments the *hounsi* throw themselves upon it or, caught in spasms of emotion, stick their heads into it as if wishing to be devoured.

Handfuls of herbs, leaves, aromatic roots and medicinal grasses are tossed into the *pie-lon*, after which two muscular young men seize wooden poles some six feet long and begin a frantic pounding of the contents. The *pie-lon* becomes the mortar, the solid poles, called *mash pie-lon*, are the pestles. The floor shakes beneath the rhythmic thud of their relentless churning. All is synchronized with the drumbeats and the dance, and the room seems suddenly in motion. At a time like this it is not unusual for the *houngan* to lie on the floor and command that the burdensome *pie-lon* be placed on his abdomen. Once underneath it, he cushions the shocks of the *mash pie-lon* with his body while the men continue driving the poles to the terrifying clamor of the drums.

The *hounsi* take this willing torture as their cue. They now invite and receive "possession" until the ritual has been generated into a Voodoo holocaust. All of which is quite enough to persuade interpreters that the intention is to unleash primitive emotions under the guise of religion. It is, however, a good deal more than that. For a little while the *houngan* is the symbol of the Earth Mother, and the *hounsi* are supposed to represent the cosmic dance.

Promptly at midnight the salvo of the drums signal the begining of the sequence toward which all that has transpired is merely prologue. The *houngan's* helpers have set a wooden tub on a bench and filled it with water. The mashed contents of the *pie-lon* are scooped out and placed into the tub where it is thoroughly mixed by the busy hands of the *hounsi*. The mood and tempo of the scene have changed from the pandemonium of possession and the syncopated tangle of the drums to the sombre quiet of reflective worship. The *hounsi* who, a short time ago, were the wildly rotating puppets of the *loa*, now reverently form a semi-circle while the *houngan* makes the inevitable *veve* upon the greenish water in the tub.

This done, the mothers make their way to where the *houngan* stands. Bearing in their arms their recently born infants, they come to offer them for baptism on this holy night. They are dedicating their children to the *Gran Infant*, Jesus, and to the Voodoo gods whoever they might be. As each tiny naked form is offered to the *houngan*, he lifts it high in presentation to the four cardinal points. Then with equal solemnity, he dips each infant into the tub. The stolid mothers smile as though Voodoo were all tenderness and as if the *Gran Mait* is as fatherly as the God of Christendom. Once more, in their minds, both gods are one.

Christian leaders in Haiti are quite convinced that the sect is dying out, although they admit that still today there are "Christian Voodooists" who worship both in church and *hounfort*, who sing both Voodoo songs and Christian hymns, and who offer their children for baptism both to Christian clerics and the *houngans* of a primitive faith. But, they insist, that as the black man of Haiti becomes more educated, the superstitious lore of the serpent religion will completely disappear.

Though this may be their hopeful wish, and though the government has officially outlawed Voodoo while still countenancing Voodoo services, a famous *houngan*, Ti Cousin, speaking for his fraternity, had this to say, "It does not follow that the most intelligent person is best qualified for spiritual experience. Whatever limits a man's nature retards him spiritually. If learning binds man to that which is physical, learning is bad. If ignorance binds him, ignorance is bad. Voodoo is a process to loose man and lift him. Voodoo is an expression of interest in everything from earth to eternity. If you say it is primitive, if it appears to you that it is crude and emphasizes the *gran mystere* of sex, all I can say is that the soul that moves in the consciousness of the universe has its own standards."

This is the point of view which many secretly hold who follow Voodoo in Haiti, in Africa, or wherever the *loa* may lead.

6 § SEX AND MODERN RELIGION

IF THE GODS OF FERTILITY—Baal, Osiris, Shiva, Legba—have been watching us, as we have been watching them—they may be wondering who is the more strange or curious, they or we. Like many modern observers, they must realize it is still a very moot question just where religion stands on the matter of sex and how it intends to deal with the new problems which are continually arising to challenge its old views.

The problems are couched in sensational phrases: *exploding population*—what will the church do about birth control and planned parenthood; *miscegnation*—should Negroes and whites marry; *compulsive morality*—can people be coerced into being good; *religion of the libido*—is psycho-analysis the new way to "salvation;" *crimes of passion*—does religion have a responsibility beyond the parish level; *our modern mores*—should the churches be concerned with the report of the Institute of Sex Research that one of two American husbands has sex relations outside of his marriage, that one of four American wives commits adultery, and that one of ten American women is pregnant before she marries? What will Christianity do with these problems now that the cult of sex, driven out of religion by religion, has flourished quite apart from any ecclesiastical jurisdiction?

Recognizing their dilemma, the churches of Christendom have reacted in a variety of ways. Catholicism has barred the teaching of sex hygiene in its schools on the basis that such information destroys modesty and a sense of shame, both of which are said to be natural guardians of chastity. Liberal Protestantism has called in specialists from highly secular camps: Sigmund Freud, Edvard Westermarck, Havelock Ellis, Bertrand Russell, Alfred Kinsey. Fundamental Protestantism has emphatically redefined sex as sin and has condemned the sex emphasis of our time as a sign of spiritual decay. The Christian faith may have routed Dionysus; it may be shaming Shiva and crowding out Legba, but what can it do about the gods of sex on Main Street?

Most churchmen contend that in no other religion has the sanctity of sex been so clearly defined and so sincerely interpreted as it has in Christianity. In no other religious culture has the individual conscience and the moral sense of the community become more discriminating. Christianity has idealized love as the highest spiritual expression and has elevated marriage to the status of a sacrament. In the best of primitive religions only the germinal principles of this kind of morality existed. Despite this emphasis on morality, the Christian church stands like an island within a growing sea of secularism, seeming at times almost to be inundated by the rising tide.

There are those who from the watchtowers of their faith are taking a long, reflective look at the path over which Christianity has come. They want to know where the church has failed. Is it possible that the old fertility religions had emphasized sex too much and Christianity has stressed the nature of its importance too little? Has the churches' aversion to sex merely perverted and activated the subject and given the secular, materialistic world a chance to exploit it? Has the idea grown that since Christianity has implied that sex is sinful, sex is now beyond the jurisdiction of any moral code? Lurking in the shadows of

Christian history are interesting telltale episodes which are now being re-examined.

First there was the matter of Christian judgment on sex itself. In the very earliest days of Christendom, even before the church was fully formed, the elders of the faith counseled together to decide what ought to be done with this subject. "There are many ways in which sex can be interpreted," they seemed to say. "It can take the form of love or sin, of sacred passion or lust, of a gift of God or a snare of the devil. Now that we have so recently conquered the pagan religions, what shall our advice to our people be? How far can we trust them with so potent and explosive a force?"

The Old Testament gave them good cause for wonder and concern. Overburdened with eye-witness accounts, Biblical literature recorded sexual perversions for all who had access to the written Word. Judges 19 reported the story of a householder who turned his concubine over to a mob of young men of Gibeath who "so abused her all night" that in the morning she lay dying on her master's threshold. When the householder saw her there, he took a knife and, "laying hold on her, divided her, together with her bones, into twelve pieces, and sent her into all the coasts of Israel. And it was so that all that saw it said, there was no such deed done nor seen from the day that the children of Israel came up out of the land of Egypt unto this day. Consider of it, take advice, and speak your minds."

Genesis 19 gave the account of Lot who offered his daughters as whores to the men of Sodom. Second Samuel 2 recounted the adultery of David and Bathsheba, the wife of Uriah; and II Samuel 13 chronicled the lust of Ammon who forcibly seduced his sister Tamar and then hated her with a "hatred greater than the love wherewith he had loved her." Genesis 38 unashamedly described the trespass of Onan who "spilled his seed upon the ground" in penalty for which God struck him dead. When Michal, the daughter of Saul, reprimanded David for dancing naked before the ark, God was so displeased with her, He punished her with barrenness until the day of her death.

(II Samuel 6:20-23). Who was to say what it all meant? Jehovah's will was not always clear.

Rightly perplexed, the fathers of the faith reviewed the Old Testamental record, text by text, and found it teeming with sodomy, lust, adultery, and perverted love among the children of men. With new concern they read again the canticles a poet of Israel once sang,

> My beloved spake and said unto me,
> Rise up, my love, my fair one, and come away.
> For, lo, the winter is past, the rain is over and gone;
>
> The flowers appear on the earth;
> The time of the singing of birds is come,
> And the voice of the turtle is heard in the land.

Beautiful it may have been, but it was too Baalistic. It could only increase the flames of sensuality which the newborn faith, Christianity, sought to check. People were already justifying their actions by a dangerous rationalization, "Unto the pure all things are pure." In opposition to this, the fathers recalled Jesus' unequivocal pronouncement, "He who looketh upon a woman with lust hath committed adultery already with her in his heart." And thus the fathers of the faith concluded that an emphasis on words like these was the better part of wisdom.

Whether or not the early church deliberately planned it so, the phrase about looking upon a woman with lust was seared into the minds of men. Out of this emphasis emerged the image of an intolerant Christ, a Prophet who, born without sin, condemned in others a passion He had never felt. And with this unyielding approach began the first real estrangement between the institutionalized Christ and mortal men. No longer was Jesus recognized as a man of peculiar tenderness, of sensitive understanding, and of divine capacity for tolerance and love. Gone was the gentle Galilean who, hating sin, had dined with sinners, had forgiven a prostitute, and had pardoned a woman taken in adultery. He had now become instead a judge to be feared and a moralist to be avoided, a preacher who uncompromisingly proclaimed, "If thine eye offend thee by bringing lust into your heart, pluck it out!"

The church-at-large made little attempt to set the record straight. In fact, it proceeded even further in its unremitting attitude toward sex. For nineteen hundred years it impressed upon its followers the concept that men are conceived and born in sin. The text upon which this ominous declaration was based was penned by a Psalmist in a moment of despair when the weary wasteland of the world enshrouded him. With aching heart, he moaned, "Behold I was shapen in iniquity and in sin did my mother conceive me!" It was a lonely man's lament, but the churches took it up and made it a preferred tenet in their commentary on the fate of man. The all-engulfing power of the words hung over Christendom like a choking vapor. A strange and curious emphasis was placed upon this text. Hymns intoned the plight of every child born into the world, sermons deplored man's lost estate, and rituals were prescribed to rid men, if possible, of inborn sin, a sin interrelated with Adam's fall—and sex.

The inter-relation was never clear. Apologists said that although God had commanded the progenitors of the human race to be fruitful and multiply, they sinned because they made sex pleasurable. Theologians, casting a backward glance toward Baal, concluded that love in the garden had become lust. Others insisted that God was jealous of earth's first parents because they loved each other more than they loved Him. Purists defined original sin as a sin of pride, as the transgression of a divine mandate, or as an act of concupiscence.

Whatever inborn sin may have meant to Biblical scholars or the proponents of the faith, to the average Christian the "forbidden fruit" was synonymous with sex, and immorality was linked to the symbol of the apple and the snake. Man's conflict resolved itself into a struggle between his divine nature, at times dimly recognized, and his lower, physical self, the needs and cravings of which were all too conspicuously felt. How to reconcile the two was the problem. Ever in the background was the slimy serpent sex and it became fixed in man's mind that every evil was somehow derived from this primary impulse. Pleasure and sin were always inter-related, and sex, as such, was far too pleasurable to be divine.

Back along religion's path lingered another concept which many Christians had uncritically accepted. Through centuries of spiritual monitoring the church implied that God's admonition to Eve was a sinister and universal warning to every expectant mother, "I will greatly multiply thy sorrow and thy conception; in sorrow shalt thou bring forth children." (Genesis 3:16.) Whether it was so intended or not, the ominous promise became an unflinching part of doctrine. In the minds of millions of Christians the conviction persisted that the pain accompanying childbirth was mysteriously involved with the nature of God's wrath. Was this in itself a pagan point of view which had stealthily found its way into the Christian frame of reference?

One thing is true. When the first Christian missionaries took the gospel into primitive societies, they found "the heathen" possessed by the same belief that some divine power needed to be appeased through the use of rituals, charms, and rites to induce a painless delivery. The Burmese untied all knots, opened all doors, and loosened all garments to make the birth pangs less agonizing; the Indonesian placed a flower, the Rose of Jericho, in the maternity room, believing that as it opened the child would more easily be born; the husband among the Australian aborigines walked back and forth some distance from where the mother lay, in the belief that he could induce the unborn child to be born quickly and easily by following him. Christians resorted to prayer. They devised all sorts of divine petitions to take away the curse of suffering, and there were many who believed that since God had ordained the travail and the pain, He must look with displeasure upon childbearing itself.

Had not the Apostle Paul implied that marriage lowered a man a good fraction in the scale of godliness? He told the Christians at Corinth, "I say to the unmarried and widows, it is good for them if they abide even as I (celibate). But if they cannot contain, let them marry; for it is better to marry than to burn." (I Corinthians 7:8, 9.)

True, he may have been engaged in spiritual polemics when he said this as he was when he spoke of men becoming eunuchs for the Lord's sake, but the conviction persisted that the most exalted state of sanctity was celibacy, and the most acceptable vocation in the sight of God was the sublimation of sexuality in a religious vocation. Such was the true "imitation of Christ." In the Book of Revelation, St. John added his testimony to the case when he described the choicest corner of heaven as being inhabited by those who "are not defiled with women, for they are virgins. These follow the Lamb whithersoever He goeth. These were purchased from among men . . . they are without spot before the throne of God." (Revelation 14:4, 5.)

So the repugnance to sex grew. So hypocrisy about sex increased, and a sense of fear and frustration became intimately involved with the sexual act. It often caused men to believe themselves guilty of crimes which they had not actually committed. Growing in the mind of nearly every Christian was the belief that sex was sin. No doubt the churches were sincere. It was the past they feared. It was Baal, Osiris, Shiva, Legba who haunted them.

In order to define its position, the church laid down certain regulatory acts. Roman Catholicism made clerical celibacy an obligatory law of the church, officially introduced in the 4th century with the insistence that the practice is not contrary to human nature and that it is highly acceptable in the sight of God. Eastern churches were less strict. Although celibacy was advocated, it was not strenuously enforced and existed more in principle than in practice. Eastern priests who were married before their ordination continued to live with their wives, and Nestorians allowed priests to marry after they had been ordained.

Sects among the Eastern Church were, however, rabidly inclined toward glorifying virginity. During the 17th and 18th centuries, Russia was swept by dissident groups called Chlists, who staged wild dances and demonstrations around celibate leaders designated as "Christs" and "Virgin Marys," who remained passively seated as the dancers whirled around them. Paradoxically, these ceremonies, designed to honor chastity, only aroused sexual passion among the worshipers and ended in orgies reminiscent of the Bacchanalia. There was also a Russian society known as the *Castrati*, consisting of men who had mutilated themselves in the belief there could be no higher expression of devotion than to interpret literally Paul's injunction about becoming enunchs for the Lord's sake.

As for the non-Catholic groups, denominations like the Anabaptists, the Moravian Brethren, and other pre-Reformation cults and sects, had views on sex which were extremely moral. In fact, they considered themselves the guardians of morality and realized that problems of sex involved the disciplines of self restraint and prudence. Marriage was the divine ceremony which sanctioned sexual relations, and it is safe to say that these independent movements believed that the sexual act had other aims than reproduction. They were of the opinion that an enduring love is the animating principle of marriage and that sexual attraction could play its part without outraging the "divine life." Idealistically, they regarded the love act as one to inspire and give passion, while yet retaining a purity of morals and an emphasis upon the rich development of human life.

The celibate life was openly rejected by Martin Luther. The reformer married an ex-nun, Katherine von Bora, and sympathetic interpreters have sought to show that the event re-instated marriage to its rightful place in the institutionalized church. Celibate clerics did not agree, however, at the time, and their attitude has changed little since the 16th century. Protestant ministers, on the other hand, are quite convinced that the "natural and honest" wedded state represents the kind of permanent values to which the Christian life should be committed, and that the parsonage or manse should provide an example for the Christian home.

Yet despite the high walls of sanctification—or taboo—which

each Christian group built around its sexual ethic, the ancient pagan gods consistently broke through. They crashed the gates of celibate-minded-monasteries and parsonages alike. Reports of illicit sexual encounters shocked the outside world, and it became apparent that neither nuns nor priests nor ministers were spared the passion which once had given homage to the ancient gods of sex. Baal, Osiris, Shiva, and Legba were successful in perpetuating their presence in half-disguised Christian symbols, like the Alpha and Omega, the *Crux Ansata*, the *vesica piscis*, the lotus blossoms, the lilies, the fleur-de-lys, and the "womenly garments" worn by ministers and priests. Or is the relationship carried too far, for is there any object which, with a little imagination, cannot be likened to a sex symbol? Or is there any religious group which has ever been spared the scandal of unmitigated sex?

Consider the march of faith across the American frontier. The revival hysteria which was bent on saving sinners created a goodly crop of new sinners along the way, particularly during the "Great Awakening" of the mid-18th century and the "Great Revivals" of the first half of the 19th century. The theme of these evangelistic extravaganzas which shook the country from New England to Kentucky was fear: fear of judgment, fear of God's wrath, fear of hell. Powerful preachers like Increase Mather, Jonathan Edwards, George Whitfield, James Davenport, and James McCready whipped the people into such emotional frenzies that Baal himself would have been pleased with the results. Granted that this religion of the pastures and the plains was the forerunner of the constructive expansion of Protestantism, it, nonetheless, left in its wake an emotionalized religion which still affects many faiths today.

The outdoor meetings were frequently staged under the stimulating light of the full moon. Often they were conducted on a round-the-clock basis continuing through many days and nights. They were the sporting events of their time and thousands of people came to spend a weekend or longer on the camp grounds, sleeping in their wagons, in improvised tents, or on the open ground.

A plank platform was built to hold the stentorian exhorters, the gospel singers, and the ranters of the Lord. Around this rostrum, far as eye could see, the worshipers stood or knelt together, or reclined on heaps of straw while the evangelists spun their magic. From low-murmured invocations to the mighty thunder of prophetic cries, the exhorters called down Jehovah's wrath and glory. They urged and ordered the erring saints and the penitent sinners to board the "glory train." To reach the destination, the holy ghost baptism, was the ultimate goal of the evangelistic episodes. When the converted were possessed by this religious rapture, they were as fanatical as Voodooists. People sang and wept and "spoke in tongues" and danced and rolled until the camp grounds trembled beneath the stomping of the holiness-baptized-children-of-God. Like an epidemic, the baptism ran through the crowds, sending ordinarily reserved men and women into a satyr-like spell. Several jerked so violently they snapped their necks and died. Others lay in a state of shock while the leaping, shouting, hand-clapping, anointed-of-the-Lord danced over them.

Conservative theologians, viewing this from afar, complained that the revivals were more nearly the work of the devil than the doings of the Lord. Observers, too worldly or too strong-willed to be caught up in the experience, described the affairs as sexual orgies and avowed that "more souls are made in these revivals than are saved." Even the hymns became enchanting parodies:

> Come hungry, come thirsty, come ragged, come bare,
> Come filthy, come lousy, come just as you are!

Thoughtful students of religion saw a similarity between the revival grounds and the trysting groves of Baal. The communion services and the love feasts which were part of the Sunday festivities were sacred for many, to be sure, but they also aroused others to the emotion of fertility rites. As for the testimonies of the saved, these frequently deteriorated into boasts about the sins which the convert had engaged in during most of his life. He was now reliving them to the pious delight of his enraptured audience. Even some of the ranters seemed to gratify their sexual desires by damning sex, and satisfied their frustrated longing for rum and tobacco by roundly condemning their use.

Some said it was revolt against Puritanism, while others insisted it was a defense of it. The early Puritans had put sexual promiscuity high on their list of divine transgressions. Those who broke the Seventh Commandment, (Thou shalt not commit adultery), were the most serious offenders, and the penalties they received were sharpened by threats of ostracism from the household of faith. Yet even among the censorious Puritans, sex knew no season. Certain elders decided it was God's will to condemn the entire subject, and it was considered the better part of modesty to avoid it as though it did not actually exist.

Sexual revolt persisted, however, in many forms among God's people as, for example, the early 19th century experiment in selective mating conducted under the label of Perfectionism. Inaugurated by a Dartmouth College graduate, a Congregationalist named John Humphrey Noyes, this was one of America's most classical examples of a revolt against prudery in the church. In 1848 Noyes, a Vermont-born Biblical scholar, believed the time had come for someone to set Christianity straight on the relation of the sexes. The church-at-large, he declared, had been altogether too unrealistic in its approach to this subject and too timid in its treatment. Himself a highly moral man, Pastor Noyes let it be known that he was inviting Christians to join him in a life of perfection, or near-perfection, in which the subject of sex could be openly discussed and in which mature men and women could engage in "scientific propagation."

In an essay on the subject, Noyes presented the thesis that the attachment of two people in "selfish love," that is, the desire to possess each other and to build a wall of exclusiveness around each other is as sinful as not loving at all. "Exclusive attachment is a form of idolatry," he said, and some three hundred men and women agreed with him sufficiently to embark on a communal venture at Oneida, New York. They represented Protestants exclusively, although Catholics and non-Christians were not barred. Agriculture and a printing establishment sustained them, and the manufacture of silverware, known as *Community Plate,* gave them a reputation for craftsmanship which has continued until today. They referred to their colony as a church of the apostolic tradition, in which perfectionism meant the immediate and total cessation of sin.

But the sin, as far as the church-at-large was concerned, was inherent in the Oneida marital adventure from the very start. The basis of the Noyes' experiment was that within the limits of the community membership there was to be freedom of co-habitation based upon consent. If any man or woman, having affection for another, could gain that person's approval through the counsel of a third person, they were permitted to become partners in the "planned mating program."

"We make an attempt," said Noyes, "to produce the usual number of offspring to which people in the middle classes are able to afford judicious moral and spiritual care, with the advantage of a liberal education. Engaged in this attempt are men and women who have been selected from among those who have most thoroughly practiced our social theory."

Opposition from the institutionalized churches, dissension from within, and the gradual waning of religious fervor among the participants, brought the Oneida experiment to a sombre close in 1880. After a thirty-two year period of planned parenthood, said by many to have been a hundred years ahead of its time and producing a community of exceedingly moral and intelligent progeny, Perfectionism died almost simultaneously with the death of its founder.

It was a transitional movement, a link between the inhibited thinking of the past and the free and modern thinking on the part of those who were more concerned with the question, "What does reason dictate?" than with, "What does the Bible say?" Not that J. H. Noyes and his spiritual demographers were directly responsible for trends that developed, for relatively few people took his bold Oneida experiment seriously; he was, however, the reflection of those who brush aside, for a time, conventional acceptance of tradition and re-examine age-old beliefs in the light of current spiritual and social environment.

Noyes once said he wished only to alert the churches to the need for bringing religion to bear upon life's most essential concerns which he enumerated as sex, birth, and demography. There are modern critics who hold the same wish. They say that the church all too frequently avoids these knotty problems or turns them over to secular authorities with the excuse that, "Sex is outside our province. See what you can do about the fact that illegitimacy has increased 133 percent in the past two decades, that venereal diseases are striking 200,000 new victims every year, and that there are currently 220,000 illegitimate births annually in the United States."

The secular press has taken over where the churches have been silent and is trying to educate the public by way of such sensational titles as: *Late Blooming Females; How To Be Happy With Sex; Books, Beds, and Bromides; Help Cupid Shoot Straight; Susan McViddy Finds Out What She's Been Missing!* The consensus seems to be that the Bible's teaching on sex must now be filtered through popular publications and true confessions, and that the public should be assured it need have no fear that God is annoyed with this commercialized approach. After all, what thinking modern person would dare say that the Bible is infallible, and where is the theologian who today would take the Scriptures literally? Biblical students have found its texts filled with meanings within meanings, and churches have discovered disclaimers upon disclaimers. Hence, secular analysts advise the public, "Do not worry. The strange and curious process of time is distilling Scripture's truest meaning."

Oddly enough there is no essential quarrel between religion and the world on this point. The warning in Matthew 5:28,29, for example, which speaks about a man committing adultery in his heart if he looks upon a woman with lust and which stipu-

lates that an offending eye should be plucked out, is now merely
an axiom and not a divine command. Philosophically it means
that the world of thought should be as real and hallowed as the
world of deeds. Since few Christians feel they can ever reach
absolute perfection, they have adjusted Christ's injunctions to
fit their disciplines. This happy rationalization has become an
accepted practice in western Christianity. And since neither the
churches nor the ongoing translations of the Bible are in agreement, who is to play the role of infallible judge?

In the King James version of the Bible, for example, we read,
"But if they cannot contain, let them marry; for it is better to
marry than to burn." This text, in which "burn" was construed
as "burning in hell," has now been mellowed in the Revised
Standard Version to read, "But if they cannot exercise self-control, they should marry. For it is better to marry than to be
aflame with passion." Every new Biblical translation comes up
with the startling discovery that the Lord is more contemporary
and less condemnatory than previous translators ever suspected.

All of which, it is said, is a good and healthy trend. "Neither
do I condemn thee," has certainly become a truer modern image
of the Christ than the frightening, "Thou shalt not!"

Many other "misconceptions" are also passing. The insistence
that childbirth must be accompanied by travail and pain has
been solidly refuted, not only by medical science but by a new
generation of ambitious young mothers. The ghostly God of
vengeance, who demanded recompense for the sin of Eve from
every mother everywhere, is dematerializing in the light of modern thought. The miracle of birth is sacrosanct these days and
has been romanticized in theatres and boldly televised into
homes. The characteristically modern claim that motherhood re-
juvenates the face and figure has also forced religion to embar-
rassingly relinquish another ancient "truth."

The Psalmist's insistence that man is conceived and born in
sin is not yet gone, but it is going. It is being crowded out of
traditional Protestantism by contemporary religious movements
which have vigorously shaken off the implication that the bio-

logical process is evil, that God abhors the procreative act, that sex is sinful, or that the Psalmist had modern man in mind when he voiced his lamentation three thousand years ago.

The irony of the situation is that the secular approach to sex is becoming the prophetic voice to which the churches, generally, are adjusting their thinking. Has religion become a listening post, a monitor, rather than the spokesman in this field? Is it true, as some contend, that in another fifty years our altars will be completely secularized? Or are we finally coming out from behind our facade of prudery and make-believe?

It is being whispered that Christianity can never challenge or absorb the total life of man until it admits that the mystery of life is the supreme mystery, that moral standards must be developed which will sanctify sex behavior, and that true religion began when the seed of spirit, sown in the womb of matter, brought forth, by an immaculate conception, the children of God. Remove from the Christian church, they say, all emblems and symbolisms and references to sex, and nothing is left. Advise people clearly and honestly how inherent sex is in worship, and man will once more be drawn to the 220,000 half-filled churches across America.

All of which must surely be causing the gods of fertility—Baal, Osiris, Shiva, Legba—to wonder what will happen next.

PART

TWO

 ────────────────────────────

THE

CONSCIENCE

CULTS

7 § THE CONSCIENCE CULTS

SOMETHING WITHIN MAN is a monitor, a thing called conscience. It rings a bell when things are well; it sounds a gong when things are wrong.

Where is it located? When did it first appear? No one knows. All we know is that most of us have a sense of obligation to do or to be that which is just and good, and when we fail we suffer with a sense of incompleteness or of guilt.

In ancient faiths, man directed his conscience toward pleasing or appeasing the gods. His actions were right when they produced the desired results. This was the way of the people. Then came a time when it was impressed upon man that his actions were right only when they were good. This was the way of the priests. Then came the gospel which insisted that man's goodness is never good enough. This was the way of the saints.

These three levels of consciousness still persist and each man still lives according to the light of his own understanding. One thing, however, can be said of every stage: when man became conscious of conscience, he searched for a means of appeasement, and in that moment a form of religion was born.

How much of conscience is innate and how much of it has been incorporated into man's thinking remains a riddle. Some metaphysicians contend that man's seat of awareness of what is right and what is wrong is located in that elusive instrument of knowingness, the pineal gland, which may be the mysterious "third eye," a remnant of an ancestoral sense-organ which once provided man with divine insight. This pineal gland which is the home of conscience is deteriorating, they insist, and therefore it is easy to see why men's consciences are on the wane, and why it is no longer safe to say, "Let your conscience be your guide!"

Certain religionists, on the other hand, believe that conscience was first awakened in Eden and that it has never slumbered since. And there are other theories. The intuitionalist explains this oracle of right and wrong as a perceptual agent; the social scientist sees it as the expression of environmental pressures; the empiricist calls it the voice of experience; the philosopher says it is the application of intellectual judgment; the psychologist finds it a process emerging out of the maturing of life's motives.

Still others wonder whether conscience was ignited by law by a Haamurabi or a Moses, or by an ethic by way of a Zoroaster or an Aknhton, or did it evolve out of a quest such as that made by a Buddha or a Pythagoras? Or did it all begin with the Testament of the Twelve Patriarchs who in 100 b.c. held up to the startled eyes of men the Seven Deadly Sins: fornication, gluttony, strife, vainglory, pride, deceit, injustice?

When Christianity further sensitized conscience by adding sins more grievous than even the seven deadly ones: murder, suicide, and particularly the unpardonable offense against the Holy Ghost, man's only hope lay in the gift of grace and the assurance of God's everlasting mercy in His dealings with the children of men.

Upon the razor-like edge between visions of purgatory and paradise, man groped his way with but the beclouded light of conscience to guide him. With rites and rituals, forms and phrases, manuals and magic, he fearfully sought to maintain his straight and narrow way. But as time went on, the deadly sins became less deadly and a line was drawn—so fine it became invisible—between sins that kill the spirit and sins that destroy the flesh.

Through the pain and travail of wanting to do what was right, but often not knowing what was right to do, man's conscience became a heavy load. It blessed and cursed him, inflicted peace and punishment, drove him to joy and grief, and caused him to rely more and more upon those who claimed they had the skills of faith and the power of mind to know what God commended and what God condemned.

While there were persons with amazingly flexible or easy consciences, consciences whose slate could be wiped clean with one stroke of an ecclesiastical rite, there were others whose consciences allowed them no rest until they took a more drastic, personalized approach. Absolution, restitution, or other assurance of spiritual restoration were not enough for these people. They believed that a clear conscience could result only from an extreme commitment and some inordinate devotion, even though these meant the scorn and ridicule of church and state.

They were willing to pledge themselves to this uncommon way of life in order to appease the monitor and keep the bell a-ringing. We may dismiss them as strange and curious people, but even the best or worst of us often glance their way a bit wistfully, wondering if, perhaps, their consciences are clearer than our own.

8 § THE PENITENTES

THE FINAL REMNANT of those who practiced the old world forms of penance is slowly passing from the American scene. Here in the new world where religious martyrs are few and where God is strictly a Servitor to man, the Penitentes of New Mexico are revising their primitive rituals and will soon be little more than a legend.

In the back country of the Sangre de Cristo (Blood of Christ) mountains during the forty days of Lent, you may still occasionally hear the eerie piping of the *pito* (flute), the wailing chant of a marching procession, or the clatter of a *metraca* (wooden rattle). It is even possible that you may catch the sound of savage whips as they slash the crisp night air and land with a stinging thud upon a half-nude body. But for the most part, a guilty conscience among the Mexican-American Brothers Penitent is now assuaged by less barbaric practices.

In the olden days, the Penitentes adhered to the belief that "without suffering there can be no salvation." By this they meant physical suffering and they meant it realistically. Because most sins are flesh inspired, they must also be exorcized by way

96

of the flesh. Hence, the whips. Any type of whip would serve, such as a piece of rope or a black snake or a piece of braided yucca. The more ingenious brothers used strips of crawling cactus or affixed sharp bits of metal into whatever *disciplinas* they chose to use. The idea was to suffer, to bleed, and, sometimes, to die.

There were other devices of torture, some mechanical, which will one day find their way into museums when the last of the Penitentes has succumbed to less vicious forms of penance. For example, there is the *Caretta del Muerto,* the cart of death, a heavy plank-and-timber conveyance set on wooden axles and equipped with wobbly, wooden wheels. Built low and close to the ground, as death should be, it carries an effigy: a black-shrouded skeleton with a skull or a mask for its face; its bony hands grip a bow and arrow, which is aimed toward its willing victim. The "victim" is a Penitente, a man who believes that God will honor his suffering, be pleased with his practice, and understand his heartfelt sorrow for his sins. The pain administered by the *Caretta del Muerto* does not come from the arrow however, for this is merely a symbol that every man must die. The torture is inflicted by a rope affixed to the cart and which passes around the Penitente's bare chest. The cart, loaded with stones, is the burden the seeker after peace drags behind him as he trudges barefooted through the hills, trudges until his feet are red and his breast is bleeding from the rubbing and the cutting of the rope. Meantime he constantly wails and pleads, *"Penitencia! Penitencia!"* This is a cry echoing back through time and vibrating to the same primitive key found in most of the world's religions. In Christianity, particularly in the 13th century, Europe had its men and women who scourged themselves or were scourged in propitiation for real or imagined misdeeds. There were public processions in those days, particularly in Italy, in which the marchers furiously whipped one another as they wended their way to a church or a shrine. The practice later developed into a religious order, a brotherhood of masochistic sufferers called Flagellants, whose symbol was the whip and whose rite was self-castigation.

They did penance not only for themselves but for the sins of the world, becoming, in their minds, replicas of Christ. The Roman Catholic Church, of which they were members, frowned on their exhibitionism and sought to stop them by Papal decree. While penance could be understood and the infusion of grace was recommended, the idea that ordinary men should torture themselves was beyond the purview of common sense or even uncommon faith. In a saint the action might be condoned, but such self-torture was surely never recommended to the laity by either scripture, church, or state.

Still the practice persisted. The Flagellants believed that tragic visitations were the "acts of God." An earthquake or a devastating storm were manifestations of heaven's wrath which demanded penitence. At no time was this more clearly demonstrated than during the 14th century when the Black Death, which ravaged Europe and parts of Asia, reduced entire cities to cities of the dead. In England, too, the black-spotted-scourge, which ran its devastating course for more than a year, was not halted until the eve of Michaelmas in 1369. The plague was, to the Flagellants, either a judgment of God or a momentary triumph of the devil. But in either case, it was an indication that man needed to appease the One or shame the other.

Who was to judge the efficacy of penance or the means by which it might best be induced? Penance was one of the sacraments which some believed needed to be sedulously involved with the suffering of Christ. Penitential physical torture was practiced in some lay orders in Catholicism, called tertiaries, which consisted of people who, although living in the world, were seeking to be as devout as priests or monks or nuns. The Third Order of St. Francis was such a group, and it was this Order that brought flagellation into the American southwest in 1598, when the conquistador Don Juan de Onate, with his soldiers and his friars, properly fortified with the sword and the cross, marched up from Old Mexico. In the wake of considerable slaughter of the natives, Don Juan built the first Christian churches in New Mexico, blessed rivers, and christened villages with the melodious names of saints. As he subjugated the heathen, he gave God the credit for overcoming the enemy who were equipped only with native spears. His friars recited their rosaries amid the plundered villages and augmented the kingdom of heaven by great numbers of war-stunned prisoners and tortured slaves.

It was on a night during Holy Week, at the height of his conquest, that the valiant Don Juan proclaimed a period of fasting and prayer to show the Lord that he was indebted to Him for past victories and to invoke His aid for future conquests. It was near Good Friday, when the wages of sin are usually expected to be paid, that the quixotic Don was impelled to set his own conscience free.

While the soldiers and Franciscan friars knew of Onate's valor, only he knew his sins. Even in the midst of his conquests, Don Juan longed for the scourge; even while his spirit was being lifted up, he vowed to discipline the flesh. And so he went out from the camp with only his captain, Gaspar de Villagra, into the lonely, moonlit desert where he fashioned a whip from the catcus and the fiber of aloe and stripped his body to the waist. Clutching this flagellum in both hands, he struck himself first over his right shoulder and then over his left, whipping and weeping and crying out to God for mercy as he shed his own blood for the remission of his sins.

The lowly Franciscans, when they heard his wailing supplications and cries, came to where he was. They made crowns of cactus and pressed them down on their heads so that they, too, might show their leader how greatly they sympathized with him. They threw off their mantles and begged for the lash as they chanted and wept. Then the soldiers came and lacerated themselves; the women and children walked barefoot over the cactus-covered ground; and Captain de Villagra himself took up the whip of his beloved Don and laid it fiercely upon his own body. All their cries, mingling in a single word, *"Penitencia!"* rose as an offering from the altars of their pain.

Today most of the flagellentes who trace their history back to the Third Order and Don Juan and who are known as *Los Hermanos Penitentes* (the Brothers Penitent) are found in towns along the Rio Grande between Santa Fe and Taos and in villages hemmed in by highways #85 and #64. They are no longer able to escape the prying eyes of those who consider them strange and curious.

For years they have been forced by Penitente-peepers, made up of tourist and townspeople, to carry their sanguinary rituals back into the hills, farther and farther from the public eye. Although they have never sought publicity, they are too sensational to be left alone. They have shown their resentment toward the invasion of their privacy in various ways. In the late 1900's an adventurous investigator and writer, Charles F. Lummis, who tried to photograph their ceremonies, was shot in the neck, but he lived long enough to tell his experiences in *The Land of Poco Tiempo*. Some years ago a man working on a Penitente story was killed by his houseboy and, although the Brotherhood was blamed immediately, it was later shown to have been a case of robbery and unmitigated murder. Nonetheless, the Penitentes have been as tolerant as the average religious group would be whose services have been subjected to ridicule, investigation, raids, and the persistent pursuit of men with high-powered cameras and recording instruments. Although legislation against them has been advocated and threats of excommunication from the Roman Catholic church have been made, the priests will tell you, "The Penitentes are good Catholics, but they have their own peculiar emphasis on worship during Lent."

Just how peculiar it is depends upon the observer's point of view and whether or not he believes that self-torture might carry within itself a cleansing pain. That many Penitentes are often caught up in the mob emotionalism of their sadistic rites goes without saying. That some are pre-fortified with drink has also been confirmed. But the true Penitente, of whom at least a thousand still remain out of an estimated twenty thousand of some thirty years ago, believes that without suffering there can be no salvation. For him it is incongruous to confess one's sins and assume a form of penance merely by an act of will. To him the issue is clear: suffering should be as intense as the act of sinning had been real. There must be a discipline of the body equal to the discipline of the mind before the conscience can truly be appeased.

And so the Penitente fashions his own form of chastisement: the whip. And the Cart of Death. And sometimes the cross. Some of these heavy-timbered crosses, weighing three hundred pounds, may be seen stuck in the sands near the *morada* (Penitente chapel) or propped against the aging adobe walls. To do a special penance, an indulgence of merit, a Penitente will on occasion during Lent, drag one of these crude crosspieces across the desert until he falls exhausted beneath its weight. This kind of self-punishment, he believes, will provide an abiding grace. It is all very well for a worshiper to pray before the stations of the cross in Catholic churches and to feel contrition in his heart, but it is only when a man falls, as Jesus did along the way of sorrow, that he enters into a true communion with Him. Only one act assumes a greater meaning than this solitary and torturous journey: crucifixion itself. This, too, has not been omitted from the ritual of the Brothers Penitent, and even today persists in remote mountain retreats, far from unsympathetic eyes.

It was crucifixion even more than flagellation to which the church and the state objected. The monstrous reports that in remote areas in the American southwest, crosses, on which living sacrifices were bound, were lifted on some barren *Calvario*, were enough to scandalize any staid official, ecclesiastical or political. To him it was barbarism; to Penitentes it was the highest possible emulation of the Christ.

Los Hermanos Penitentes is a fraternity, highly organized, and not a group comprised of fanatical exhibitionists eager to see which one can outdo the other in acts of mortification. These people are, as has been said, "good Catholics." Their village life is tranquil, simple, and sincere. Some work at farming, ranching, or sheep herding. Others may be storekeepers or mechanics. Many of their children have "gone on to school," and are interested in getting on in the world. When their young men were called into military service, they were different only in that many of them bore the mark of the whips across their backs or carried the scars of small crosses, which had been cut into their flesh with a piece of flint.

The leader of a local Penitente group, known as the *Hermano Mayor* (elder brother), was, in the olden days, also the mayor of the village or an important town official. Serving with him at the *morada* services is the *Celador* (doorkeeper) and some ten devoted brothers who constitute a kind of governing board or consistory. In addition to these there are other important officials: the *Maestro de Novios,* who instructs the novices; the *Rezador* (reader of prayers); a *Coadjutor,* in charge of the *disciplines,* and an *Enfermero,* whose task it is to treat the wounds of the victims of the macbre rites.

Throughout the year, the Brothers Penitent operate as a fraternity, engaging in charitable work, cooperating with the churches, and, occasionally, holding services of their own in the *moradas* or conducting memorial rites at the death of a member.

So it is really not until Ash Wednesday therefore, at the beginning of Lent, that they become a strange and curious people. But even then, the public Penitente processions are innocent enough, for the ordinary visitors see only the pilgrimages which are devoid of the whippings, the crosses, or the Cart of Death. They may witness the orderly march of worshipers who bear images of Christ and statues of the Virgin and reverently chant *alabados,* their quaint old religious hymns. The only distinguishing feature of the procession, which leads from the *morada* to the village church, is the cacophony of sounds coming from the shrill piping of the flutes and the rattle of the *metracas.*

It is not until night that the bizarre rituals begin. It is only on Fridays that the sound of the yucca whips can be heard. And it is only during Holy Week that the unprecedented ritual reaches its appalling height. What happens then resembles a Passion Play enacted by zealous participants who are not interested in commercialism or in fame. It is an American Oberammergau dramatized for itself alone. Instead of its being a public performance with seats provided for spectators, it is held clandestinely to escape any prying eyes. To foil the tourists and defeat the newsmen's cameras, it is held at night instead of at the traditional three o'clock hour of Good Friday afternoon.

It is preceded by a worship service in the *morada* conducted by the *Hermano Mayor* and the *Rezador* at a crude, candlelighted altar. The Brothers Penitent, some with whips clasped in their brown hands, sit or kneel on the earth which forms the *morada* floor. The *celador,* guarding against intrusion, sits at the door, while other guards who have been posted in the shadows around the windowless *morada,* patrol the grounds. The area around the *morada* is crowded with Penitente families, the women heavily shawled, and the children wrapped in *serapas* against the chill night air.

The *Hermano Mayor* begins the ceremony with a sermon on the sacrament of suffering. "Penance," he says, "is born of pain of the body and of the heart. Of what meaning is the whip if the heart is not broken? What is the cross if the spirit is not bruised? These holy days of the Passion of our Lord are the days of our fellowship with Him. Blessed is the Brother who praises Jesus with heart and spirit and honors Him anew with the blood of his discipline."

The service is deceptively innocent. It is difficult to imagine that in a little while, after words of contrition, a chant, and a prayer, these men will emerge not as worshipers, filled with the peace of Christ, but, instead, inspired by His suffering, they will be fired by the passion of medieval flagellants. Ominously armed with whips of various sizes and shapes, which have been given to them by the *Coadjutor,* they create the feeling that all that has transpired is merely a prologue to the coming drama in which they will participate with an intensity unequaled by any actors anywhere.

Among them, as they step out into the beckoning night, is a young, barefooted man, wearing only short, white *calzones*. His head is covered by a black gallows mask into which holes have been cut for the eyes and his back is crisscrossed with recent wounds. And as the *Hermano Mayor* assists him, he braces himself to receive the heaviest of the crosses. He tenses his body and tightens his muscles as the burden is so placed on his shoulder that the crosspiece will pinch and cut into his bare flesh.

As the scream of a fife cuts through the quiet of the dark night and the rattle of a *metraca* calls tantalizingly from afar, the women and children begin a wailing chant. A group of some thirty of the Brothers Penitent, brandishing the whips they carry, indicate that they need room so that they may begin to beat themselves across their already disfigured backs. As an elderly brother, slowly swinging his lantern, starts forward on the trail, a procession forms behind him. The first sharp swish of the flailing whips sends convulsions through the bodies and causes the men to flinch against their will. The night is filled with the echoes of Golgotha. The march to *Calvario* has once again begun.

It is the young man with the hood, *El Cristo* (the Christ), who carries the cross, who is the focal point of the procession. This masked figure, selected for this high honor by the fraternity of the Brothers Penitent, will remain unknown until after his "death" and "resurrection." Having prepared himself for this ordeal all through Holy Week by fasting and self-inflicted whippings and prayer, he has so emulated the real *El Cristo* that he has in fact relived every detail of Christ's last week. He has symbolically been tried before Pilate, realistically scourged, ritualistically initiated with the flint-scarred cross upon his breast, and now, as he makes his way to Calvary, he feels he is truly the Chosen One. His progress is not made in silence, for the siren call of the *pito* lures him on, the chatter of the *metraca* invokes his faith, and the chants of the women drown out his cries if any there should be. But there will be none. He is *El Cristo*, ready to be crucified 'for the sins of the world.

El Cristo rarely dies. Nonetheless, his suffering is real enough. The entire march along the *"Via Dolorosa"* is cast in the starkest of reality: the lantern bearer is followed by the *Hermano Mayor* and the *Rezador,* who endlessly intone their chants amidst the reverberations of the *metracas.* Then comes the *Pitero,* who sends out the shrill, siren call of the flute, followed by the masked and anguished form of *El Cristo,* dark and wraithlike under the tottering cross. He is urged on by a frequent stinging blow of a whip in the strong hands of the *Coadjuter.* Stumbling and falling either out of sheer exhaustion or by design because he remembers that Jesus fell three times, *El Cristo* is flanked by the group of men steadily flogging their own naked backs, their lacerated bodies taut and tensed against the throbbing pain. Behind them march the women and children, murmuring prayers and "Hail Marys" as they trudge on, camouflaged against the night.

On a knoll about a half mile from the *morada,* a hole has been gouged out large enough to serve as a resting place for the cross. The *Hermano Mayor* and the *Rezador,* who have already arrived, wait in the lantern's light while *El Cristo* falteringly climbs the hill, staggers to the ground with his burden, and kneels unsteadily in prayer. The fife and the *metraca* are stilled. The whippers, some with kerchief-bandaged heads, rest, limp and bleeding, from their purgation, while the women gather silently behind them haunted by the breathless cries of *"Penitencia!"* and over-awed as if they themselves are standing as once the Virgin Mother stood.

Members of the Brothers Penitent now gather around "the chosen one." Strong men pick him up and lay him on the cross, stretching out his arms and making straight his legs. Although he may plead to be nailed, his wish is seldom granted. Wordlessly the crowd watches, transfixed, while *El Cristo's* hands and feet are tied to the roughhewn cross with buckskin thongs which are laced so tightly his hands stand out like claws. As the cross is partially lifted up, a crown of cactus thorns, pressed down on the young sufferer's head, causes a shudder to convulse his already tortured body. The cross with its human sacrifice is raised high, but only for a moment, for it is then let fall into the hole with a sickening thud. *El Cristo* hangs by his wrists, a living corpus on an American *Calvario*.

Nearly everyone is kneeling now. Women bow their heads or cover their eyes with their black shawls. The *Hermano Mayor* and the *Rezador* remain standing, gazing at the hanging figure as they carefully watch and listen for any especially painful intake of breath from within the shrouded mask. From the kneeling group a tender chant rises caressingly:

> Christ is now dead
> And all are worth saving.
> Give Him your soul
> For which He is calling.

Endlessly long moments pass. It is a belief among the Penitentes that no one should suffer more than he can bear, and it is with this kind of instinctive timing that *El Cristo* endures his agony. It is with this kind of faith that the worshipers bear with infinite patience the eternity of twenty minutes before the *Hermano Mayor* says, "It is enough."

Then the Brothers, lifting the cross from its setting and carrying it like a pallet on which *El Cristo* lies, begin their soundless retreat back to the *morada*. Halfway down the trail a chant is begun. It grows in exultation and intensity until by the time the procession has reached the *morada* door it is a song of triumph and victory. Reverently the cross-bearers carry both the cross and the crucified inside and tenderly place them on the ground before the candle-lighted altar.

The worshipers, crowding in, kneel or sit on the ground or stand against the walls, willingly and sympathetically making room for any man with a whip who feels the need of one more lacerating blow. But the *Rezador* is quick to begin the chants which are used for the *tenebrae*, the commemoration of the suffering and death of Christ. Here, in the shadowy chapel where the ritual began, the Passion Play of the Penitentes reaches its logical conclusion. Since *El Cristo* has "died," he must also rise again; sorrow must be turned to joy, and the scripture must be dramatically fulfilled.

Solemnly extinguishing a candle after each chant, the *Hermano Mayor* reminds the people of the sacredness of this hour. Fourteen times he pinches out a flame with his fingers, and then, after the final chant, he takes the one remaining lighted candle and conceals it behind the altar. Having so symbolized Christ's death and burial, the Brothers now simulate the earthquake which, according to the Scriptures, was heaven's rebuke to man's infamous deed.

The *morada* seems suddenly to spring to life, shaken by a charivari of screams, *metracas*, rattle of chains, pounding of pots and pans, and the ear-piercing shriek of the *Pietero's* fife. This is *tineiblas*, the earthquake and the dark. The cries reflect the agony of souls in purgatory; the wail is that of mankind aware of his sins; the reverberating *morada* is the trembling earth.

And then comes the resurrection. It is symbolized not only by the lighted candle being lifted to the top of the altar, but by the removal of *El Cristo's* mask and the freeing of his hands and feet. His crown now is the narrow ring of blood where his head has been pierced by the cactus thorns. He rises to his feet and lifts his hands in blessing over the murmuring, swaying, joyfully weeping Brothers Penitent, as the *Hermano Mayor* majestically proclaims, "He is risen!" To which the people reply, "He is risen indeed!"

Early on Easter morning many of these Brothers and their families will make their way to church, dressed in their Sunday best and carrying their rosaries and their missals. They will participate in the ecclesiastically prescribed way of worship with all dignity and reverent grace. The soft-spoken priests, the spotless vestments, the solemn sacrament, are as much a part of the Penitente tradition as is the Good Friday crucifixion. The sign of the cross which the *padre* makes over the kneeling people is a benediction which brings them peace and quiet joy.

Yet, often, as they perform their acts of devotion and join in the graciously enacted symbolic rites, their minds wander back to the *morada,* to the night marches, to the sound of the *disciplinas,* and to the sight of a man very much like themselves, who staggered beneath an actual cross and who was hung upon it while they chanted in the night. Calvary is more real to them because of their *Calvario,* and the resurrection of Christ more meaningful because of their *El Cristo.*

Some people say it is just as well that *Los Hermanos Penitentes* are dying out and that their strange and curious rites will soon be only a legend. But there are others who feel that in this last remaining stronghold a symbol is passing, the symbol of *"Penitencia."* Penance with pain, they say, will finally be discarded in the desert and the hills as it has been discarded elsewhere in the world. And when this is gone, where, then, will those who still believe there can be no salvation without suffering go to appease their stricken consciences?

9 § THE APOCALYPTICISTS

Belief that the world is coming to an end has tormented the mind of man ever since the first mysterious darkening of the sun during an eclipse, the first earthquake, the first volcanic eruption, and the first great flood. Paleolithic man gouged out shelters in the rock, caves of refuge against the day when the gods would destroy what the gods had made. The people of Baal built the massive temples at Baalbek as lookout stations for the interstellar destroyer whom they believed would come. And Noah built an ark.

Apocalypticism, by which is meant the probing into the future of this old world's fate, caught the imagination of religions all the way from the ancient Aztecs to the equally ancient Zoroastrians. At the time of the Babylonian exile, some 600 years before the birth of Christ, the Hebrew people comforted themselves in their miseries and endured their oppressions bcause of their faith in a God of righteousness who would eventually triumph over the forces of evil. They were confident that He would renew the earth with justice and peace. Hebrew prophets—Daniel, Enoch, Moses, Baruch—sustained their people in the darkest hours with the light of apocalyptic hope.

It remained for Christianity, however, to give apocalypticism its greatest emphasis. The apocalyptic writings—Daniel, Ezekiel and the Book of Revelation—became the texts for a timetable in which men claimed to read the mind of God. Nor did the followers of Christ think it strange and curious that they, the most enlightened among the seekers after truth, should teach, confidently and without equivocation, that the world would one day end. Most of the sacred Christian writings had as their purpose the revelation of events which were to happen at the end of time. Even the gospels are largely apocalyptic books. Jesus himself looked for the end of the world within His time.

"Tell us," the disciples implored, "what shall be the sign of Thy coming, and of the end of the world?" And Jesus said, "Ye shall hear of wars and rumors of wars. . . . . nation shall rise up against nation, and kingdom against kingdom. . . . . the sun shall be darkened, and the moon shall not give her light, and the stars shall fall from heaven, and the powers of the heavens shall be shaken." (Matthew 24.)

Then Jesus went on to say, "There shall be weeping and gnashing of teeth. When the Son of Man shall come in his glory and all the holy angels with him . . . and before him shall be gathered all nations; and he shall separate them one from another, as a shepherd divideth his sheep from the goats." (Matthew 25.)

In his second epistle, Peter added his ominous note, "The heavens shall pass away with a great noise, and the elements shall melt with fervent heat, the earth also and the works that are therein shall be burned up." (2 Peter 3:10.)

Awed by the far-seeing eyes of their apocalyptic seers, the early Christians staked their messianic hope on Christ. He was their God of the Apocalypse. Less than two hundred years after His death, apocalyptic groups were flourishing wherever Christianity was preached. There were, for example, the Montanists, followers of a "pagan" priest, Montanus, who had been converted to Christianity after serving for many years in the temple of Cybele (Aphrodite). He claimed he had a vision in which the Lord revealed to him that men were living in the latter days. Frequently seized by the spirit, Montanus proclaimed in a loud voice that the days were numbered. Virgins followed him, wearing heavy veils so that no man could see their faces until Jesus came and first looked on them. Wives lived apart from their husbands so that the Lord would find them pure. Men gave up all their worldly goods so that they might meet God empty-handed. Secular education, science, art, and worldly pleasures were renounced, and Montanism became a movement of fasting and prayer, with pilgrimages to the tops of Phrygian hills to wait the coming of the Lord.

In the third century other enthusiasts grouped themselves around Novatian, a Roman presbyter, labeled a heretic, who preached that the second coming of Christ was imminent and that the church had better prepare itself and warn its people. Great crowds followed Novatian as others had followed Montanus, chanting their favorite prayer, "Come, Lord Christ, clothed in all Thy wrath and judgment, come with all Thy vengeance, come."

In the fourth century, Novatianism gave way to the Donatists who, fleeing the world of men in order to embrace the world to come, set their hopes on the prophecies of Donatus of Africa. Among other things, he reminded his followers that the Scriptures limited the specially chosen of the Lord to 144,000. These represented the inner circle spoken of by that greatest of all apocalypticists, John the Revelator, who said, "I looked and, lo, a Lamb stood on Mount Zion, and with him an hundred and forty and four thousand, having his Father's name written in their foreheads." (Revelation 14:1-3.)

The church branded Donatus a heretic, as it had Novatian and Montanus in the fourth century, and as it was to do with the many other chiliastic souls who down through the centuries claimed divine revelation hostile to the culture of the institutionalized faith. Anabaptists, Waldensians, Albigenses, Moravian Brethren, Swiss Brethren, became links in an unbroken chain of apocalyptic advocates. They divided into many fractional groups and movements all of which seemed strange and curious to the institutionalized faiths. There they were, making religion seductively simple, thinking more about the life to come than about this life, waiting for Christ's return, warning men of it, casting anxious eyes to the heavens, and stubbornly declaring they were ready to die for what they believed.

They came to be known as millennialists, and soon there were pre-millennialists and post-millennialists with many other factions ranging between these two extremes. The pre-millennialists believed that Christ would descend from the skies in a cloud of glory and set up a perfect kingdom over which He would rule for a thousand years; the post-millennialists insisted He would appear *after* a thousand years of peace had been instituted by man himself. Both groups, however, like the church at large, were united in one point of agreement: they professed belief in a literal heaven and a literal hell and in a literal devil whose forces would be vanquished by the armies of the Lord. They foresaw an actual, inevitable encounter between Logos and Lucifer, archenemies since time began. They had a name for this conflict, the Battle of Armageddon, and it was foretold in the infallible apocalyptic record: the Book of Revelation.

Every period in religious history had its millennialistic groups which stubbornly insisted that Armageddon would occur within their time. These remnants of the faith asked the question which apocalypticists are still asking today, "If you were convinced that the world is coming to an end, wouldn't you begin examining *your* conscience?" Perhaps it is this, this secret awareness of his own sinful nature that has made man continually fear and anticipate the end of the world. The haunting thought of retribution has lurked in the heart of Christian and non-Christian alike, and the spectre of man's sins catching up with him has, at one time or other, haunted every soul. "The end of the world" is fully as thought-provoking a phrase as "Ye must be born again," and as disturbing as the words, "Be sure your sins will find you out."

Two apocalyptic groups are especially worthy of review in

the light of modern times. The first is a movement which, a hundred years ago, was known as Millerism. Its founder, William Miller, born in Pittsfield, Massachusetts, on February 15, 1782, saw military service in the War of 1812 and came out of it shaken by the brutality and suffering he had seen. For many years he had been an atheist, but now he found no rest until he was converted in a Baptist revival service. At this time he was thirty-four and, inspired by the life of Christ and Christ's promise to return to earth, he began an exhaustive study of the Bible. Finally, licensed as a preacher, he launched a forceful ministry, made magically impressive by his prediction that the Second Coming of the Lord would take place between March 21, 1843, and March 21, 1844.

Date-setting always caught the imagination of religious enthusiasts, and this time it seemed that the stage of the world had truly been prepared for a spectacular apocalyptic prologue. "Signs and wonders" had been seen in the heavens, including an unusually large meteoric shower and the flash across the skies of the great Faye comet. The years preceding Miller's prophetic dates were also marked in America by the rise of the Mormons, the coming of the Spiritualists, the growth of Shakerism, and the increase in Christian communal experiments such as the Ebenezer Society, the Bethel Community, and others.

Miller found himself the focal point in this religious extravaganza. People followed him wherever he went. They organized themselves into groups and found leaders among themselves who spurred them on. Soon the established churches were aroused. They began expelling members who followed "Mad Miller," and Protestant and Catholic groups alike condemned Millerism as a modern heresy. But as the year 1843 drew near and as the prediction was intensified that time was running out, rabid apocalyptic believers gathered on hilltops, on haystacks, and climbed trees to wait the coming of the Lord. Donning white "ascension robes," they sat like yogis, facing eastward in preparation for the ecstatic event.

The months dwindled away. The portentous year went by.

March 21, 1844, came and went, followed by but one earth-shaking event; on May 24, a message was sent over a wire strung from the U.S. Supreme Court room in Washington to inventor Samuel F. Morse in Baltimore. It said, "What God hath wrought!"

Miller conceded that he had made a miscalculation. He set a new deadline: October 22, 1844. Some doubted. A number turned away from him in disillusionment. But many continued to believe. In the winter of 1844, however, when the Lord had still not appeared, Miller was forced to check his calculations once more. In the meantime, his followers, breaking up into various factions, were disputing among themselves over such things as the sleep of the soul from the hour of death until the judgment day, whether Saturday or Sunday should be observed as the true day of the Lord, whether the rite of baptism should be administered through sprinkling or immersion, and whether anyone should ever again presume to set a date for the second coming of Christ.

Heavy of heart, but still convinced that Armageddon was near, William Miller went to meet his Lord in death five days before Christmas in 1849. Though he was considered an unscholarly theologian by most church historians, he left a heritage to American faith which today is known as Adventism and whose influence upon religious culture is incalculable. Devout and consecrated people, the Adventists have for many years been an example to Christendom by their holy living, simple faith, and benevolent giving. They are the world's most conscientious tithers, setting aside a generous portion of their incomes for the Lord's side of the ledger. Morally responsible, possessed of an exceptionally selfless ethic, they have established hospitals, orphanages, and schools in many outposts of civilization.

True, they have many beliefs which still make them appear strange and curious in the eyes of the more traditional churches. The Seventh-day Adventists, numbering some 300,000 members, observe Saturday instead of Sunday as their Sabbath. They believe death is an unconscious sleep; that all men, good and evil alike, remain in the grave until the resurrection; that the resurrection of the just will take place at the second advent of Christ; and that the judgment of the unjust will take place a thousand years later, at the close of the millennium. All of the Adventist groups—the Advent Christian, the Church of God (Adventist), the Life and Advent Union, the Primitive Advent Church—are highly moral, believing that Jesus wanted His followers to refrain from alcoholic drinks, from the use of tobacco, and from the eating of pork. Down through the years they have kept the whispered warning, "Get right with God, for the end of the world can come at any moment."

Oddly enough, the warning is not as anachronistic today as it might appear. Apocalypticists have a new and staunch supporter in an area quite unrelated to their speculative hope. Science, which many men have learned to trust and believe in more than they do in religion, has soberly warned a nervous world that the power of total annihilation now exists. Modern apocalypticists have been quick to hint that this may be the form the end of the world will take. They are almost persuaded to begin date-setting once more, for they believe that the clock of God is running down. It will not be the benevolent Creator who will destroy the world, they say, but, rather, malevolent man himself. God did not foreordain the end of an era, but God foreknew. Ever since Adam, man has been spinning the web of his own destruction and, as more than one prophet of this doom has warned, "Adam's end may be the atom."

This is the alarm loudly sounded by a modern group fully as vocal as were the Millerites a hundred years ago. It goes under an impressive name, Jehovah's Witnesses, and is one of the most powerful and fastest growing religious groups in America. Its nearly 1,000,000 members believe unqualifiably that we are living in the last days and that it is their assignment to summon the faithful into the living ark of the Lord, the ark in this instance being the Jehovah's Witnesses' organization with headquarters at 124 Columbia Heights in Brooklyn, New York.

So sure are they that the end of the world is near that they are willing to stand on street corners and silently witness, despite the ridicule and the abuse they receive from the passing crowds. The indoctrination goes even deeper than this. Every true Witness is a minister and is dedicated to give his time and his life, if need be, to the fulfillment of Jehovah's work. Because they do not believe or trust in world governments, they refuse to pledge allegiance to the flag. Having renounced worldly kingdoms, they will not take up arms in defense of any country, submitting to imprisonment rather than induction into military service. Convinced that all other religions are false, and confident that churches are a subtle device by which the devil seeks to delude men, they have become an insular, anti-religious, anti-social group, accepting as literally as life allows the Master's injunction, "Be ye in the world and not of it."

They claim a spiritual connection with other witnesses of Jehovah: Abel, Abraham, Moses, Daniel, Enoch. They say they have no earthly founder and no mortal leader, but religious scholars insist that the movement began with Charles Taze Russell (1852-1916), a Pennsylvania businessman, owner of several clothing stores. In turn a Presbyterian and then a Congregationalist, he found his real need of religious certainty sparked during an argument with an atheist whom he was trying to convert to Christ. So effective was the non-believer's defense and so weak was Russell's persuasion that the infidel almost converted him. Stung by this close skirmish which almost cost him a complete loss of faith, he began a thorough study of the Scriptures in the course of which he was influenced and helped by the Adventists.

Adventist books and pamphlets, as well as their ability to "prove" their claims, helped Russell formulate what he believed to be an iron-clad defense against the most thorough-going unbelievers. It is not known whether he ever encountered the atheist again, but his apocalyptic platform had been well established. He was now able to affirm on Biblical grounds that at death the soul sinks into a state of unconsciousness, from which it will be awakened during the millennium and judged and sentenced either to everlasting life or complete annihilation. He declared that God had shown him where the Adventists had erred in their calculations and stated that he had been given the proper key to unlock the mysteries of the apocalyptic kingdom.

Russell based his theories on three dispensations: the first extended from the time of creation to the time of Noah; the second from the time of Noah to the death and resurrection of Christ; the third from the resurrection to the year 1914, at which time, Pastor Russell predicted, the souls of those that sleep will arise in order and be judged. His followers, known as the Russellites, interpreted his remarks to mean that the end of the world would come in 1914. He let the matter stand and the movement grew until, at the dawn of the 20th century, it numbered some 300,000 enthusiastic souls. His *Watch Tower* magazine was their house organ, his *Studies in the Scriptures* their texts, and his organization, spreading over the world, was known as the "International Bible Students Association."

The year 1914 became their target date and for a moment it seemed that Russell's prophecy was to be proven terrifyingly true. On June 28, 1914, when an unknown Serbian terrorist in Sarajevo, Bosnia, killed the Austrian Archduke Ferdinand and plunged Europe into war, the Russellites declared it was the beginning of the end. Then nation rose against nation, just as the Scriptures had predicted, and a cry of "Armageddon!" swept through apocalyptic ranks. In many cities around the globe, the International Bible Students were besieged with converts, and for a little while even the most skeptical theologian wondered whether Pastor Russell might actually have had divine inside information.

The fury of war increased, but the year was running out. Perhaps, the Russellites said, there had been a slight miscalculation. A difference of one year, two years, what did it matter? Then when the Middle East became a focal point and there was fighting in Jerusalem, no more telling signs were needed, for apocalypticists had always vowed that here in the Holy Land the final slaughter would take place. They watched and waited, but the world dragged through its years of carnage without any intervention from a cosmic power.

The war had not yet reached its climax when Pastor Russell died on October 31, 1916. When he passed away on board a train in Pampa, Texas, while on a preaching mission, it is said that a traveling companion invited the Pullman porter to, "Come and see how a man of God can die."

He died courageously, and his followers praised him even though his prophecies remained unfulfilled. They found a reason for their unfulfillment, however, as devotees usually do in these matters, and upon it the faithful fastened their hopes. The end of the world *had* actually begun in 1914, they said, but mankind was not yet fully aware of it. Christ, they insisted, had entered His kingdom, had subdued the forces of Satan and driven the unseen hosts of devils out of their invisible habitat once and for all. The reason for a deteriorating world culture, a rise in crime, a trend toward world unrest and war could be found in this very fact: devils which had once lived in the nether-nether land of a spiritual realm now lived on earth among the children of men, as retribution for man's sins.

As this supposition grew, a new and vigorous leader arose in the person of J.F. Rutherford, a judge in the 14th Judicial District of Missouri. Born in Booneville, Missouri, he was forty-seven years of age when his spiritual teacher, Pastor Russell, had died, An able executive and a forceful leader, he seized upon a new name for the group: Jehovah's Witnesses, an identifying mark for all those who would champion the apocalyptic cause. Some of the International Bible Students refused to accept either him or his new name, but there were many who saw in Rutherford exactly the type of leadership they needed and who felt the name was prophetic of the power of his leadership. Jehovah's Witnesses! The title linked them with the Biblical heroes. It gave them blood relationship to Abraham, who was prepared to slay his own son in order to testify that he was a faithful witness. It identified them with Noah, Moses, David, Daniel, Isaiah. Wherever the word "witness" appeared in the

Bible, there they saw their prototype. In league with such a cloud of immortals, Rutherford built the organization into a religious theocracy. At its Brooklyn headquarters, he established a Bible College, dormitories, refectories, bookshops, and a printing plant operated by a staff who labored without salary for Jehovah-God.

Day and night the new organization worked and witnessed, fighting against time, they said, calling out God's anointed before the dreadful day of Armageddon. They canvassed villages and cities across America with the thoroughness of census takers. Not a house was missed, not a person was neglected. Every family could expect a rap at the door and find a man or a woman standing there carrying a bag of books and magazines and a portable phonograph on which the messages of Judge Rutherford were played.

"Good-day," the Witness was trained to say, "I am a minister and if you will let me come in for a moment I will teach you truth. We are living in the latter days. I am one of Jehovah's Witnesses. . . ."

Slammed doors were merely part of the promise that there was to be persecution for righteousness sake. Ridicule was proof that the Lord chastened those He loves. Charges of "racket" and "heresy" were obvious signs that the people feared "the truth." Doggedly, Rutherford's relentless apostles continued witnessing without salary, without reward, expecting no compensation excepting that which would come to them when the end of the world vouchsafed their claims. On that day they would stand up boldly before Jehovah God and say, "We have been obedient to the heavenly vision."

Occasionally the rap at the door was answered by a seeking soul whom the churches had passed by or whom institutionalized religion had disenfranchised. One out of every hundred calls resulted in a convert. That meant a thousand converts out of every 100,000 visitations, or a million out of every 100,000,-000. It was a statistical certainty that Jehovah's Witnesses could not fail if enough Witnesses rang enough doorbells.

And they did ring the bells.

Books were sold and magazines were placed and the movement grew. Whenever a prospect was discovered, he was provided with literature and given free private tutoring in the Scriptures, especially in the apocalyptic references of Daniel, Ezekiel, and the Book of Revelation. Soon the new recruit, converted to apocalypticism, indoctrinated in the faith, assured that he was on the Lord's side, went out to ring doorbells on his own and to tell others of Rutherford's claim that, "Millions Now Living Will Never Die." The words became a saying around the world. People took them to mean that, though the Witnesses were cautious not to set a specific date, they, nonetheless, knew that this generation would not pass away before the Master came.

Then mortality caught up with Judge Rutherford. On January 8, 1942, he died, but not before he had crystallized a religious movement of phenomenal power. Welded by spiritual bonds so strong that they defied intrusion, the Witnesses respected only those laws which did not contravene the laws of God as Rutherford interpreted them. They refused to salute the flag or serve in the military forces. They would not consent to vaccination or blood transfusion. They maintained strict neutrality in respect to voting and practically avoided voting altogether. They canvassed in towns and cities where canvassing was forbidden and, almost without exception, Witnesses were legally supported in their views and practices by a constitution pledged to the American ideal of freedom in the pursuit of spiritual faith.

Slowly, against great odds, the Witnesses were accepted by the institutionalized churches as a contemporary movement which was here to stay. They called their meeting places "Kingdom Halls" so as not to be defiled by the word "church" or "chapel." Their services consisted of a thorough study of lessons prepared and published at the Brooklyn headquarters. All services were alike whether they were held in a vacant store building in America or in a thatched hut in an African jungle. Submission there must be, the Witnesses declared, submission to divine authority channeled through the Brooklyn headquarters where a president and a board of directors worked with Biblical scholars to formulate the teaching. Gilead Bible School trained more than 3,000 ministers. Every moment of the day the Brooklyn presses piled up staggering production figures: *One World, One Government,* 4,800,000 copies; *The Meek Shall Inherit the Earth,* 4,900,000; *A Commander to the Peoples,* 3,000,000—books bearing as their dedication: "To Jehovah and His Messiah."

Strange and curious? They are. And they rather enjoy it. They believe that Jehovah's people must be strange and curious in the eyes of the world. No one can outquote them when it comes to Scripture. Few can withstand the steady bombardment of their references from Holy Writ. Biblical knowledge, accepted uncritically and with eager passion, is the power that holds them together in one of religion's most closely-knit organizations.

They have concluded from their studies who will be "saved" and when. They are convinced that only 144,000 will be invited by the triumphant Christ to share His glory in the highest heaven. Others will reign on "an earth remade among men reborn." The Witnesses are even now dealing with the question of what might happen if, when the end of the world comes, some of the earth's citizens should happen to be on the moon or Venus or some other planet. They have concluded that men will be judged wherever they are because Jehovah God's presence fills all space.

In the early days of Rutherfords's leadership, the devotees fully expected that Abel, Noah, Abraham, Samuel, David, Daniel and others would some day walk American streets. So they built a house for them, a mansion on a lovely ridge in San Diego and named it Beth-Sarim, House of the Princes. Here Judge Rutherford lived and died, and, since Armageddon seemed to have been indefinitely postponed, Beth-Sarim was finally disposed of through a real estate agency.

Undeterred, the Witnesses persist in their predictions that the end of the world is near. Unofficially, the year 1972 has been suggested as the fateful date, though they are not given to date-setting. Militant vigilance is their watchword, and it is registered in every phase and aspect of their work. They have assured the world that they are pacifists *only* in relationship to wars among men and nations. Let the battle of Armageddon come and you will find them fighting on the Lord's side, armed with whatever weapons Christ may choose. Even the songs they sing in their Sunday services are built around the theme of warfare with the world:

> Up, every soldier on Christ's side enlisted,
> Aye, gird for the fight!
> Mount Salem's ramparts, fight, shoulder to shoulder,
> With all who lift up the standard of light!
> See, all the nations in tumult assembling,
> Against God's Anointed their rulers are set;
> Satan, their prince, gives defy to Jehovah,
> Short is his time ere he suffers defeat.

And the hymn *Armageddon* foretells what is to happen to the institutionalized faith:

> The sun and moon are darkened, the ocean depths are stirred,
> The age abiding mountains are scattered at God's word.
> The nations rent asunder, did not of him inquire;
> He stands the earth to measure, in flaming judgment fire.
> The forces of religion, God's covenant have transgressed;
> And the abomination have they set up and blest;
> While to the wind they're sowing, Jehovah sounds alarm,
> He'll make them reap the whirlwind of Armageddon's storm!

Meantime the mighty presses are thundering out the warnings in millions of books and hundreds of millions of tracts, proclaiming to a world engrossed in selfishness and strife, "The Kingdom is at hand!" Each year some 200,000 delegates from the continental United States and foreign lands make their pilgrimage to the annual conference of all Jehovah's Witnesses. Phenomenal meetings are held at Yankee Stadium, Madison Square Garden, or, perhaps, at Soldiers' Field or the Hollywood Bowl. The place does not matter, for the earth is the Lord's and the fullness thereof. The Witnesses—a cross-section of American life—come by plane and train, by car caravans, by bicycle, and on foot. Wherever they hold their conferences, they witness, trudging from door to door whether the city is New York or Los Angeles. Nothing deters them. Neither weather, nor law, nor persecution can stay them from their appointed rounds. Each year they become more powerful in the eyes of an uncertain and often aimless world. The traditional churches are giving them a second glance to see what it is that makes individuals dedicate their loyalties to a "strange and curious faith" and rise from listless listeners of the gospel into doers of the word.

Insular and stubborn though these Witnesses may be, paradoxical as it may seem that they enjoy the protection of governments while still opposing governments, or that they condemn religions while they themselves are a religious movement growing more like a denomination every day, they can never be accused of being neither hot nor cold. They are the modern zealots who, had they lived in the days of paleolithic man would have gouged out caves of refuge in the rocks or, in the days of Noah, would have helped him to build the ark.

For although scientists may assure men that the earth is an old and rugged planet, that it has been around for billions of years and has withstood the cosmic buffeting of time and space with dependable fortitude, the apocalyptic devotees look to the sky. "Is man indeed competent and worthy to inhabit the world God gave him?" they ask. "Or is the earth merely a temporary home, as mortal as man himself?" Strange and curious is the fact that through all the years during which men contemplated on the end of things, no words ever seemed quite so filled with meaning and so contemporary as those which say, "The heavens shall pass away with a great noise, and the elements shall melt with fervent heat, the earth also and the works that are therein shall be burned up."

So said Peter in his second epistle, the third chapter, the tenth verse, and so say Jehovah's Witnesses today.

10 § FATHER DIVINE

"I<small>F YOU WANT</small> a clear conscience and a heartful of peace, see Father."

This prescription has been filled for literally thousands of Americans by a fabulous dispenser of hope and joy: Father M. J. Divine. In fact, so many people have been helped by this man of middling height and giant personality that a great deal of early defamation about him has changed to praise. So many lives have been transformed from a meaningless existence to lives full of purpose through Father's techniques, and so many down-and-outers have been rehabilitated that investigators are now convinced that something spiritually and psychologically sound must be stirring behind the bizarre facade of the Peace Mission Movement, Divine's pretentious religious organization.

This movement had always been considered absurd and for good reason. Father's ardent devotees had not only spread preposterous claims; they were enthuiastically prepared to back them up with facts. They were saying: the Peace Mission Movement now has more than 1,000,000 members scattered throughout the United States, Canada, England, Australia, Switzerland,

Austria, and West Germany; Father has all the money in the world; whenever he needs money, he simply *thinks* money and it materializes; he owns hotels, farms, businesses, apartment houses, and country estates; the touch of Father's hand changes lives, Father's smile can melt your heart, Father's displeasure can kill you; Father's banquets are free; they are on-the-Lord and consist of forty, fifty, and even sixty courses; Father's schools have teachers who have their Ph.D's but still they teach for nothing; Father has already converted all the people on the other planets and that is why he is now working on this one; Father, you know, is God.

There were any number of things the public could do with this plethora of claims: ignore them, discount them as the ravings of deluded fanatics, write them off as heretical, expose them as propaganda for a religious racket, or investigate them in the spirit of research. If, for instance, you as a courageous researcher were to conduct your own investigation, you might be surprised, as many like you in the past have been.

At the Broad Street Headquarters in Philadelphia you would meet executive secretary John Germaine, a capable, quiet-spoken, matter-of-fact businessman, quite willing to answer any questions about the Peace Mission Movement. With facts and figures, he would persuade you that the Divine kingdom is huge, active, and financially sound. It is, in fact, not merely solvent, but it is wealthy, consisting of thirty apartment houses in such cities as Newark, New York, Philadelphia, and Los Angeles; a dozen city hotels, fourteen residence clubs, twenty properties in foreign countries, some twenty luxurious country estates, several schools, churches, and business establishments "too numerous to mention."

Mr. Germaine would explain in technical detail how this imposing empire functions as a well organized cooperative, built upon a system almost monastic, in which the employees, provided with room and board, are quite content to work "for humanity," even as monks work in monasteries or as nuns serve in their respective orders, different only in the fact that these dedi-

cated members of the Peace Mission Movement have not secluded or isolated themselves. Actively engaged in the world of
men as farmers, service station operators, hotel managers, cooks,
clerks, maids, store-keepers, and professional people, they are all
employed in the paradisical kingdom of Father Divine. Over this
industrial Eden, Father rules as an infallible adviser. Owning
nothing, he owns everything; wanting nothing, he has everything; asking nothing, he receives everything. And, if this is
difficult for people outside the kingdom to comprehend, well-
qualified John Germaine makes it easier by saying, "As you
know, Father is really and truly God."

With this ambiguous encouragement, you would visit the
hotels and mansions and farms and business places and talk to
the Divine workers, only to discover that the assumptions are
more than correct. The enterprises of the Peace Mission Movement represent a vast cooperative conducted on a spiritual ideal;
the employees working not for wages, but for love—Father's love.

In true monastic fashion they have assumed self-appointed
vows with such sincerity that some observers wondered whether
this might be a Catholic movement. After all, Divine's title of
"Father" was enough to suggest something of the sort. The matter, however, was immediately clarified. The Peace Mission
Movement is neither Catholic nor Protestant, nor is it exclusively
Christian. It is a spiritual approach to life in which they, as true
believers, take literally the injunction to seek first the kingdom
of heaven, which, to them, is Divine's "heaven." For Father Divine, although he has been endowed with the titles—Bishop,
Founder, Pastor, and Reverend—is something more than a mere
ecclesiast. According to his unabashed and joyous coteries, he is
Father God M. J. Divine, Dean of the Universe.

So the followers, those who have been "reborn," take their
vows, one of which is celibacy. For, as many an eager zealot will
tell you, "When you are really born again, sex is out." Like other
investigators, you would find evidence of hundreds of "broken
homes" as a result of a convert giving up husband or wife. You
would also discover that frequently both parties, deciding to

change their marital status to a brother-sister relationship, have joined the Divine Kingdom together, both aspiring toward "angelhood."

Angelhood does not mean wings; it means work. It means close fellowship with Father, full-time service in a cooperative enterprise, and a communal life in a "kingdom home" where all of God's children dwell together in peace. Angelhood means a new moral code: no more sexual intercourse, no more smoking, no more drinking, no more hob-nobbing with the world, no more sin, and, so far as the true aspirant is concerned, no more sorrow. Angelhood demands a life of discipline, and this discipline is taken as a vow. So is poverty a vow, but theirs is a rich kind of poverty with an unusual kind of food and fellowship that the world can never give. Living in poverty under Father Divine results in living like the child of a king.

Coupled with the change in life's direction is another unique religious practice: the "angels" change their names to show they have been reborn. Mortal monikers like Joe and John and Mary give way to Full-of-Joy Joseph, John of Meekness And Light, and Faithful Mary. There are others: Honey Bee Love, Ima Light, Glory Sun, Pearly Gates, Live Dove, Violet Ray, Smile-The-While George, Noah Frankness, David Peace, and thousands more. Said Joyful Job, "In Bible days, changed lives always brought new names—like Saul, who became Paul on the Damascus Road; like Jacob whom God named Israel; like Peter, who got to be known as The Rock."

These rehabilitated, reborn, renamed angels of Father Divine have come from many religious backgrounds, from many social levels, and from many walks of life. Any preconception about their intellectual status, or the lack of it, has to be discarded when you actually find accredited Ph.D's teaching Negro and white children in Divine schools because of their love for the Peace Mission Movement. They will tell you that here they have found an opportunity to make a contribution to a program where true integration is born of the spirit and not of the law; where there is no distinction between races or classes; and where the terms: "white," "colored," and "Negro" are never used. Here, too, are bonafide psychologists and highly skilled sociologists giving their services free of charge, inspired by the contributions the Divine program has made in critical areas. Impressed by the evidence that here is an organization sincerely committed to service to others rather than to self, that is engaged without fanfare in slum clearance, that lives as well as talks Americanism, and that wants to create better working conditions for all people, you begin to reappraise the entire movement.

You discover that the thirty Divine Missions in New York, the twenty-five in Pennsylvania, and the seven in California all sponsor Peace Centers with recreational facilities, orphanages, homes for the aged, and employment agencies—free for the needy and indigent. Divine evening schools offer courses in "all academic subjects, with practical classes in Americanism, Christianity, and Brotherhood." These are also free, and why not? ask the assiduous angels, since God is at the helm.

The *bizarrerie* deepens when you sit in on the extraordinary "Communion" services which are held whenever the spirit moves Father to gather around the table with several hundred members of his flock. It is not a eucharist of wafers and wine, but a feast, a festival, a banquet, the like of which few churches of the traditional order have ever spread. Unstaged for the public, unrehearsed for investigators, the meals more than approximate the exaggerated reports. Held at the Philadelphia headquarters or at a country estate or, occasionally, on a Sunday, in Harlem, or at the opening of a new hotel or apartment house, the "Communion" is partaken of at a huge U-shaped table set with all the decor of a formal banquet. Linen tablecloths, luxurious stiff linen napkins, sparkling dinnerware, brightly polished silver, and fresh-cut flowers are the rule. At Father's place are twelve silver serving sets for coffee and tea. Nearby are some sixty serving forks and spoons, and on Father's chair three gold letters are inscribed: G*O*D.

The "communicants," Negro and white, stand packed against the walls singing and clapping their hands as they tell the world they love "Father Divine, Master of Omnipotency, greatest of all the *intelligency!*" Or they cheer for America with, "We'll keep the flag of freedom and liberty waving high, by living our Constitution and the Bill of Rights, by fearlessly standing for the rights of every man, by establishing justice and peace as real Americans!"

Suddenly there is a hush. A psychical impulse passes through the singing crowd and is registered by those who are in tune with Father. In a moment a song of intensive love bursts like a Halleluiah Chorus accompanied by applauding hands, tear-dimmed eyes, and earnest shouts of "Thank you, Father dear!" and "Peace!" and "Isn't he sweet!" and "He's here—God Himself is here!"

He is a stocky man, a bald, stocky man, pleasantly brown, and of indeterminate age. Some say he was born in 1880 on a rice plantation on Hutchinson Island in the Savannah River, but there is no record of his birth. He is dressed well but not expensively. His rounded face is a study of prophetic brooding, deepened by a misty, dreamy look in his almond eyes, and a thoughtful concern which his half-smile only intensifies. With masterly poise, he walks to his place and stands for a moment while his young white virgin wife, Sweet Angel, charming in her innocence, gives the impression, through solicitous concern, that she, perhaps more than anyone else, knows that she is in the presence of "God Almighty, Author and Finisher of All that was, is, and is to be."

Oddly enough, this adulation does not seem either ludicrous or sacrilegious, though it constitutes the apotheosis of a man whose name was once simply George Baker and who is believed to have started his evangelistic career at the turn of the century when itinerant messiahs were conjured up by the sorcery of revivalism. Now the worshipers bow to the mystery surrounding this implacable figure. Not one of his followers would hesitate to do his bidding, whatever the command might be. Not a single one doubts him or his claims or denies the deification with which he has been enshrined, and even you might admit that all the cavil is now modified as Father, seating himself, wearily, humbly, and almost sadly, gazes tenderly at the lost sheep who have wandered into the green pastures of his selfless love.

Who are the lost sheep? You see dignified men of middle age and several sedate old ladies, well-dressed young men and women, and several others who might have strolled in off the streets of the needy. The ever-present secretaries, some eight or ten, Negro and white girls, with stenographic books, take their places on either side of the Divines, while across from Father a group of "Rosebuds," the girls who make up the Divine choirs, take their seats. When some 200 have been seated, the doors are closed, and those who could not find room at the long tables are requested to wait quietly in ante-rooms for the second serving. It will be a long wait.

For now the fabulous provider of his people's needs gives the nod to the head waitress who, in turn, transmits the command to her staff of immaculately dressed women in white, and the supernal fare begins coming in on silver trays. Each tray is first presented to Father, who blesses it with upraised hand, adds a serving fork or a spoon as needed, and sends it on its dignified way around and across the table. Everything is here: chicken: fried, fricassee, a la king—meat: steak, roast, cold cuts—potatoes: boiled, mashed, creamed, or scalloped, and candied yams—fresh vegetables to meet every taste, and crisp, cool salads of many kinds. It is like a setting for a Hollywood extravaganza, and it is free, the gift of "God" who, it is said, has no bank account and has never needed to pay any personal income tax. Why should he, when he owns nothing? "Nothing," as his followers say, "but everything!"

Father is not materialistically inclined. The kingdom, as far as he is concerned, cometh not by observation. The "Promised Land" of the Peace Mission Movement consists of a chain of farms in Ulster County, New York, as well as Pennsylvania. They provide poultry, cattle, and farm produce for the restaurants, hotels, and banquets in the Divine domain. When Father bought the fashionable million-dollar Brigantine Hotel near Atlantic City, he redecorated and reconditioned it and dedicated it as one of the better "heavens" in his kingdom. Some of the suites had previously rented for ten and twelve dollars a day, but Father scaled the whole lot down to a straight two dollars a week. Then he sent out embossed invitations to his followers and re-opened the Brigantine with a banquet of a hundred and five courses—all free.

His purchase of Newark's Riviera Hotel for $500,000 in 1948 was newsworthy because it was paid for in cash—as are all of Father's transactions—in one to twenty dollar bills. A group of his followers brought the money in suitcases, disdaining the use of guards or police for protection. "We trusted," said John Germaine, "In God." He meant, of course, Father Divine, for Father is their shield who says, "Permit me to be transmittible, permit me to be reincarnatable, permit me to be reproducible. When this is done you will see God in all mankind!"

Father is their crusader: "It is immaterial to me what man or men may think or say. I am going on!"

He is their hope: "I have even greater discoveries for you than the Atomic Bomb!"

He is their wonder-worker: "I cause your prayers to be heard and answered before you pray them!"

He is their messiah: "I produce God and shake the earth!"

And he is their ruler, for he has told them that America is God's throne and democracy is His crown.

To publicize his basic tenets, Father publishes a sensational fat tabloid called *The New Day* with the date line carrying A.D.F.D. (Anno Domini Father Divine). This is a weekly which sells at the nominal fee of five cents a copy or two dollars a year. Father's messages signed by spiritual aliases such as: King Sweet, Kind Beloved, Lord of all Lords, Omnipotent Monipresent, True and Living God Father Divine, are all here for the public to read and for his devotees to praise. Here, too, are songs —new songs, passionate songs which are memorized by Father Divine followers wherever they may be:

> We thank you, sweet Father,
> For your love and care.
> We thank you, sweet Father,
> We know you are here!
> We love you, we praise you,
> We thank you, our God;
> We live in secureness
> By trusting your love!

Or,

> Oh, can't you see he is God to you and me
> He's the one who came to set us free.
> I want to be rolled up, wrapped up, tied up in his love
> And let the rest of the world go by.

Inasmuch as practically every word spoken by Father is recorded by his ever-attendant secretaries and since his interviews and sermons are also stenographically immortalized, it is to be expected that the bulk of *The New Day* copy should be given over to this material. At first glance, the outlandish use of coined words and phrases might tempt you to discount Father as a clownish figure. You are confronted by such expressions as, "I visibilate God!" or, "I tangibilitate! I materialize every assertion, for God is the materializer of all of His Earth's Creation!" or, "I come to all men and all nations that they may be well, healthy, joyful, peaceful, lively, loving, successful, prosperous and happy in spirit, body, and mind, and in every organ, muscle, sinew, joint, limb, vein and bone and even in every atom, fibre and cell of My Bodily Form!"

But turning the pages of *The New Day* and digging ever deeper beneath what you thought was religious frippery, you encounter the testimonials of people whose lives vibrate to the idioms of Father's language no less than to the magic of his presence. They have listened to his words and something has happened in their hearts; they have read his messages and they want more to read; they have longed to know what they needed to do to be saved, and Father had the answer.

It is an answer that has intrigued every sincere inquirer who-ever stepped behind the so-called pearly gates of the Divine kingdom. Even you would have to admit that the little man who plays God has hit upon a most cogent technique for rebuilding lives. It revolves around a single word: *restitution*. Once this fact is understood, the magic of Father's influence becomes clear.

Here is how it works. Somewhere along the way of his upward climb this Savannah revivalist learned that an individual's major problem consists of living at peace with his conscience. Whether Divine experimented first with himself in this realm is not known, but that he hit upon a psychological truth with shatter-ing conviction is evident. He puts it this way: you can never realize your true self—the God within you—while you have un-requited sins locked up in the closet of your soul. You must drag them out into the full light of truth. You must come clean. You must make restitution.

This powerful approach to a revised way of living is instituted behind all the sensationalism and folderol of Divine's subtle in-sinuations that, in some special sense, he is God-in-the-flesh. The question, "Is he sincere or insincere about this self-canonization," cannot be answered. It is not a matter of sincerity. It is a case of a "Divine" obsession. He clothes himself in the consciousness of a God whom he has made in his image, a brooding, visionary, affluent, infallible, omnipotent, anthropomorphic God, five feet three, dark complected, bald-headed, and with a secret weapon for changing lives: restitution.

Whoever comes to him, whether it is a bum off skidrow, a Philadelphia industrialist, or a New York politician, Divine's prescription is the same, "You must make good for the sins over which the grass has grown. You must stop living a lie. You must come out from behind your false front. You must face yourself and begin to clear up your life." So powerful was this stereotyped formula, so universal were men's cloistered sins, so effective was the wonder-working-power of "coming clean" that the reborn souls were soon saying, "If you want a clear conscience and a heartful of peace, see Father."

What actually happens when you see Father? In effect, he persuades you that you are now sitting down with God. He has a saying, "See God in somebody, for until you see him in somebody you cannot find Him in yourself." So he is God's proxy, and in a day and in a land where it is surprisingly easy to join a church, Divine makes it difficult. Not that he asks for money. He doesn't. Getting converts is by no means a way of financing his religious movement. Nor is getting converts an IBM process with him. He uses none of the evangelistic cliches like, "Hit the sawdust trail—won't you come, beloved—Jesus is waiting—all you must do is believe."

None of these idioms clutter the mind of this obdurate judge of righteousness. He tells his spiritual clients that getting right with God means *work*. It requires a re-examination, a change in life, a new moral standard, but, most of all, it requires *restitution*. Many a Divine convert actually takes pencil and paper and, going back over his life, jots down all the half-forgotten sins, all the unpaid bills, all the unrepented deeds, all the venial and mortal acts which have blocked his way to inner peace. This vivid document then becomes a working sheet for his rehabilitation, and he begins to make restitution.

How seriously do his followers take this restitution requirement? They take it in desperate seriousness. With some it becomes a matter of life or death. All who embark on the excursion work as if God were watching. And "He" is. Etched into their tarnished but aspiring minds is Divine's warning that, "Even when I am not with you in my bodily form, I am with you in my spiritual presence. Aren't you glad?"

And the converts are glad. Disenfranchized, as many of them have been by the traditional churches, suspicious of the ease with which other professed Christians rationalize their questionable deeds, weary of the commercialism and form of institutionalized religion, and annoyed by the evidences of cultural and color consciousness in the major faiths, they are convinced they have finally found God sure enough. They like most of all the fact that Father has provided them with a tangible, usable, workable, and challenging technique to live by: restitution.

Even in the days of the depression, many large corporations began getting letters. Checks came to Sears and Roebuck, Montgomery Ward, the telephone company, J. C. Penney Company, and many more, accompanied by a memorandum saying, "I have met God and am paying up my outlawed bills." A New York firm at 364 West 121st Street advised Father, "This is to acknowledge with grateful appreciation the sum of $310 paid to us by Ruth Smile. This was a debt all but forgotten." The Unity School of Christianity in Kansas City wrote in to say, "At the request of Miss Glory Sun, we are writing to acknowledge receipt of a money order from her for $25 in complete payment of a debt she felt she owed us, although we had released her previously from any further obligation." Goodwin and Goodwin, New York realtors reported, "Dear Father Divine: We are pleased to inform you that one of your followers, Faith Faithful, has paid up an old debt of back rent. . . ."

One Divine convert testified, "Twenty years ago I stole a hundred dollars from the lady I was working for. When I heard Father God I knew I had to make that good even though nobody knew I had stole it. I earned a hundred dollars. Then I went to look for the lady I worked for. She had died. I told Father. He said I had to give the hundred dollars away somewhere just the same, because it didn't belong to me. I said I would give it to him. He refused. I looked around where to send it and thought that there wasn't anybody who had done more for me than my country. So I sent the hundred dollars to the Treasurer of the United States down in Washington, D.C."

Stolen goods were being returned. Lost and found articles took on the aspect of holy obligations. The smallest detail of life became opportunities for demonstrating self perfection. As an investigator you might be tempted to admit that the probity and candor of Divine followers are phenomenal and that when a convert reaches the "name-changing-stage" he can very probably be trusted with anything excepting—and this is the annoying anomaly—his relationship with Father. At this point, all researchers contend, the angels have a blind spot. Some observers suggest that Divine uses hypnosis to influence his subjects, that he keeps his followers under a post-hypnotic spell, that he is actually with them even though he is not present in the flesh.

This God-obsession is dangerous, objectors claim, because the illusion has been built up through the years until it has become a psychosis of misguided hope for many thousands of enthusiasts. Zealots, believing blindly and implicitly that Divine is God, point to their legends to prove it, legends which go back to 1919 when Father and Mother Divine (Peninah who passed away in 1942) opened their first "heaven" in Sayville, Long Island. Here Father and his first wife, a Negro, fed the multitudes "without money" and began establishing missions in Harlem, Newark, and in Philadelphia with "buildings just materializing as he had need of them." It was impossible even in those days to convince the "angels" that Father's income came from a cooperative system in which people contributed their time, from people who passed away and left their money to him, or that people, like themselves, had put money into a cooperative enterprise and had permitted Father to manage it. Fathers' followers simply wished to believe he was God and believe it they did.

Then there was the heavenly proof of his "Deityship" in Nassau County, New York, in 1932. Father had been preaching and changing lives and conducting great meetings filled with much power when he was arrested for disturbing the peace. This was because his followers, becoming so filled with his spirit, sang and shouted their praises as they crashed through to victory. Unbelieving neighbors notified the police and Judge Smith sentenced Father to jail. Although the judge was a hale and hearty man and not at all superstitious, five days after he sent this man Divine to prison, his honor died of a heart attack. "That," said Father's followers, "is what a man gets for fooling around with God!" And Divine, in his jail cell, shook his head and shyly said, "I hated to do it."

Followers still relate how Father sent his messengers of peace down to see Huey Long and how they were refused a hearing and how subsequently Mr. Long met an untimely death. Not through any fault of Father's; it was God at work. Will Rogers did a take-off imitating Father and Father said, "Stop it!" But Mr. Rogers saw nothing offensive in his act and kept on. Then there was a plane crash, and Will Rogers was killed. And everyone knew what happened to Senator Bilbo whom the Divine people had tagged as a racial bigot and about whom they sang in Father's presence, "D-O-W-N, down with Bilboism!" He died. Furthermore, there was one of Father's most beloved angels, Faithful Mary, who said that Father was immoral and who threatened to expose him. On her way to a radio broadcast, Faithful Mary was accidently struck by a car. Lying on her hospital bed, she had to admit that Father was God.

Father, himself, in a sermon had this to say, "You might not be amused, but you may be surprised to know, that just one year ago when we opened the Divine Greenkill Park in Ulster County, near Kingston, a boy was drowned in the pool. The coroner came and was very antagonistic and very malicious to me, even tried to personally stop my car and tried to take the key of the car, and spoke of what he would do. I gave him to know he did not know who he was fooling with. Thursday I saw an article in the paper where he had been killed instantly. They said he was driving his car, and that his brother was with him. Without a collison, colliding with any other car, the car just merely left the road and smashed into a tree and was cut in two. Both he and his brother, the two men, were killed instantly, and many other such things have happened with those who maliciously make attacks upon the FUNDAMENTAL."

"And so," the angels say, "you may rest assured that Father *is* God and if you start playing around with a live wire, what happened to others can happen to you."

But what will happen to Father? And what will happen to those who are convinced that nothing *can* happen to him? For as there is reasonable proof that he *was* born and equal evidence that he has been subject to the aging process of time, just as any other apparently mortal man, and since it is assumed that one day he must bow to the King he seeks to emulate—what then?

Followers will not speak on this subject. They know that there are miracles all around them, and who is to say what the final miracle will be? Even though there have already been frequent reports of Father's demise, as if roundly to refute them, he still appears in all his glory at the communion table. He comes, accompanied by his lovely bride and attended by the young virgins, his Rosebuds, to be acclaimed by his ever trusting flock. Smiling benignly, he accepts the adoration, nods understandingly as he hears the songs of love, the sighs of passion, the testimonials of those who, but for him, would still be lost in sin and still be conscience-weary.

"Thank you, Father," they say, "for setting me free, for taking me into the sanctuary of thy love and closing the door so that only you and I, Father, are there together, and there is no one there besides."

"Bless you, Father dear, for taking this life of mine and making it as bright as crystal and as pure as snow and for showing me the only way to peace."

"You are my all-in-all, Father; my love, my life, and my hope. I was lost. I was adrift. I was floundering in sin and wickedness, and you took my hand. You took my hand and set me on the high place where there is only glory and joy. Oh, that all might find you, Father mine, as you found me!"

Hardly able to escape the web of rapture spun by such believing hearts, you, as an investigator, might yourself be ready to believe that even when Father is no longer among his followers, he will still be there! Having looked at the Peace Mission Movement from the inside and having judged it by what religion can do in the lives of men, several researchers have ruefully been forced to say, "If, for many a questing soul, God is a symbol for goodness and love, then Divine is a symbol for God."

11 § THE OXFORD GROUPERS

WHAT Father Divine did for the uneasy consciences of the down-and-outers, Frank Nathan Daniel Buchman did for the troubled minds of the up-and-outers, and he did it with such dramatic effectiveness that his method has aroused both the praise and the condemnation of the church at large.

Because Buchman himself, at the age of twenty-seven, was in need of conscience therapy and, because he found it, he was able to help others in their search for cures. Born in Pennsburg, Pennsylvania, in 1878, into the family of the local hotelkeeper, he grew up in a Lutheran home under the discipline of a deeply religious mother. At an early age, he was slated for the ministry and was educated at such bonafide schools at Muehlenberg College in Allentown and Mt. Airy Lutheran Theological Seminary in Philadelphia. It was during his pastorate in Overbrook, a little parish near Philadelphia, that he came to realize he was a soul-sick man. Searching for the reason, he delved into himself for the answer and decided that he was trying to give his parishioners something he himself did not have: a clear conscience.

There undoubtedly are many ministers who preach goodness,

but they themselves are not as good as they know they should be. There are others who advocate tithing, but do not tithe; and some who admonish their people to be virtuous but who are far from being paragons of virtue. They do all this, however, without realizing their schizophrenia. But Buchman was different. He was a strange and curious man who was bothered by the fact that his pastorate had the appearance of success without actually being spiritually successful. Because he himself lacked a religion of depth, all he was able to give his people was a religion of impulse.

In Philadelphia, where he distinguished himself by building the first Lutheran settlement house, his brooding over religion-preached and religion-practiced was intensified during a tiff with his board of trustees. Although stung by their rejection of some of his ideas, he continued to preach love while he himself harbored bitterness, and told his flock to walk with Jesus while he, like the very least of the disciples, followed Him from afar.

So he left his church and he left the city of brotherly love to begin a pilgrimage that eventually took him to England. It was there, in a little wayside church in Keswick, on a Sunday afternoon in 1905, that he listened to a woman preacher sermonize simply and impressively on the "miracle of the cross" and its "power to save."

Now it is no secret that ministers dislike to listen to sermons, often even their own, and especially sermons by women, and Frank Nathan Buchman was no exception. But as he sat in the intimate surroundings of that small chapel, he mingled his own longings with those of the speaker, and for the first time in his life religion took on the form of a living experience. He later described it as an explosion in his soul. Suddenly he discovered that what he had been unable to find in his own pulpit, he had now found in a foreign pew, and what he had been unable to give others he was now able to give himself.

The experience was actually so imperceptible and so lacking in any visible manifestations that none of the other worshipers or the female ecclesiast was conscious that a man's life had been completely changed and that the echoes of this change would some day be heard around the world. Quietly, Pastor Buchman sat there analyzing himself, taking an inventory of his iniquities, tugging away at his sins until he felt himself purged of pride, selfishness, ill will, and a stricken conscience. As far as he was concerned, the power of the Christ had reached down to him from Calvary and transformed his life.

That night he wrote some letters. He sent each of his former board members back in Philadelphia a note saying in effect, "I have borne you ill will. I have been headstrong and sinful. I ask your forgiveness and I am ready to make restitution."

He received no replies. But that did not matter. Confession of sin and an attempt to right a wrong carried their own reward: a sense of complete adjustment to God and man. The assurance of freedom, a kind of "washing out," and the cleansing of the spirit that came to him after he had faced himself and declared his own shortcomings, caused him to reflect on the miracle-working-wonders of the Christian faith whenever that faith is translated into action.

What, he wondered, would happen if Christianity became a formula to live by instead of merely a philosophy to talk about and a theology to listen to? What if men could be persuaded actually to become doers of the word! Never in all the years of his seminary training, throughout all of his courses on church history, homiletics, Biblical literature, or during all the toilsome months of his ministry had it ever dawned on him that Christ's principles were applicable to the contemporary life of the individual. So phenomenal was this discovery that Buchman was a changed man. So compelling was his experience that he had a divine hunch he could change others. In short, the triad upon which "Buchmanism" was to be raised for all to see embodied exactly this: a man can be changed; the changed man can change others; change enough men and you change the world.

Himself a changed man, Buchman was no longer the parish pastor who had drifted into obscurity at Overbrook and into hostility in Philadelphia. It was a transformed Buchman who was now guided to Pennsylvania State College and to the job of secretary of the campus YMCA. Here his new principles of faith made their debut on the wild stage of student affairs. He was all for being honest, open, and above board with every aspect of life.

One of his first bombshells exploded on the campus when he pointed out that students were more interested in sex than in the spiritual life and more concerned about money than about an education. Why not drag these indignities into the "light of the cross" and take a look at them? As part of the development of a technique, he introduced a "morning watch," an "hour with God," which was a time for self-examination and spiritual adjustment. He urged the young people to come to him with their problems and their sins, promising emancipation and the activation of the spiritual impulse. Although not a great speaker or an outstanding educator, he had an uncanny, almost psychic, sense for being able to see what was lurking in men's consciences. It was this talent which was to become one of his greatest assets in the development of his new evangelistic technique.

Nonetheless, Buchman's mastery at changing lives unfolded slowly and undramatically on Pennsylvania State campus. In fact, he devoted seven years to little more than preparing for the spiritual windfall that would one day be his. His one great gesture was the initiation of a Student Christian Movement that brought to Pennsylvania State such spiritualized personalities of the World War I era as John R. Mott, Robert E. Speer, Henry B. Wright, and Sherwood Eddy. This turned out to be an exciting episode in campus religion, and the most inspired participant was Frank Nathan Buchman himself. Sensing the possibilities of a world wide revival, he joined globe-circling Sherwood Eddy on one of his tours in which meetings of an evangelistic type were held in various parts of the world. It was during this period (1918) that the full impact of man's hunger for something-to-live-by struck the imaginative Buchman. The realization that men were fed up with apathy in the church and longing for usable spiritual techniques was all he needed to make the nations his campus and to approach all men as he had the students back in Pennsylvania.

Now it must be remembered that the erstwhile parish pastor had the one basic ingredient for success: self-discovery through self-examination. Or, as he phrased it: Christ-discovery. Either way, the end was the same; the Christ in self was the true Self, and its capacity for goodness and truth was unlimited. Having found this path to peace: peace of mind, peace of soul, peace of conscience, he set up a guidepost which clearly and concisely charted the way for every seeker, "Come clean!" Using this as his directive, Buchman fearlessly ferreted out the sins of others with amazing skill. Once, at a Sherwood Eddy rally, a heckler disrupted the meeting by shouting forth the demand, "I'm an atheist. Prove to me there is a God!" When Eddy's attempts to answer the man had worn themselves out against the wall of unbelief, Buchman took over. Fastening his diagnostic gaze on the man, he charged, "It is not unbelief that keeps you from God. You're an adulterer! Let's clean that up first and then we'll get around to the God business!" And even as the heckler capitulated under this line of attack, so thousands of others were eventually to fall helpless before the modern reformer who "looked not on the outward appearance."

It was in 1921 that Christendom began hearing of Dr. Buchman as a man who fearlessly pronounced his judgments on campus life and sent them reverberating around Oxford's ivory towers. The war, which many religious leaders had predicted would bring nations to their knees and start a wholesale revival, had brought only disillusionment and cynicism to many who had seen its carnage and lived through its godless horror. Students, particularly, were living on the edge of unbelief. Anglicanism in England was bemoaning the fact that its young people were defecting from the ranks of the true faith. Evidence of this was to be found at Cambridge and Oxford, and so it was into this strategic religious battlefront that Buchman made his way, bringing with him his proven triad: man can be changed, the changed man can change others, change enough men and you change the world. Drawing up his most formidable weapon, he challenged students and the world to, "Come clean!"

Soon he was conducting a one-man revival that caught the attention of Anglican leaders. With remarkable skill, he introduced workable techniques, smoked out men's hidden sins with his insistence that they "turn to truth for God's sake!" and changed lives. His converts banded themselves into an energetic, soul-winning organization and, taking full advantage of the classical title and tradition of their institution, called themselves the Oxford Group or, simply the "Fellowship."

The secret of success, insofar as the operational pattern was concerned, centered in the "house-party" technique, an outgrowth of the experimentation which Buchman had instigated in his "morning watch" at Pennsylvania State College. House parties were, of course, more pretentious than the campus-conducted hours with God. They were exactly what the name implied: occasions where fun and fellowship were sparked by music or triggered by philosophical discussions. They included games and buffet luncheons or dinners aimed at uninhibited camaraderie between the sexes with an emphasis not on sinning, but on SIN: the confession of sin, the washing out of sin, the forgiveness of sin, and the resolution to sin no more.

This was done in various ways. These house parties offered an opportunity for each guest to seek out someone to whom his sins could be confessed, and Buchman himself served in the capacity of "Father Confessor" and advised the person how penance should be effected, how restitution could be made, and how the glory of the "washed clean soul" would be manifested. Or confession was made to the entire group assembled at the party, and attitudes toward sin and sinning were candidly discussed. Usually, quiet times were provided during which the guests would sit in Quaker silence or go their individual ways into the out-of-doors, seeking fellowship with God and inspiration for their needs.

House parties were Buchman's idea of how Jesus would deal with individuals and change individuals if He were alive today.

And as far as Buchman and the Groupers were concerned, He was very much alive and walking and talking among them. As of old, He was calling them to penance and to change their lives. The lakeside where He once had trod was now a living-room in a swank mansion, where successful business and professional men and women listened to His words as eagerly as had the lowly fishermen of Galilee; the home of Martha and Mary where He used to visit was now a country club in Los Angeles or Cleveland, Ohio, where the Groupers were ready to sit at His feet just as the wayfarers in Bethphage had done; and the Upper Room where once the Pentecostal fire had raced among the hopeful searchers after truth was now a plush banquet hall at the Statler or the Biltmore, where the students and young people, enjoying much the same fellowship, were Christendom's modern disciples seeking guidance and new power for service. It was religion in the style of the roaring twenties—the days of the Scopes' trial, Lindbergh's flight, and the scandal of Teapot Dome.

House parties, however, had such a powerful effect that they outlasted the feverish pace and prosperity of this period. They outlived the stock market crash in 1929, the advent of Hitler in 1933, and the death of King George V in 1936. In fact international Buchmanism was so potent that a diplomat, C. J. Hambro, president of the Norwegian Parliament, testified that as his life had been changed by the Groupers so it might also be possible for all of Norway to be changed.

An Episcopal rector, Samuel M. Shoemaker of Calvary Church, New York City, was so won over that he not only united actively with the movement but permitted his parish house to be used as a headquarters for the work. An educator, Dr. Christian Richard, at the University of Iowa claimed that he had found inspiration and guidance in the Group teaching which surpassed many spiritual helps he had found in Catholicism; and Professor B. H. Street, Provost of Queen's College, testified that he was compelled to lend his support to Pastor Buchman because of the profound conviction that the Oxford

Group held the secret for changing lives and giving people new hope and faith.

Lives were being changed and the movement invaded the highest political and social strata to work its miracles. "Change enough people and you change the world," was the apothegm; "God has a plan for every man," was the call to arms; and the "Jesus-way" was the command for conquest. In 1935, when ten thousand enthusiastic Groupers assembled for a meeting at Oxford, it looked as though Buchmanism could conquer the Christian world. As "Frank," or "F. B." as he was affectionately called by his loyal followers, looked out over that enthusiastic group of influential converts, he could see the reflection of his Keswick Chapel experience being relived in nearly every heart.

Delegates had come from around the world, the result of the Oxford Group evangelistic teams. Most of them had been washed clean, changed, inspired, enflamed by the power of the house party technique. Now they sat together in an international "house party" and listened to one another's confessions, or unabashedly admitted their own half-remembered immoral acts, their sexual perversions, or their lapses from grace. Together they testified about triumphs over self and went on record to say that Groupism works as nothing else had ever worked in religious regeneration. With consummate skill, they not only talked about but lived through the five Buchmanite C's: Confidence, Confession, Conviction, Conversion, and Continence.

Best of all was the fact that being born again the Buchman-way was *fun*. It was religious gravity decked out in modern robes of gaiety. It was fervent faith geared to the life and pattern of the time. It was religion sought, caught, captured and made personal without going behind monastic walls or giving up anything—excepting sin.

The churches watched and wondered. While some ministers, predominantly those of the Anglican and Congregational communions, endorsed and embraced the movement, the majority of the clergy remained wary of the Groupers. They were suspicious of Buchman because, despite all his claims, he was apparently not averse to having the program built around Frank as well as Jesus. He said he wanted the movement to revitalize Christianity through the churches, but all too often Groupers left the churches never to return. Buchmanism, the church at large concluded, was not complementary to organized religion; it was competitive.

Furthermore, there was a growing conviction among conservative pastors that the Groupers were sensationalists, using their house parties not for the repenting of sin but for boasting about it and often committing it. Sex was talked about so freely and couples discussed their intimate affairs *de amour* so openly that one minister who observed, "Buchmanism is not agape, but Agapemone," voiced the criticism of others who felt that it was not the love-feast of primitive Christianity that Buchmanism had revived, but the love of primitives.

What critics in the traditional church failed to realize, however, was that the secret of the Oxford Group's success lay in its fundamental awareness that man's conscience is troubled, troubled with fears, frustrations, guilt, superstition, and unrequited sin. Buchmanism insisted that the battle for a man's soul must begin in a man's mind, and that the triumph of the mind cannot be effected without first achieving the conquest of the conscience. "To *be* right with God you must *get* right with God" was a basic working slogan.

Therefore, to achieve this rightness, the Oxford Groupers devised concise and usable procedures which could be followed and understood by the very least among the distinguished Buchmanites. Whereas Protestantism, generally, had left its people stranded as far as "self-help" in religion was concerned, Groupism provided them with a veritable "do-it-yourself-kit" for the development of the spiritual life. The steps, based on the premise that "when a man listens, God speaks," required each Grouper to set aside a portion of every day for inner examination. This, of course, was a practice as old as faith itself, but F. B. gave it a modern touch when he advocated listening to God rather than talking to God. And how does one listen? By putting the mind at rest and making the soul receptive for divine impressions.

So the Oxford Grouper went "into the silence" either by himself or with others of kindred inclinations. He literally closed the door on the world and remained "waiting on God." Whenever a thought broke through, he jotted it down on a clipboard or a notebook which he had brought especially for this purpose. At the start, the messages so received might appear trivial, but as the participant developed, he learned to tune in on the God-given impulses and tune out what was obviously merely a self-induced idea.

To check the validity of these silent-time messages, Buchmanism provided its followers with a four-way test. It was suggested that each perception be judged against four absolutes: absolute honesty, absolute purity, absolute unselfishness, absolute love. If the flashes of insight could stand the test of these four touchstones, it was believed that they represented God's directives.

The simple poignant fact of doing something with one's religion proved to be such a powerful force in the life of the individual that many theologians stood aghast. Was it possible, they wondered, that mature men and women could be so naive as to sit in the silence with pencil and paper and wait on God! They called it Voodoo, self-hypnosis, and wrote the Buchmanites off as strange and curious people. But the Groupers simply asked the theologians, "What practical application of religion do you have to offer in its place?" Men's consciences, they went on to explain, were troubled and people wanted to *do* something definite with their faith, something more than just listen to religious platitudes or hear rhetorical sermons only dimly related to contemporary life. They asked, "How *does* God make His will known to modern man?" "Through history," retorted the theologians, "through history and the prophets and intellectual expressions and sacred writings," and they defended their position by drawing a sharp distinction between theology as the *possession* of truth and philosophy as the quest for truth, and ended by concluding that Buchmanism fitted neither the one nor the other.

It did not matter to the Groupers. They knew what they had found. They had "inside information" and also a growing supply of empirical proof that, "When man listens, God speaks; when man obeys, God acts; when men change, nations change."

It was not the theologians, however, who despoiled the Oxford Group, nor was it the growing accusation that sex and the talk of sex were being overly stressed at the house parties and at the college meetings. It was true, Buchman had been ordered out of Princeton as early as 1924 for saying that sex ruled the campus life, and it was also true that some Groupers had become so conscience-stricken when they tried to ease their consciences through public confession that they had broken under the strain. An Oxford campus paper, *Isis*, had once gone so far as to accuse the Groupers of being psychopathic. But none of these things actually accounted for the decline of the fellowship. The cause lay deeper: even though Buchman really believed he could save the world, the world was neither ready nor willing to be saved, and that, in short, was the situation. There is an individual conscience and a world conscience, and the technique that worked effectively for the former broke upon the obdurate stubbornness of the latter.

There will always be the question whether Buchman had the capacity for the greatness and acclaim that came to him. There is also a question whether his instinctive talent for reading the ways of men was lost when he attempted to read the ways of nations. Whatever it was, however, the Oxford Group died when it changed its emphasis from man to the masses, and when it changed its name from the Oxford Group to MRA—Moral ReArmament.

The transition took place in a series of events in the late 1930s when time was reckoned in terms of the actions of men: a Franco in Spain, a Hitler in Germany, a Mussolini in Italy, a Chamberlain at Munich, a Stalin in Russia. And, as if wagering that these men could be "changed"—these leaders in whose hands a tottering Europe was destined for demolition—Buchman called his followers out from their house parties and morning watches with God to save the world.

It was at a spectacular meeting in the Hollywood Bowl on July 19, 1939, that the man with the Keswick Chapel experience proclaimed to 30,000 spectators, "Tonight you are witnessing the preview of a new world order." It sounded like prophecy. It looked like the hand of God. For ten days this world assembly at Del Monte, California, held the spotlight and caught the fancy of the press as it endeavored to arouse a staid and not-yet-world-conscious Christendom with flaming slogans:

The plus of the character is the plus that will change the world.

The quality of the individual is the quality of the nation.

MRA: scientific medicine for the moral ills of the world.

Buchman read messages from King George VI and from Queen Elizabeth, from premiers of every nation where MRA banners were waving, and from governors of thirty-three American states. He read a message from President Franklin D. Roosevelt which said, "The underlying strength of the world must consist in the moral fiber of her citizens. A program of Moral ReArmament for the world cannot fail, therefore, to lessen the danger of armed conflict. Such Moral ReArmament to be most effective must receive support on a world-wide basis."

Following President Roosevelt's lead, many other national and international figures endorsed the general principles of MRA. Buchman made it appear that their endorsements were tantamount to membership in the program, and it was as Harry S. Truman later said, "Being for MRA is like being against sin." Undaunted and inspired, F. B. challenged the entire world. His goal was to mobilize a world-wide army of 100,000,000 spiritually inflamed followers by December, 1939, a hundred million men and women who would "listen to God!"

But before even one million could be enlisted, the world exploded. There were Munich and a Soviet-German pact; there were declarations of war that darkened all of Europe and Great Britain. The threat of war cast its shadows over the Middle East and the Far East and eventually over America. It was a race against time to remake the world, and Buchman lost. Wherever MRA was strong, war's threat was stronger, and something happened to the consciences of men in the roar and tumult of battle that destroyed both the quiet time and the four absolutes. What MRA had confidently predicted could not happen, did happen, and even Chamberlain, who had believed in MRA, was disgraced. And Pastor Buchman, who had doggedly held to hope for the redemption of Hitler, discovered that Hitler could not be redeemed. In the holocaust of disillusionment and the conflagration of ideals, the ranks of MRA were thinned as men put aside their faith in God for faith in guns.

The homeless remnants of the Oxford Group-MRA were gathered up by Buchman on Mackinac Island, Michigan, during the years of the war, and there they plotted their strategy for the days to come. They inaugurated road shows, thesis dramas built around the theme of how lives can be changed. They sent young actors with big names and royal blood on the road with these productions to testify to the power of Christ in their lives and to pay tribute to the man who had left the pulpit long years ago to find a faith. They also developed techniques for mediating labor-management disputes—the "mediation of the Jesus-way"—and looked forward to the time when they could make their influence felt at international tribunals in settling world affairs.

But even while the road shows played such naive and hapless productions as *You Can Defend America*, a patriotic musical revue, and *Drugstore Revolution*, a story of the rehabilitation of young lives, and *The Forgotten Factor*, an industrial drama for national teamwork, there were other "dramas" being played upon the fiery proscenium of the international stage: Pearl Harbor, planes over Tokyo, the Death March of Bataan, Corregidor, Stalingrad, Coventry, Kassel, D-Day, Iwo Jima, Okinawa, Hiroshima, Nagasaki, the execution of Mussolini, the suicide of Adolf Hitler, the rise of Russia.

Even so, the aging, but apparently ageless, Buchman has survived through all of these changing scenes. Traveling between Mackinac Island and his London center and the sumptuous quarters of MRA in Caux, Switzerland, he has never wanted for recognition and support from his devoted band of faithful whose changed lives are his handiwork. How many of these there are is indeterminable; perhaps 10,000, perhaps 50,-000. They are loyal to the core and will continue to explain and exploit MRA through many new and historic epochs in world history. In fact, the true MRA devotee insists that all that has gone before is merely a prologue to the great drama of brotherhood which is even now unfolding on the international scene. To this conviction many of them give of their time, talent, and fortune. Who is to say that they may not be right or who is to deny them their good intentions?

Call it Oxford Groupism or MRA or what you will, there is always a need for that something or someone with sufficient courage to challenge a man's conscience and to supply him with techniques whereby he can wash away his sins and "come clean" with himself and his several worlds. With such conviction, these faithful may yet, with their simple and alluring triad, prepare the world for what Buchmanites refer to as the *New Day*. Certainly, the formula is well phrased and wholly valid: man can be changed; the changed man can change others; change enough men and you change the world.

12 § PSYCHIANA

THERE ARE AT LEAST half-a-million people in the world who owe their peace of mind to Frank B. Robinson. The number includes men and women of many religious persuasions who often felt like sinners when they went to church and were told that, "You are conceived and born in sin," "There is no soundness or health in you," "God gives everyone a cross to bear," "The day of miracles is past." As these seekers after truth heard these dire sermonic assertions, something in their hearts rebelled and they said, "This is not true." Yet, as a result, their consciences became uneasy.

Robinson came to their rescue. Authoritatively and with dynamic conviction, he eased these harrowed minds with a fearless declaration, "I don't believe these things either! From the moment I threw these negative concepts overboard, life became a blessing and religion became my joy!"

It was not "church religion" he was talking about, however, and therein lies the story of one of America's most phenomenal contemporary movements. Nothing like it had ever been seen before and it is safe to say that it marked a transition in the field of religious promotion, with the result that the techniques it presented are now openly employed by some of the groups which once were Robinson's severest critics.

The Robinson religious movement had a prophetic name: PSYCHIANA. In 1928, when this coined word was first announced, terms like psychism, psycho-analysis, psychosynthesis, and psycho-therapy were known but not yet in vogue. Psychiana, which had the subtle nuance of something spiritualistic, became even more mysterious when Robinson affirmed that the name had been revealed to him in a dream.

In this dream he had found himself in a room with a dead man. Standing over this corpse was a stranger who made mystical signs and murmured whispered phrases as the cadaverous form began to stir. When Robinson asked him what he was doing, the stranger replied, "You should know. I am using Psychiana to bring life back to a spiritually dead world."

And that was exactly what Psychiana set out to do. In Robinson's words, it was designed to "awaken the world for God." It consisted of affirmations, instructions, parables, testimonials, and spiritual concepts organized into progressive courses of lessons which were sold through the mail. Psychiana was, in reality, a mail order religion, a correspondence course "guaranteed to help you find the Power of God or your money back!" To publicize it, Robinson advertised in every type of magazine, all the way from *Police Gazette* to *Psychology*. He brandished his ads in newspapers, did a direct mail order business of staggering proportions, and created what one advertising agency called the greatest selling-line ever written: I TALKED WITH GOD— YES, I DID—ACTUALLY AND LITERALLY! AND SO CAN YOU!"

The base of his operations was Moscow, Idaho, home of the University of Idaho, and, in 1928, a town of some 7,000 souls. When tall, dynamic, handsome Frank B. Robinson came to Moscow that year from Los Angeles to work in a drug store as clerk and pharmacist assistant, he was forty-two years old, married, the father of one child, a son, and he had twenty-five dollars to his name. Because he was a newcomer and, obviously, a strange man when it came to religion, people began checking up on him.

They learned from hearsay that he had been born in New York City in 1886, but that there was no actual record to prove this. They discovered that his boyhood had been spent in England where, apparently, he had lived with his Baptist preacher father and his stepmother, his own mother having died when he was a child. His memories of parsonage life and the merciless discipline of what he later referred to as the "pseudo-godliness that is actually worse than godlessness" were things he discussed freely over the drug counter. He was frank to declare that "church religion" had never given him a "break" or showed him any Christian mercy.

He told inquirers into his past that when he was fourteen, he had been shipped off to Canada with a younger brother, Sydney. They had passage on a steamer, five dollars in spending money, and a letter of introduction to a Baptist clergyman in Belleville, Ontario. But when they arrived, this preacher, the Reverend Henry Wallace, turned them over to the Salvation Army because he did not want the boys on his hands. When Sydney contracted pneumonia and hospital care was needed, Brother Wallace refused to help, and Frank, in desperation, wired his father for money, only to receive the laconic reply, "Secure best medical advice. Sorry cannot help financially." After his recovery, Sydney left town never to be heard from again.

His father's indifference, coupled with the heartless attitude shown by Henry Wallace, created in young Robinson's mind a bitterness he never forgot; he called it the "callousness of the so-called men of God." The disillusionment deepened, he claimed, because he himself desperately needed help in finding peace of soul. The institutionalized churches, Protestant and Catholic, left him cold. The Salvation Army, with all its "gospeleering" and its beating of drums and the rattle of tambourines did not bring his diffused image of God into focus. All anyone had ever offered him was rhetoric and speculations on what the will of

God might be. Throughout these unsteady stages of his spiritual search, he defied ministers with the charge that, "Unless God is a discoverable, knowable reality, He is nothing."

During his teen-age years, when he worked on farms around Belleville, Frank discussed religion with other hired hands. He talked about it with customers in a Belleville drug store where he was employed as a clerk. He made it a conversation piece with his fares during his period as a hack driver, and he needled churchmen into telling him in what way they were better or different than he.

A well-to-do, imaginative Baptist businessman, however, saw young Robinson as a Saul of Tarsus on the Damascus road. Like Saul, Frank was fighting the Christian church, but perhaps all he needed was a sudden "flash of light" to change him and make him bless those he now was persecuting. Recognizing this, the businessman forthwith sent Frank to a Bible Training School in Toronto, confident that his protege would one day be an evangelist within the framework of denominationalism.

The well-meaning philanthropist, however, was never more mistaken. In a rebellious moment at the Bible School, Frank told the teachers he was now more than ever convinced that organized religion could never point the way to a knowable God. He left before the end of his first year and began to pursue what, to all appearances, was an aimless quest. Wandering from one job to another, he worked on farms and in various stores; served for a brief time with the Royal Canadian Mounted Police; then migrated to the States and enlisted in the United States Navy. After this discipline he reverted back to his earlier pilgrimage, took a job as a drug clerk in Portland, Oregon, put in a stint as a whistle-punk with a lumber company near Klamath Falls; and held several odd jobs in California.

Each step, however, was leading him toward his destiny, for throughout all these years he never ceased "looking for God." Sporadically he returned to the well-beaten paths of Protestantism, only to discover that whenever he needed help, ministers disappointed him and Christian organizations offered him stones for bread. In later years, as he tabulated his indictments against the churches, he included: the preacher father who had beaten him until the blood flowed; a Salvation Army lass who had tried to seduce him; and a church elder who, when asked for advice about entering the ministry, had said, "Frank, you never appeared to be much of a damned fool, but you are certainly making one out of yourself now."

Then one Sabbath morning in 1928 he felt impelled to attend a service in a large and beautiful church on Wilshire Boulevard in Los Angeles. In the foyer he was greeted by an usher with a fresh carnation in his lapel who handed him an expensively printed church bulletin and said with a laugh, "Go right in, there is plenty of room."

As Robinson stepped inside the auditorium and walked down the thick-carpeted aisle, the organ music lifted his soul to what he described as "tremendous heights." But as he sat down on the cushioned pew, he realized that he was one of only twenty-six worshipers. Twenty-six worshipers in a million dollar church! As he looked over the remnant of a once virile congregation and studied the people, mostly elderly women, his antagonism against the church and its ineffectuality to hold its members became even more intense. Nor could he find in the sermon any hope or clue as to where and how the living God could possibly be found.

To the dinner guests who were waiting at his home at 500 Laurel Avenue, he vehemently described the lifelessness of the morning worship. Loudly he proclaimed that either God lives and can be found, or else He is dead and institutionalized religion is merely perpetuating a fraud. To these diatribes a guest laughingly replied, "Frank, you take religion too seriously. The church is a good thing even if it does nothing more than just stand on its street corner. Every town ought to have a church, same as every town ought to have a school or a jail. It's part of the system."

Later that afternoon, Robinson, alone in the house, went

into his room and closed the door. His outcry during those moments, which he later reported in many of his books, became the lamentation of a modern prophet. "O God," he exclaimed, "if I have to go to hell, I'll go with the consciousness that I went there earnestly trying to find you!"

As the moments passed he stood perfectly still, hopefully waiting for he knew not what. Then he fell to his knees, closed his eyes, and heard himself say, "The spirit within me is the Spirit of God, the same spirit that has moved in the lives of all great men. I have confessed this Spirit for many years, but I have also suppressed it. I want to express it from this moment on—fully, completely, perfectly."

Kneeling there, he felt his mind cleansed of every thought save the thought of the presence of God. His eyes filled with tears and he found himself breathing deeply, repeating with every inhalation words which seemed to have been whispered to him, "I believe in the Power of the Living God!"

He had the vivid feeling that he was not alone in the room. He could sense the Presence of something or someone, although he could see no one nor hear anything but the words he so earnestly repeated. Yet something had drawn aside a curtain deep within him and he seemed to be standing face to face with the Power that is life. No longer, he said later, did he feel a limiting consciousness; he felt only a single, specific sense of complete unity with God. In that flashing moment of insight, he realized as never before that he was the inner counterpart of a divine creative power. From then on he was convinced that he was the personalized activity of cosmic force. Those who have experienced something smiliar call it conversion. Others refer to it as a religious experience, or the Baptism of the Holy Spirit. Robinson called it "talking with God" and after that Sunday afternoon he was a changed man.

In the past, he had wandered about a great deal as if to escape from himself. He confessed that he used to try to forget his troubles in drink, that he envied people whom fortune had blessed, and that he doubted his own destiny. Now all was transformed. He wanted only to trust in God, to face himself, and settle down. So he began looking around for a job that would permit him time to develop the religious truths that were begging for expression. He found himself "guided" to Moscow, Idaho, where Charley Boles had a drug store that "closed early" and that needed a clerk. Robinson applied for the job and moved to Moscow with his family.

It was at this point that the town picked up his story. Moscow was suspicious of him because he talked about religion in the same way that high-powered salesmen talked about their wares. God, to Robinson, was apparently a commodity that everyone needed and that no one could live without. He evidently believed that religion should be advertised and sold across the counter. Some Moscowites knowingly touched their fingers to their heads when they observed the athletic, modestly dressed figure walk briskly along Main Street. They lifted their eyebrows when they saw him pause and energetically grab a notebook from his pocket to jot down a sudden idea. Robinson carried an assortment of sharpened pencils in his lapel pocket and when he wrote he had a habit of pushing his hat back on his head and listening, almost as if he heard a voice.

Midnight strollers could look up to a room above the drug store and hear the clatter of a typewriter and a mimeograph machine. Neighbors who noticed the light in the Robinson home which burned long into the night gossiped about these strange and curious new citizens.

"He pounds the typewriter hunt-and-peck till his fingers bleed. Then he tapes them up and types some more."

"Mrs. Robinson is as bad as he. They're both hepped on whatever it is they're doing."

"I've seen him walk through the wheatfields and the potato patches, just walking, and writing things down."

"He often takes his son for a walk in the woods. He tells him to listen and see if he can hear the voice of God."

The grocer, the banker, the butcher, and the clothier reluctantly advanced credit to the Robinsons, saying, "As long as you're working for Charley Boles, it's all right, but we never know how long folks like you will stay in Moscow."

Then one day an announcement in the *Star-Mirror* invited the public to a series of lectures on the "God-Power" in the dining room of the Moscow Hotel. Newspaper readers called their friends' attention to this newest piece of evidence that Charley's new drug clerk was really up to something. That evening some sixty people, out of curiosity, made their way to the place of meeting, among them several professors from the university, a number of farmers, and townspeople, mostly women. As they sat on the dining room chairs in the room where the tables had been shoved against the walls, they glanced surreptitiously at one another, some amused and some abashed. To begin the service, the drug clerk sat down at the piano and played a solemn gospel hymn and, to everyone's surprise, he played it well. Then he played another and another from memory (he couldn't read a note) and when he had finished, he got up. He stood before them simply dressed in a worn but well-pressed suit, his blond hair freshly cut and an expression of eager, deadly earnestness in his blue eyes.

"Ladies and gentlemen," he said, "the old songs are beautiful and I love them. People have been singing them for a long time. For nearly two thousand years men have professed belief in what Christianity teaches, and yet the world is going to hell. Fast. The reason is plain. We have worshiped the Messenger instead of living His message. The Christian church, driven to desperation as it is, will do one of two things; it will either die in its tracks, in which case another religion will step into the picture, or it will discard completely the foolish notion that God Almighty was crucified on a cross. That theory of God will have to go. It is going. It was a man who was crucified there, a man who came to make God real and living in the hearts of men. Most ministers have already discarded the Jesus-God theory, but they are hiding behind the fear that if they tell their people the truth, their position will be endangered. But truth should make men free! And that truth is that the same power which

Jesus taught and used and demonstrated resides in you and me!"

For an hour the fascinated audience sat and listened to the emphatic and confident voice of this inspired speaker. To several it was a new voice, strangely prophetic. To others it was heretical. To some it was the raving of a religious fanatic. Then, as if to mystify them even further, he told them a strange story. He related how he had walked along Market Street in San Francisco one night and felt the "awful loneliness that everyman feels when he is truly seeking God." But as he had walked, he had suddenly felt that he had the power to be whatever he wished to be and to accomplish whatever he set his heart upon. Even though it occurred to him that he had only five dollars, his sole possession, for some curious reason he felt as if he had just inherited a fortune. Under a street lamp he met a bum and stopped him, saying, "Can you use this?" The bum's eyes moved slowly to the extended hand and fastened themselves on a five dollar bill which lay there. "Take it," Robinson urged. As the bum stretched out a dirty hand toward the money, he asked suspiciously, "What's the deal?" When Robinson assured him, "No deal," the bum had grabbed the money and dashed off into the shadows and out of sight.

And as the little Moscow audience sat and listened, trying to understand, they were almost as suspicious as the bum had been. But they were engrossed as the drug clerk went on to tell them how his steps then took him to the far end of a deserted street where he found an abandoned livery barn. Opening the door which creaked on its rusty hinges, he went inside and lay down on a pile of hay, penniless but exalted, seeing God wherever he looked in the dark shadows of that deserted and dusty room. The veil between the visible and the invisible had been drawn aside, he said, and he had learned a truth which all the riches in the world could never buy: *The way to find God is to believe you have found Him.*

He concluded his remarks by saying, "A knowledge of the availability of the Power of God can supply every need in life. It is given to us in proportion to our capacity and our willingness to put it to use. A new light and a new faith are going out from Moscow to everyone who is willing to join me in this great adventure."

A stranger "church service" had never been held in this Idaho town. There had been no songs, no prayers, no texts from the Scripture, and not even an offering had been suggested! As the people began to depart, some thoughtfully, some confused, and others offended, one man asked, "Is it your idea to start a new church?"

"No," Robinson told him, "there are too many churches already."

"Well, what do you really have up your sleeve?"

"Didn't I make it clear?" the drug clerk exclaimed. "There is a way for every individual to come into a consciousness of the presence of God in his life."

"Sure, but isn't that what the churches have been trying to do all along?"

"Has the church done it for you?" Robinson demanded. "How aware are you of God's nearness? I'm trying to cut through to the actual living power of God here and now. This power will help you meet every emergency."

"I haven't any emergencies," said the man. "And I don't understand you."

And Moscow never did understand Frank B. Robinson. He was always looked upon as someone apart, someone outside and beyond the intimacies of the local scene. All that Moscow knew was that suddenly, almost overnight it seemed, the lecture lessons appeared in mimeographed form, then in neatly printed form, and soon Psychiana had its own printing establishment! The light that had burned late in the Robinson home was now transferred to a Psychiana office building where some eighty girls sat at lazy-susans and assembled material, sending circulars into every civilized country around the globe. And in an executive office the former drug store clerk typed furiously, sending out positive thoughts, breathing in the "God Power," and promising success to those who felt they were failures, friendliness for those who were lost and lonely, and health instead of sickness—all guaranteed.

Whatever the power, however real or imagined, it began to work miracles in the lives of the thousands of people who enrolled for the courses at $26 for a series of 24 lessons. Some even wired for the lessons, so urgent had been Robinson's appeal in his printed ads. Moscow predicted that it could not last. The town was convinced that this so-called God Power was simply a brazen confidence which Robinson was generating through his own dramatic and dynamic personality. No longer a drug clerk, but now a phenomenally busy religious teacher, he was now Dr. Robinson, with a degree from a metaphysical school in Indianapolis. He worked as though he were personally in God's employ. His day began early, no matter how late into the night he had labored. He breakfasted at home where his wife, Pearl, managed a busy household which now included a daughter as well as their son. Here in his den, on a portable typewriter, he hammered out the Psychiana lessons in the white heat of his conviction, wrote some twenty books, and reeled off affirmations which became guidelines for ministers who openly opposed him but who often secretly used his material.

Each affirmation, intended to solve a particular problem, was to be repeated aloud by the student at specific periods according to his individual needs. Psychiana believed there is a mystical power in the spoken word, and that any thought sent out into the void in faith must be fulfilled. Some of the most popular affirmations were:

GOD CAN AND MUST WORK CONTINUALLY FOR GOOD IN MY LIFE.
THE LIFE SPIRIT WHICH IS GOD LIVES IN ME AS MY OWN LIFE.
IT IS IMPOSSIBLE FOR A MAN TO DRAW UPON THE SPIRIT OF GOD
FOR ANYTHING AND HAVE THAT SPIRIT FAIL.
THE SPIRIT OF GOD IN ME CONTROLS MY PERSONAL AFFAIRS.
I BELIEVE IN THE POWER OF THE LIVING GOD.
THE CONSCIOUSNESS OF THE SPIRIT OF GOD NEVER LEAVES ME.
I AM REVEALING GOD TO THOSE AROUND ME.
NOTHING IS IMPOSSIBLE FOR ME TO ACCOMPLISH BECAUSE THE

SPIRIT OF GOD IN ME WILL ACCOMPLISH ALL THINGS.
I SHALL LIVE FOREVER BECAUSE GOD LIVES FOREVER.

Affirmations of this kind with minute instructions on how to use them comprised the lessons and were then presented in such a personal way that their popularity was insured. For example, Lesson One in one of the courses began, "My dear Fellow-Student: You and I are about to begin a wonderful journey together. We shall travel the most beautiful path you have ever known. Little did you suspect that such a journey as this could be possible on this earth. . . ." Lesson Two began: "Two weeks have passed since your first lesson. This lesson was the first step you have ever taken into the mystical, superlative, glorious Realm of the Spirit of God. I know just exactly how you feel, for every step you will take, I have taken before you."

Students were more than willing to enroll for advanced lessons after the first course had been completed. They bought Robinson's books and frequently sent unsolicited donations to the Psychiana movement. As a religious corporation, Psychiana was affiliated with the Byzantine American Catholic Church, Eastern Rite, into which, Robinson claimed, he had been invited and which offered him a connection with a hundred million Eastern Catholics. In view of his aversion to institutionalized religion, this affiliation was never understood even by Psychiana's most loyal supporters. Intimate friends, who saw the large portrait in the Psychiana office showing Robinson decked out in the full regalia of "Archbishop of the Byzantine Order," shook their heads in unbelief. A huge gold cross dangled at his breast and an ecclesiastical collar made him look very unlike the prophet his students visualized him to be. Few people, however, actually knew Robinson or presumed to understand him. He rarely met his students. Only occasionally did he speak at religious gatherings. Psychiana had no ministers, no fieldworkers, no churches, no chapels. Uncle Sam's postal employees were the missionaries who carried the correspondence lessons to students in more than 12,000 American cities. Los Angeles had 14,000 enrollees for one particular series of lessons; Birmingham had 13,000; Detroit 18,000; New York 24,000; Des Moines, Iowa, 9,000. Mail carriers in 74 foreign countries delivered the electrifying announcement, often in three-colored flyers, "I Talked With God—Yes, I Did—Actually and Literally. So Can You!"

At its height, which extended from the bleak years of the depression in the early thirties straight through the period of World War II, Psychiana was mailing out more than 500,000 letters a month. When the movement began in 1928, the Moscow post office had been second class; but when it became first class in the thirties, Robinson attributed this directly to his activities.

He was a changed man in many ways. No longer the eccentric drug clerk, he now was a confident diagnostician of his students' needs, a man of profound confidence and a seemingly inexhaustible reservoir of faith to effect notable cures among his followers. He drove a Cadillac, dressed immaculately, wore a big Stetson hat, and was not averse to smoking cigarettes. He was a dramatic figure as he strode purposefully down the streets of Moscow, seemingly unimpressed by the fact that the little town had not fully capitulated to the Power of God.

He donated a park for the betterment of the city's life, founded a youth center for the people of Latah County, joined the local Rotary Club, was elected a member of the Mark Twain Society, and became president of the News Review Publishing Company, publishers of *The Daily Idahonian*. Although some people recognized his frequent and unpublicized philanthropies and there were those who admired him for his devotion to the principles he preached, the majority of the Moscow citizenry and most of the farmers of the Palouse country were determined that the broad-shouldered, six-foot religionist remain a prophet without honor in his own community. They put him down as "not of our kind" and a fellow who "made religion big business." To which a minister added his opinion that any man who made religion big business made it a bad business.

But out in the romantic world of the unsatiable quest for truth, things were different. To his more than 800,000 active students, Robinson was a man of God, a miracle worker, a kind of saviour to those whose lives were rehabilitated through the power of his printed word. These people wrote to him constantly, addressing him as, "Dear Doc," "Wonderful Teacher," "Dear Prophet." "Dear Friend: On Thursday I telegraphed you that I needed help due to what I was afraid would be a terrible sickness. It must have been that you no sooner got the wire than I was already getting better." "Dear Helper: Only God knows what you have done to me. My husband was out of work, we were hungry, we did not know where to turn. You told us that God would supply all our needs if only we visualized the fulfillment of those needs. A miracle happened. My husband got work. . . . We are so grateful to God and you."

Long letters, postcards, poorly written letters, well written letters, and the honest expression of believing hearts no less than sentimental trash all made up the incredible correspondence that reached the "Man Who Talked With God, Idaho." An ardent, down-to-earth disciple in Montgomery, West Virginia, wrote, "All Hail to the Spirit of Life! Your wonderful teaching has blessed me with a typewriter maching i dont know much about typeing so please excuse all unspelt words. Writing to try to express my thanks for the man of God who delivereth us from poverty and want through teaching of that great providing spirit of life in us. it has been manifested and proven to me and they all around me can see how prosperious i am since ive been taking these lessons. they make remarks about it i got a referagtour two weeks ago and they all ask me how is it that you can get a new frigadair an no one else here can. i ansered well i turst the GOD who never did die and he has all things in his hands. say some of them call me crazy and others believe."

Although some letters bristled with condemnation, these did not come from the students, for, after all, they could get their money back if the courses did not appeal to them. They came instead from ministers who saw in Robinson's denunciation of the churches and in his de-deification of the Christ a case for heresy. They had good reason to be shocked, for in the pages of his

Strange Autobiography, Robinson said, "I have seen lots of 'religion' in my day. I have seen religion in action. I saw it nearly beat its own sons to death. I saw it guzzling beer. I saw it having illicit intercourse with members of its own church. I saw it lie, under oath. I saw it steal. I do not want that sort of religion, for religion, or what masquerades as religion, has not changed for the better since my boyhood days. It has gone so far that the whole world knows it for what it is—a ghastly sham perpetrated on the world by the church in the name of God."

As for Psychiana's views on Jesus, these were blunt and clear. The Galilean, according to the teaching, was a man like any other man, a man like any Psychiana student or like Dr. Robinson himself who realized the Power of God. And because Jesus recognized this Power and this oneness with the divine source of creation, He was able to perform miracles, just as any Psychiana student could do if he advanced as deeply into the God-consciousness as Jesus had done. The "redemptive plan of salvation" was scrapped, so far as Psychiana was concerned, as being pure fiction. In fact, Robinson wrote a book entitled, *Crucified Gods Galore* in which he sought to show that twenty world saviours had suffered martyrdom before the time of Jesus.

"As for Jesus," said the lessons, "he was the greatest of all spiritual pioneers. We cannot and do not accept the Immaculate Conception, the Virgin Birth, or the Vicarious Atonement. We doubt whether Jesus would have accepted them himself. The poor, lowly, lovely Nazarene never wanted any man to build a monument to him. What do you think Jesus would say if he returned to earth and saw cathedrals built in his name while people lie sick and diseased in sin? What would he do if he saw men and women prostrated before his statues without recognizing the Power of God which he tried so desperately to bring to them? For the great master did know spiritual truth. His message was so potent that had not the churches cast it aside and worshiped the messenger instead of his message the world would now know God. People are sick and tired of traditions of Jesus.

They are sick of church theology. They want God. They want a spiritual Power they can use now."

In the thirties, when this teaching was being broadcast, it was heresy. Billy Sunday wrote Robinson saying, "For God's sake, stop driving men and women out of the Kingdom of God. As fast as I save them, you drive them away." An irate minister, who had seen two of his "best families" leave his congregation after they took up Psychiana, threatened to shoot Psychiana's leader if he ever stepped foot inside his town. "Be thankful it's the twentieth century," a theologian warned Psychiana's founder, "or we'd burn you at the stake!" The term antichrist was a synonym for Frank B. Robinson among many religionists. Postal authorities, alarmed by claims that Psychiana was using the mails to defraud, investigated. The Better Business Bureau vowed that Psychiana was a racket. Many church groups warned their people to destroy Psychiana literature as speedily as it came to them. All of which seemed to Psychiana to be "good advertising." On the wall of Robinson's office was a conspicuous statement which informed visitors: "In Washington not long ago, the Postmaster General said to Dr. Robinson, 'We have never, in seventeen years, received one complaint from a member of your organization.'" As for the Better Business Bureau, it became a target for Robinson's righteous wrath. He sent millions of circulars through the mails which declared:

When Jesus walked the earth some two thousands years ago, he brought to humanity a message of staggering import. He brought the very same message that Dr. Robinson is bringing today. But "reformers" crucified him. They never let up until he was safely in the tomb. They thought they were doing good, because Jesus Christ was certainly unorthordox, just as Dr. Robinson is unorthodox. There was not a "Better (?) Business Bureau" operating in that age; but had there been, you may be sure it would have been in the vanguard of those misguided people who, because Jesus refused to operate according to their traditions, killed him. . . .

As he walked the borderline between near-deification by his devoted students and the defamation of the church at large, he declared, "The Power of God always works best in an emergency! When you are troubled, threatened, or disturbed, go into a quiet place. You will be strengthened and filled with power. There are no greater words in the Bible than these, 'Be still and know that I am God.' Like the tornado with the space of calm in its heart, so the restless, ever-throbbing and heaving rhythm of God is eternal peace."

Some of the suggestions designed to induce this "eternal peace" were simple to a point of naivete. For example, a standard "Procedure for Psychiana Students" prescribed:

1. Before beginning the day's work, close your eyes and say, "Spirit of the Living God. I begin this day recognizing your presence in me. I'm going to let you guide me every moment through this day. Thank you for being so close to me."
2. At breakfast, smile.
3. At noon, repeat the statement made earlier and express gratitude to God for being so close to you.
4. In the evening read your Psychiana lesson and recognize that the Spirit of God is in you.
5. Before you retire, don't get down on your knees and ask God to forgive you all the sins you have committed that day. Thank Him that you have committed no sins for which you need to ask pardon. You can sin if you want to, but if you do, don't come sneaking around to God at night and ask forgiveness. If you really are sorry for what you've done, you won't do it any more. Then, before you retire, think of a few names of those you have spoken to about Psychiana or those who would be interested in having our lessons started to them.

The powerful appeal of the Psychiana movement resided in Robinson's unshaken conviction that every man is on a spiritual quest. His constant complaint was that the churches blamed everyone and everything for their own failure to attract people and never once would admit that they themselves might be at fault. His lessons told his students, "If the philosophy which the church of today brings to the world does not attract modern man, that philosophy cannot be of God. By the very nature of man, man wants God. He belongs to God and he instinctively wants to turn to God. When the history of this age is written we will need to include a remarkable paradox: everybody agrees that religion is the only thing that can save civilization and last Sunday a hundred million Americans stayed away from the churches' services."

An appeal even more potent than the spiritual quest was the search for miracles of healing. This possibility drew many thousands into the movement, for Robinson had dynamically publicized the fact that, "There can be no problem in your life that you cannot solve. There can be no lack that you cannot fill. It is utterly impossible for you to draw upon the Spirit of God in you for anything and have that Spirit fail you."

He had testimonials of healing miracles to prove it. During his Portland meeting a telegram was handed to him stating that a boy in Tacoma, named Corwin Hull, was dying of tubercular meningitis. Robinson read the wire to the audience and announced that the boy would not die but would recover through the Power of the God-Law. Ten days later the mother of the boy wrote saying, "All the doctors gave him up. Now they cannot understand why he is getting well. They say it is a miracle. We know we would not have him but for you."

From Aurora, Oregon, a student reported, "Before I took up this study I was X-rayed and found I had a spot on one lung. The doctor was afraid of cancer. Yesterday I was X-rayed again and the spot is disappearing. The doctor is dumbfounded. I understand. I am overjoyed."

An Anaheim student testified, "I had a very bad stomach and I took soda two or three times daily. After telling you about it and using your affirmations, I don't have to take soda any more."

A foreign student went on record to say, "A close friend of mine had a large goiter and was worried about an operation. It would have been dangerous. I placed my hand on her goiter and said, 'The Spirit of God is making you whole!' Sometime later her doctor examined her and found that the goiter had completely disappeared."

As Psychiana prospered and as the reports of miracles of healing increased, the Robinson files grew to the bursting point with so many testimonials that he could no longer be accused of bribing men and women into health.

But there came a time when the healer of others was called upon to heal himself. This, the nemesis of every wonder worker, of every prophet, and of every man, found Robinson fully prepared and unafraid. He had suffered several heart attacks as early as 1946, when he was sixty years of age. After one of these, when he was brought home in an ambulance accompanied by three doctors, one of whom was a close friend, he had been told, "Frank, I think tonight will be your last night on earth." Robinson replied, "Nothing doing. I shall live until I have accomplished what I set out to do." Following another attack, when doctors had ordered him to "take it easy," he got into his car and drove all night because he felt the need to visit a sick student in California. He filled these driving hours with his loudly repeated favorite affirmation, "I believe in the Power of the Living God!"

Two years later his belief in the God-Power reached its supreme challenge. Yet, in a very real way he had accomplished what he set out to do: to make religion dynamic in the lives of men and to publicize and popularize it as few contemporary religious leaders had dared to do. Assured of this in his own mind, he died in Moscow on the night of October 18, 1948.

When the news of his passing was publicized across the country via an AP release, students deluged the Psychiana offices with telegrams and telephone calls. Flowers and messages of affection flooded the Robinson home. Many Psychiana enrollees expressed skepticism about the report of their teacher's demise; they sincerely believed that he would never die. They had taken literally the unqualified statement he had made in his books, "I am a prophet of God." They had read in his lessons that death would one day be overcome.

The condolences and expressions of shock and sorrow did not come from Moscow or from the churches, but from the mail-order congregation in the great "church of the world" whose pastor and prophet was Dr. Robinson. Mrs. Robinson said, "God in His Infinite wisdom and power has let His light shine through him. I am so sorry so many people misunderstood. I am so grateful he was able to help so many. I know that he wants nothing more than to have us all practice what he taught and immortalize the things to which he devoted his life."

When Frank Robinson died, Psychiana died with him. It was only a matter of months before the Psychiana presses were still. It was only a matter of two short years before thousands of students had completed their courses and were told that there would be no more Psychiana courses, no more affirmations, no more books, and no more instruction on how to find the Power of God. But even so, many students by that time had already romanticized their teacher into a legend. He came, they avowed, into the world to teach the churches how to propagate the faith, how to use the power of positive thinking, how to rightly interpret the Christ, and how to prove to America that there is no conflict between a religion of health and prosperity and the true worship of God. Their prophet, they were sure, had lived until he had fulfilled his mission.

Today the books of Frank B. Robinson are at a premium, and Psychiana's lessons are already collectors' items, not because of their literary value, but because they marked an epoch in the Americanization of the Christian faith and another contribution to the glorification of the gospel of abundance. A remnant of the faithful still write or wire to Moscow, Idaho, hoping to receive some word or vision for their special needs, while other students leaf through their correspondence courses hoping to hear their prophet speaking to them once more. Most cherished of all, as far as Psychiana students are concerned, are the teachings which put their consciences at ease, as when Robinson said,

You ask me if it is wrong to take care of your physical and material needs? No, it is not wrong, provided you take care of them as you should through the Spirit of God. You ask me if it is wrong to believe that Jesus was born as other men are born and that he lived as other men lived? No, it is never wrong to believe the truth and to throw superstitions overboard. You ask me if there is only one way by which men can be saved? There is, but it is not by way of any church or man-made creed; it is only by a recognition of the Spirit of God living in you as your Spirit of life.

Robinson's convictions and personalized touch worked pure magic among his devotees. They had come to him with their ideas about a meek and lowly Jesus and he had told them to get that idea out of their heads for Jesus was nothing of the sort. To Robinson, Jesus was a hard-hitting prophet with enough courage to oppose the leaders of the church and state of his day. Jesus had known what he wanted to say and he had said it with all the power he had. Robinson, who had described Jesus as a big man, standing well over six feet, had always insisted that if the Galilean were living today He would employ all the modern means of communication to promote His gospel. If Jesus were living in America, Robinson had proclaimed, He would dress as well as the best of us, drive a good car, and "I wouldn't be surprised if he'd wear a Stetson hat!"

And these are but a few of the reasons that many Psychiana students still think of the "Miracle Man of Moscow" when they think of Jesus. They remember the stream of testimonials of healing, rehabilitated lives, visions, voices, and dreams. They cannot forget the comfort they received from the personalized and emotionally charged admonitions he sent them; they cannot even now divorce themselves from the belief that their teacher was a man who had literally "talked with God," and who assured them that through faith they could do the same.

Even today as they turn to the last page of his last lesson, they can find nothing strange or curious in his vivid words which said,

Standing behind you and over you and all around you, and under you for your protection and benefit, is the great Power of the God-Law. . . . I should like to talk to you about this for one solid month, or for a year, but that, of course, is impossible. So I am leaving you now and wishing for you the courage and the confidence necessary to take this great God-Power with you wherever you go and to use it for the manifestation of whatever you need. . . . Our little journey together has come to a close, and may God ever bless you and keep you until we meet again. . . .

PART

THREE

THE

SEARCH

FOR

UTOPIA

13 § THE SEARCH FOR UTOPIA

As far as utopias are concerned, America has been their most famous proving ground. One hundred and twenty-nine times in our history, people have banded together, determined to create a world within a world in which they would have friends to trust, work to enjoy, a faith to follow, and a chance to live their lives without conflict or fear.

Some of these adventures bore intriguing names: The Harmony Society, Separatism, Perfectionism, Icaria, Transcendentalism, the Aurora-Bethal Communities, Anaheim, Bishop Hill. These were projects of people who insisted that in the greater world, the world of governments and power politics, secularism, materialism, and competition, there was too great a gap between the rich and the poor, the talented and the talentless, the seemingly wise and the seemingly foolish. They felt that the good Lord wanted it differently and that man, somehow, had failed His purpose.

Most of these utopia seekers were convinced that time was running out, that God was preparing to roll down the curtain on men's affairs, and that when He did, He would look around for His elect, those who were in the world but not of it; those whose lives had been insulated by the solid walls of a righteous faith.

The attempt to establish these little utopias, these microcosms, took forms which to outsiders seemed strange and curious, but which to ardent pilgrims were in complete conformity with the highest expression of God and man.

Most of these experiments were Christian, arguing for the fact that the Christian church itself was a utopian attempt. It, too, had been built on a desire for perfect fellowship, a revolt against existing conditions, the belief in a Chosen Leader, a conviction that an era was ending and that the Lord's elect should be prepared for some great burst of glory. This "strange and curious sect" had a directive for utopia which Acts 2:44 faithfully recorded, "And all that believed were together, and had all things in common." Theirs was a communal venture.

For a brief and fleeting period it succeeded. People who observed these "cultists" said, "Behold how these Christians love one another!" They not only shared their goods; they shared their ideals. They turned the other cheek. They walked the second mile. They followed a Man whom they claimed had risen from the dead. They repeated His sayings and prayed His prayer, and changed the Sabbath from a day of rest to a day of reverence for Him. They believed they were the chosen of God. Forgiving each other, bearing one another's burdens, denying the world, they became a plain and peculiar people, neither averse to being ridiculed nor afraid to die. Freely they lived under spiritual laws which held them captive to their faith. That their utopian experiment failed is no surprise. Reality never seems able to approximate the ideal. There is evidently something in human nature which will not be regimented, and something in our divine nature that will not conform even to divine decree.

But men are bound to continue their utopian search and America is still open for the experiment, even though all but one—or two—of the 129 communal attempts have failed.

The reasons why they failed and how they failed and what

their aims and dreams have been are more than just mere slices of Americana. They reflect something in the life of each of us, a moment when, spurred by high hope or deep despair, we draw a mental blueprint for our own utopia and wonder why in the world it cannot quite come true.

14 § THE DOUKHOBORS

WHEN THE LAST Canadian Doukhobor dies on his British Columbia hill, he will carry his dream of utopia with him to his grave. For two hundred years this quest has been the ambition of his life and the hope of his people. To establish a perfect society, Doukhobors have wandered half-way around the world, have broken up into many factions, and have followed the enchanted voices of their eleven "inspired" leaders.

The story begins in the mid-eighteenth century in Russia where the word, Doukhobor, meaning "spirit-wrestler," was a nickname for a group of peasants who renounced the Orthodox Church at a time when heresies were widespread across the Slavic world. Russian church officials accused these radicals of wrestling *against* the spirit because they were criticizing and condemning the practices of Eastern Orthodoxy. The dissenters, however, declared they were wrestling *with* the spirit in order to purify the doctrines and correct the evils which they claimed were rampant in the established religion. When the church fathers demanded to know by what authority these illiterate peasants dared defy and oppose the mighty Eastern Church, the non-conformists answered by saying they did so through the power of the "inner light," which meant to them the direct revelation of God in the soul.

The Doukhobors opposed the use of icons; they wanted priests to dress like men and not like women; they refused to comply with the government's policy on military service and the taking of oaths; they did not approve of public schools because they felt these lured their children from God; they insisted on their right to build a community "where only God would reign;" and, most of all, they were convinced that the soul of Christ had the power of uniting itself with any person it pleased, and that it would always be united in whomever God sent to them as their guide.

A few villages were established in which the demonstration of these ideals was attempted, and soon Doukhoborism spread from its Kharkov homeland into the Dnieper provinces. The first leader with whom the spirit of Christ is said to have been united was an anonymous Prussian Quaker who, true to his own inner light, settled disputes in the name of Jesus, argued with ecclesiastical officials, and proclaimed that the church and its ceremonies were superfluous. For two years he shepherded his growing flock of zealous dissenters, holding them together by an authoritative dictatorship. The Doukhobors, confident that he had been sent by God, readily accepted his ultimatums. Under his leadership, they prospered and flourished. Then, one day, this itinerant evangelist wandered off as mysteriously as he had come.

His departure plunged the "spirit-wrestlers" into a period of solemn contemplation. Although they objected to state rule and church ordinances, they knew that they themselves needed leadership. Opposing education, they realized they required a man of intellect to guide them. Convinced that heaven had provided them with the Prussian Quaker, they prayed, "God, send us another Christ-inspired prophet!"

Another came on a spring day in 1769, a ruddy stranger of unusual learning and eloquence, a man named Sylvan Kolesnikof. He wandered into one of the villages and announced, "I have come because God called me. God in the soul is the only guide to action."

The Doukhobors, sure that Kolesnikof had been sent in answer to their prayers, were even more convinced of his divine right to rule when he assured them that they were fallen angels endowed with strength to rise again.

"Bow to each other when you meet," he counseled, "for you bear the image of God!"

He set a plain board table in a field and placed on it a pitcher of water, a dish of salt, and a loaf of bread. These elements, he declared, would be the symbols of their faith: the water, representing the spirit of life; the dish of salt, the essence of life; and the loaf of bread, the staff of life. Gathering around this homemade altar, the rejoicing Doukhobors lifted their voices in songs of praise. Then they bowed low to one another, fervently murmuring "Slava Bohu" (the Lord be praised). Whenever they addressed Sylvan Kolesnikof, they submissively touched their foreheads to the ground. Utopia, they were sure, was very near.

In 1780, however, this second leader died, and the Orthodox Church predicted that the schismatic spirit-wrestler-movement would perish. They were wrong, for no sooner had Sylvan Kolesnikof been laid to rest, than a bearded pilgrim strode confidently into a Doukhobor village, bearing a Hebrew Bible in one hand and a flute in the other. A strange Elijah, going by the name of Gregory Skovoroda, he declared that after long wanderings and much suffering inflicted upon him by the fathers of the Church, he had been led by the admonitions of Christ to come to them.

The Doukhobors bowed to him with their foreheads to the ground. "Slava Bohu," they said, and often they sat entranced as Gregory related how he had been trained for the priesthood, how his brilliance had confounded the theologians, and how he had "escaped" from the famous monastery at Kiev by feigning insanity. They wept and blessed him. They listened in awe as he debated with Church theologians in Latin and Greek and read to them from his Hebrew scriptures. They stood absorbed at the music of his flute. They memorized the melodies he composed and chanted his songs. Utopia was coming nearer each time they gathered around the plain board altar with its pitcher of water, its dish of salt, and its loaf of bread. But one winter's night, ten years after Gregory Skovoroda had wandered into their midst, he put down his flute, laid aside his Bible, and said, "I am going home."

Chanting sorrowfully, the Doukhoborski bore him to a mountain tomb where they laid him to rest beside Sylvan Kolesnikof. Despite their loss, they knew they were children of destiny. Their faith was clear: they believed unquestioningly in God, but denied the Trinity; they recognized the Christ in man, but Jesus was no more divine than any of their own leaders; they were pacifists and non-resistants, but stubbornly defended their way of life with passive resistance; they worshiped each other and bowed to each other, but bowing to icons was sin; they loved one another and disliked the Church; they were bound together by unbreakable filial ties, but refused to take oaths; they revered learning and despised education; they wanted to be ruled by a strong leader, but they shunned the authority of governments; they wanted utopia and they did not want the world.

In 1790 heaven sent a fourth messenger, a wool merchant, Illarian Pobirokin, from the village of Goreloe. When he told them he had "been in the spirit" and had heard a voice bidding him "arise and go to the Doukhobors," the elders proclaimed him divine and escorted him from village to village with rejoicing. More than 300 white-clad women and black-suited men followed Illarian Pobirokin through the streets, fervently singing the lovely hymns of Gregory Skovoroda.

Pobirokin's reign was short-lived. In just a year, despite his visions—or because of them—he was arrested by the Russian police, accused of inciting the people against the civil law. The Doukhobors offered no resistance to his arrest. Often entire families, charged with such subversion, had been banished to Finland or Siberia, but this, too, was part of God's plan which had promised His chosen people "persecution for righteousness' sake."

No sooner had Pobirokin been spirited away than a tall, engaging stranger, made his advent. His step and bearing supported his claim that he had been a corporal of the guards, but now he was a soldier of the Tsar no longer, for God had appointed him to the captaincy of His people. The spirit-wrestlers bowed to one another and bowed low to him. With many a fervent *Slava Bohu,* they clasped to their hearts their fifth leader, fifty-year-old Savely Kapoustin. Eloquent in speech, remarkably versed in Doukhobor history, he gathered with them at their altar in a field and said, "As truly as the heaven is above me and the earth beneath my feet, I am the true Lord Jesus Christ!"

They followed him to the region of the Milky Waters near the Sea of Azov where he promised to build utopia. He called and they came: on foot and in open wagons, bringing their possessions and the Doukhobor traits: blind faith and an unquestioning allegiance to their leader. They brought their hymns, their prayers, and their dedicated belief in the revelations of the "inner light."

Kapoustin was a dictator, demanding that the now 5000 spirit-wrestlers turn over their personal property to him. This they did, never questioning his right to rule. He bought and sold land, accepted and rejected members, made laws and broke laws according to his will, which he declared was God's will, and, under his guidance, the Doukhobors saw their dream of utopia coming true. New homes and huge storehouses were rising in one of Russia's most fertile and productive areas.

Officials of the Orthodox Church, unwilling to believe that any good could come out of Doukhoborism, came to investigate. They discovered a thriving settlement living in a "community of goods and spirit." They heard the impassioned singing of the contented colonists and the oft-repeated *Slava Bohu.* Amazed they watched as the Doukhoborski bowed to each other and bowed to them, and touched their foreheads to the ground as they greeted Savely Kapoustin. They saw the once-querulous dissenters gather in reverence around a simple board altar on which were the pitcher of water, the dish of salt, and the loaf of bread.

However, the tranquillity of utopia was soon disrupted, for Kapoustin, sensing that he was ill and would soon die, gathered twelve Doukhobor elders about him and said, "When I am gone, the power of the Christ in me will pass into my son, Vasily. Hear ye him."

It was 1820 when Vasily Kalmikoff assumed control. He bore neither his father's name nor his father's strength. He was a drunkard and so was his son Illarion, who succeeded him, but blindly the Doukhobors accepted them both as being divine. Never were they to doubt that "those whom God has sent to lead us bear the image of the Christ." Since Illarion was disinclined to take on the responsibility of married life, the elders provided him with six virgins to assure that he would produce an heir for the Doukhobor cause. When two sons were born from this experiment, it was solemnly avowed that this, too, had been the will of God.

Meantime, corruption, torture, and death swept the Milky Waters colonies and there was a government investigation. Authorities claimed they found twenty mutilated bodies buried in various fields, grim evidence of dissension and a struggle for power in utopia. However, when the Doukhoborski were interrogated, some of whom themselves bore signs of whippings, the police were unable to pry any comments out of them. It was like stepping into a family quarrel. Unified by their devotion to all they professed, the stubborn spirit-wrestlers resisted outside interference with their two most powerful weapons: silence and passive resistance.

So the government, supported by the Orthodox Church, issued a decree over the signature of Nicholas I which said, "In the name of your religion and by the command of your pretended teachers, you put men to death, conceal crimes committed by your brothers, and hide information from the government. . . ." Then followed an order that the settlement at the Milky Waters be closed and that Doukhobors who refused to return to the

Orthodox Church should be sent into exile to the desolate Caucasus.

Almost without exception, exile was chosen. Only 27 offered to return to the established religion, the other thousands gathered on a fall day in 1839 for a final service in their beloved Milky Waters community. Around their now traditional altar, they sang their thrilling hymns, bowed to one another, and murmured a tearful but confident *Slava Bohu*. With their cherished possessions strapped to their backs and following a great string of loaded wagons many of them drawn by men and women yoked together, they began their arduous trek to the isolated region which lay between the Black Sea and the Caspian.

God did not leave them leaderless for long. During their journey He pointed out to them their next prophetic guide, the eighth in what they believed was an "immortal succession." This leader was a powerfully-built young man named Peter Kalmikoff, the son of one of the six virgins, sired by the divinely profligate Illarian.

Under the indomitable leadership of Peter Kalmikoff and his wife, Loukeriya, a Doukhobor kingdom rose on a Caucasian plateau. In ten years, following their banishment from the Milky Waters settlements, the industrious spirit-wrestlers had transformed the land, built a model village, and gained so many converts that their membership grew to 15,000. The edict of Nicholas I, which had sought to banish them, spurred them on. But in 1864, three years after Alexander II had electrified Russia by granting freedom to the serfs and recognizing especially the Doukhoborski, Peter Kalmikoff lay dying of fever.

"I am mortal only when it comes to death," he told those watching around his bed. And when they begged him to indicate who would lead them when he was gone, he replied, "I give you to Loukeriya. The spirit of Christ will pass from me to her."

Doukhobors say it did. For twenty-two years she strengthened the settlements through her bold declaration that, "They who live by the laws of God do not need the laws of men." She was their beloved and honored matriarch, the ninth leader in the unbroken "apostolic chain," and they bowed before her as devoutly as any devotee of Orthodoxy bowed before his icon. But she, too, was mortal, and she died, suddenly and childless in 1884.

And then *he* came; the greatest of them all, the "truly divine," the man of whom Doukhobors still speak in hushed whispers, the chosen one about whom it is said even today, "When he spoke it was as though we heard the Christ of Galilee." Whenever they saw him, this tall, handsome, proud, indefinable man, they blessed him for blessing them. Whenever he passed, they bowed to the ground and whispered their reverent *Slava Bohu.*

His name was Peter Vasilivich Verigin, and rumor had it that he was the illegitimate son of Peter Kalmikoff. But if he was, it made not the slightest difference to the Doukhobors. Who could say? It might even have been God's plan in this way to transfer the Christ spirit to him. They loved him from the start and referred to him by the endearing term, "Petushka."

He feared no one. He honored no man above another. He sought out Leo Tolstoi for opinions on brotherhood and peace and talked to him about the basic Doukhobor beliefs: the inner light, the simple life, non-resistance, vegetarianism, and the hope for utopia. He absorbed Tolstoi's ideals and then declared that what the philosopher theorized about in words, he, Peter Vasilivich Verigin, would demonstrate in deeds through people's lives. Once, caught up in a wave of spiritual conviction, he announced to a Doukhobor assemblage, "I am your Christ, your leader, and your Tsar!"

He claimed he had found the solution to every problem by asking himself, "What would Christ do?" and then acted upon his inner guidance. This method he followed until people felt that he could do no wrong. When Petushka was arrested for arousing the people and for "playing Tsar," when he was asked what he would do now, he replied that, like Christ, he would go to prison for what he believed to be right. This time, however, the passive resistance of the Doukhobors changed to active resistance. Demanding to go to prison in his stead, they offered to protect him at the cost of their lives. Peter forbade them. They wept and sang songs of mourning; they beat their breasts and shouted to the authorities, "You are robbing us of our Christ!" Through their tears, they saw him chained to other prisoners and watched him march away, straight and proud, through the winter's snow. It was, he said, what Christ would do.

Not a day passed but what his counsel was needed; not a problem arose without someone murmuring, "What would our great leader have us do?" There was the troublesome Conscription Act which ordered all able Russian adults to be prepared for army service and which demanded that they keep guns in their homes. The elders said, "We will take the guns, but if we are ever called upon to shoot, we will shoot into the air." But would this have been Petushka's wish?

Driven by the need for guidance, the Doukhobors developed an ingenious and daring system of runners who risked their lives to bring messages to and from Verigin in his Siberian confinement. As a result, it was not long before he was once more governing his people from a prison cell. His verdict on the Act of Conscription was crystal clear, "Christ wants you to burn your guns!" he said.

The decree spread through the Doukhobor colonies, "Petushka says, 'Burn the arms!'" And heedless of the consequences, some 5000 fanatically-singing spirit-wrestlers piled their firearms high in a Doukhobor field, poured fat and oil over them, and set them aflame. As the fire raced through the heap, government Cossacks came riding in, lashing their heavy whips across the people's backs and grinding several passive objectors under their horses' hoofs. This night, June 29, 1895, was to remain forever as the occasion of "the burning of the arms," to be annually memorialized in song and celebration.

This act, however, coupled with their defiance of the law and the open deification of Peter Verigin, resulted in the confiscation of much of their property by the government. And soon, deprived of land, homes, and a means of livelihood, they wandered hopelessly wondering what Peter their Christ would have them do.

Then came 1899. Two thousand Doukhobors, spurred by Peter's message from his Siberian exile, aided from the outside by English and American Quakers and from within Russia by Leo Tolstoi, boarded ship for Canada. Actually the Russian government was driving them out with the warning never to return. The first contingent was to be followed within a year by 5000 more.

Canada was mystified from the first arrival and has remained so ever since, as far as Doukhoborism is concerned. It had seen immigrants before, but never 2000 of them, among whom not more than two spoke English. No one had ever witnessed such a landing as when the ship *Lake Huron* plowed into Halifax harbor on a bitterly cold January 24, 1900. Here was an aggregation of blacksuited men and scarved peasant women, many with children, carrying packs as if they were beasts of burden, singing the while and praising the Lord. Thirty-two precarious days at sea had only raised their hopes that the millennium must be near. A group of Quakers, on hand to welcome them, were overwhelmed when they saw the burdened Russians bow down to them with foreheads touching the ground. Then, at a signal, they arose and sang their angelic hymns, bowed to one another, saying, *"Slava Bohu,"* and wept whenever they mentioned a holy name: Petushka.

They went by train to Winnipeg, where they lived for a time in immigration halls. Here they set up an altar; a table with a pitcher of water, a dish of salt, a loaf of bread. They disdained to smoke or drink, but they were willing to trade and barter, having brought with them all sorts of possessions: jewels, rugs, and handiwork. They seemed to have no leader excepting that immortal one back in Siberia, and no plans excepting to find the Promised Land which they felt had been prepared for them somewhere in the Northwest Territory. While the government and the Quakers debated what might be done, the Doukhobors began to head westward. Some wanted to live communally because it would have been Petushka's wish. Others said they were confident he wanted them to apply for land grants so they would be financially prepared to assist him when he came.

Confused and disorganized, they looked for signs to guide them, inquiring among themselves if any of them had seen a vision or heard a voice. They pressed on westward to Yorkton, then north to the Prince Albert region and to Saskatoon. Some decided to live together under a form of communism. Those who had brought merchandise and money applied for land grants and staked out what they hoped one day would be their home. Spring found many of them in the North Saskatchewan River country building colonies, urged on by messages from Petushka, letters which were treasured as much as scripture. In some of his communications Peter told them he hoped they would live together in a fraternity and that he foresaw for them a paradise when he came.

It took no more than this to fan the fanaticism always latent in their utopian dream. Bewildered and without any clear guidance, scattered throughout the prairie provinces, driven by spiritual passion, and aroused by self-styled prophets "ordained with the power of Peter Verigin," thousands of them suddenly stampeded like frightened cattle. One proclaimed he had seen a vision of utopia in the south; another saw it in the east, eastward toward Petushka, and in the fall of 1902 they began to walk aimlessly, dream-crazed, chanting Russian hymns, trudging southeastward across the land. Never had the world seen anything like it. The flight of the Israelites, the tramp of the Crusaders, the march of the Mormons—none could compare with these utopian zealots following, they knew not whom; going, they knew not where. Every morning, the promise and the songs and the visions; every night, as the mirage faded, despair and disillusionment halted them.

"Tonight they are encamped near Churchbridge," said an eyewitness on October 21, 1902. "They are showing signs that hunger, fatigue, and emaciation have weakened their stalwart frames. Every man's face is an index, silent and eloquent, of what he has

been and is enduring. The glare of sunken eyes gives evidence
that minds are weakening. A drizzling rain is falling. Ever and
again will arise their plaintive psalms, their weird cadences rising
and falling with varying strength. Nearly all are barefooted and
hatless. All their outer clothing has been thrown away. Two
months ago the Lord revealed to them the iniquity of wearing
leather boots since they were the product of animal life. When
they marched into Yorkton they bore from a dozen to twenty
stretchers, improvised of poles and blankets, on which they bore
their sick and feeble folk. By the hand they led a man past fifty
years, born blind."

Then when all seemed lost as far as the hapless pilgrims were
concerned, Petushka came. Released from prison, he arrived in
Canada two days before Christmas in 1902. The coming of
Christ could not have provoked a more tumultuous welcome
and, because he was their Christ, they bowed their foreheads to
the ground and wept.

"Where are my people?" he wanted to know. He was told that
some of them had procured grants of land and were doing well;
others had started colonies and were awaiting him; and then
there were the thousands whose agonizing march to utopia had
brought them here on their knees before his shining boots.

He issued a decree: no one should own property in his own
name or apply for land grants on an individual basis. The time
had come for full communal living. The hour for utopia was at
hand. Assured of a token loyalty, he rallied them under a stirring
Tolstoian phrase, "Toil and the peaceful life!" Confident that all
would follow him, he organized them into an "army without
guns" under the impressive title, "The Christian Community
of Universal Brotherhood," or CCUB.

Encouraged by reports that there was rich and fertile land in
the British Columbia province, Petushka decided to move his
people. Some 3000 rallied around him at once, giving him what
money they had, and taking funds out of the colony treasury.
But others who had put their roots down as free men in a free
land remained on the farms they had started.

And so again, Canada saw a Doukhobor trek. But this time the spirit-wrestlers were not on foot, suffering hardships. They were riding in wagons and sleighs with Peter their Christ leading the procession. He drove four white horses harnessed to a shining cutter that gaily jangled with bells; and Peter himself, wrapped in a white woolen cloak like an Erlking, was followed by sled-loads of the faithful, chanting hymns of the Promised Land.

Canadians were momentarily impressed and British Columbia welcomed them to a fertile valley where the Columbia and Kootenay rivers converge. There, stretched before them, was a vast and fruitful area so beautiful it reminded the Doukhobors of the Milky Waters area about which their traditions lavishly spoke. Petushka was magnanimously acclaimed for his leadership and, with the people's money and his influence for credit, he arranged to purchase 10,000 acres of virgin land. This done, he commanded them to "Build and prosper!"

Non-resistance, vegetarianism, the inner light, the simple altar, and the inspiring chants of the Doukhobors became symbols of Canada's most ambitious communal experiment. Hard-working and industrious, feeling that at last the Jordan had been crossed, the Verigin spirit-wrestlers built their kingdom in land "where God was waiting." Under Petushka's direction, tens of thousands of fruit trees were planted and miles of roads were built. Sawmills, brick factories, and reservoirs for irrigation appeared where once there had been but barren land. Villages sprang up, each composed of two large community houses accommodating fifty people and surrounded by a hundred acres of land which was theirs to farm on a communal basis. At Brilliant stood the pride of the Doukhobor industries: an immense rectangular building which housed the B. C. Jam Factory whose products were becoming a household word throughout the Dominion.

Peter Vasilivich Verigin was known as the most powerful man in the province. When he went into a city, people pointed him out. When he wanted to borrow money, he needed only to sign his name. A town in British Columbia was named Verigin in his honor. By 1917 the Christian Community of Universal Brotherhood had been incorporated as a legal society capitialized at $1,000,000. Petushka maintained complete control of this by issuing the stock to himself and twelve hand-picked directors. Financially, utopia was booming, and so it might have remained but for a growing gap between a millionaire "Christ" and his under-paid followers.

Thousands of submissive Doukhobors were content to work and sing and live their frugal lives, returning most of their daily wages to the CCUB in the form of membership dues and gifts. They were willing to be horse-whipped by Petushka, as they often were for some slight infraction. The women were quite content for many years to be yoked together like oxen, pulling the heavy plows through the stubborn fields. All these were common practices in the Verigin design for utopia.

But gradually dissension and suspicion arose, and there developed a hard-core group called the Sons of Freedom who claimed that their inner light shown brighter than the inner light of the divine dictator. Their inner voices warned them of the need for reform, told them that Petushka was becoming worldly, that they were being exploited, and that some impending disaster lay not far ahead.

Peter Vasilivich Verigin, confident that he could pacify them and determined to hold his dissident kingdom together, invoked all the charms he knew. He sought to cajole them through flattery, promises, eloquence, fear, and most of all by frequent references to his infallibility. He met with them around their plain board altars, preached powerfully, wept dramatically, and blessed them with a solemn *Slava Bohu* when they knelt with their foreheads to the ground.

Even so, the rebellious Sons of Freedom grew in strength. In a mountain village which they had built and called Krestova—the place of the cross—their fanatical practices gained them the tainted title of "The Mad Douks." And mad they appeared. Frequently marching naked through the countryside, they chanted and sang, loudly proclaiming their belief that soon all men would have to stand naked before their God. Into the communal villages they came, preaching that worldliness was overtaking the people, proclaiming ecstatical visions, pronouncing prophecies, claiming new revelations.

Peter was suddenly a confused messiah. To add to his troubles, his wife, Dunia, whom he had finally persuaded to come from Russia so that he might show her what paradise was like, arrived with their twenty-four year old son, Peter Petrovich. The reunion was by no means what Petushka had anticipated. Dunia was not only unimpressed with what she saw, but was obviously suspicious of Peter's relationship with his "maids and secretaries." Peter Petrovich, an arrogant, bullish young man, greeted his father by demanding how much longer he intended to defraud and deceive the people by playing God. "You were always a bluff in Russia," the unfeeling son told him, "and you are even worse over here."

These accusations were but a foretaste of more to come. Wherever young Peter went, he "exposed" his father. What the Sons of Freedom had created in the way of suspicion, Peter Petrovich confirmed. By the time he returned to Russia with his mother a year later, the roots of his father's strength among many of the Doukhoborski had been cut away.

On the night of October 28, 1924, twenty-two years after Peter Vasilivich Verigin had arrived in Canada as the undisputed "Christ," he boarded a Canadian Pacific Express at Brilliant. He had purchased two tickets for Castelgar, two miles away, one for himself and one for his favorite maid. They did not get off at Castelgar. Instead, Peter purchased extra fares from the conductor and continued on with Grand Forks as the new destination. It was never reached. Beyond Farron Summit, in the quiet of the night, while the twenty or more other passengers were dozing, an explosion rocked the train. Peter and the maid were among the nine who were killed.

Attempting to reconstruct the catastrophe, the authorities theorized that a dry battery with an attached alarm clock had been responsible for setting off the explosion. The dynamite blast was believed to have originated under the seat where Verigin's suitcase had been placed. Had the man who put it there when he accompanied Verigin into the train had murder in mind? Investigation proved him innocent, although it was thought that he might have been the unsuspecting pawn in a well-devised plot. Or had the maid planned to destroy Petushka and herself? Or had Verigin himself plotted his own death? No one ever knew.

The faithful members of the CCUB, the independents, the Sons of Freedom, no less than the Doukhobors who had long ago established themselves in the prairie provinces and had watched utopia from afar forgot their differences for a brief time. They made Peter's death a form of martyrdom, and his funeral almost a march from Calvary. More than 10,000 chanted and prayed as they milled around his Brilliant, British Columbia, grave. Wherever Doukhobors lived, they paused solemnly in a requiem for their once beloved Petushka. All the devotion and loyalty which he had lost in life were restored to him for a final hour. The tomb of Peter Vasilivich Verigin was already becoming a shrine.

After his father's death and burial, Peter Petrovich Verigin came from Russia, called by the Canadian Doukhobors to be their leader. They had not forgotten his defamation of Petushka, but the magic of the Verigin name was irresistible. It was already rumored that the spirit of Christ was moving in Peter's son. So he came to British Columbia as the eleventh "incarnation," bringing with him his arrogance and his lust to rule.

The Independents were quick to disclaim him, but the CCUB put their trust and hope in him. And even though he had already labeled the Sons of Freedom "jackasses and fools," they welcomed him with promises to follow wherever he would lead. In fact, a majority of spirit-wrestlers claimed that the sins of Peter Petrovich—drunkenness, immorality, cruelty, and conceit—were, in some mysterious way, their own sins exposed and now redeemed. They called him "The Purger" because he was to purge them from all evil by living out the evil in himself. And as they gathered around their plain board altar to chant their hymns and murmur their prayers, they bowed to him as Christ, ready, they said, to accept whatever the future would hold.

It was to hold little more than tragedy. The brief respite which Petushka's death had inspired and the period of trial and error occasioned by the arrival of Peter the Purger, suddenly burst into a storm of violence. Factions developed within factions until the "army without guns" became a series of hostile encampments, out of which came a rash of arson and dynamiting of Doukhobor business places and schools. Even the pride of utopia's industries, the Jam Factory, was burned to the ground.

The police and the general public suspected the Sons of Freedom, but sufficient evidence for convictions was always lacking, and the tight-lipped "Douks" refused to divulge a single word of information. Whenever the authorities invaded the precincts of the "Sons," the members of the sect immediately disrobed. Using the weapons of nudity and "non-resistance," they fought against all the civil laws which the government sought to enforce. They refused to send their children to the dominion schools, they would pay no taxes, they would not register births, marriages, or deaths. The public sentiment of respect and sympathy, which the "good Doukhobors" had enjoyed, was replaced by public repugnance and the demand that the government "do something."

But what was the government to do? Imprisonment of the Sons offered no solution. They accepted it as martyrdom. Arrests of nudists only created more nudism until there was no longer room for them in British Columbia jails. Even Peter the Purger was baffled. One night, after a drinking party, he became so enraged at a group of the chanting nudists that he knocked the foremost man down. But even as the nudist fell, another stepped forward to take his place. The second man, also thoroughly beaten by the giant Peter, was replaced by a third, and then a fourth, who would offer no resistance but simply stood up to invite Peter's hammering fists. Finally, frustrated and physically exhausted by his futile efforts, Peter the Purger strode away, cursing all Doukhobors. As he took his leave, the naked Sons taunted him, "You are not a Christ, Petrovich, you are not a Christ!"

Steadily utopia disintegrated. The divided loyalties, the quarrels with the government, the depression, the bankruptcies, the fires, the dynamitings, coupled with Peter's own profligacy, brought about the ruin of Doukhoborism. But even then, thousands of Doukhobors still called him their "Christ." When he lay dying in a Saskatoon hospital, where he had been several times before because of "pains in his chest," the faithful continued to eulogize him. So constant were their inquiries as to his condition that the hospital was forced to issue hourly bulletins over a local radio station.

On the morning of February 11, 1939, the news of his death was flashed across the Dominion. Letters of sympathy streamed in, many of them containing money designated for the continuation of his "mighty work." His body lay in state for three days in Brilliant while a steady procession of mourners filed by through days and nights to shed tears over one who had "borne their sorrows." As the valley overflowed with grieving Doukhobors of all factions, he was reverently carried on a Sunday morning to the hillside tomb and laid to rest beside his illustrious father.

In the years that followed, the history of Doukhoborism was dominated by the obstreperous Sons of Freedom. They became Canada's major sociological problem. While some 12,000 "good Douks" became Canadianized, the reputation of the fanatical "Sons" continued to give them all a bad name. Rarely a day passed without the report of some disturbance: a parade of men and women nudists, a fire of unexplained origin, an explosion, or an inter-Doukhobor brawl. Finally, the government concluded that the only way to peace was to educate the new generation of the Sons of Freedom. Since these irrepressible radicals refused, however, to comply with the school laws and inasmuch as they concealed their school-age children when truant officers arrived, the British Columbia officials finally forcibly took the children and placed them under guard in a boarding school at Denver, British Columbia.

The Sons retaliated with a wave of bombings and burnings and nude parades. They circulated pamphlets passionately appealing to the world at large for justice and mercy in the name of God. In desperation, they threatened to leave Canada and return to Russia. This was a threat, however, to which the Canadian government reacted by saying in effect, "Go with our blessings, the sooner the better. We will happily pay your passage."

But they did not go. Most Canadians were convinced they had no intention of going. But this unconsidered declaration by the "mad Douks" became the first real victory the government had enjoyed in its more than fifty years of Doukhobor disturbances. Forced either to leave the country or acquiesce to the civil laws, the "Sons" showed signs of quieting. Reconciled to the inevitable, the once-resistant mothers of the children amiably complied with the educational policies. In September, 1959, when the children were released from their "school prison," it was apparent that a new spirit of cooperation between the Doukhobors and the government had been effected.

It is now the present. The Canadian people, resigned to the fact that the Sons of Freedom will accept the idea of naturalization stubbornly, if at all, are aware that in the villages of Krestova, Gilpin, Grand Forks, and South Slocan, the dream of a strange utopia still persists, especially among the older Doukhoborski. Sons of Freedom still have their visions and their prophecies and speak musingly of the coming of another Verigin.

Some believe that it will be a son whom Peter the Purger left behind in Russia. They feel that he is to be their twelfth leader and that God will send him, "clothed in Christ" at an appointed time.

So dreaming, they gather around their plain board altar with the pitcher of water, the dish of salt, and the loaf of bread. And as they pay homage to these elemental symbols—the spirit, the essence, and the staff of life—they chant their bewitching hymns, bow low to one another in recognition of the Christ-within, and whisper with emotion their cherished *Slava Bohu,* the Lord be praised.

15 § THE SHAKERS

IT IS REGRETTABLE that the Shakers are dying out. They were good for America and good for the world. Rarely has any group had higher ideals and the will to live them; seldom have there been people so well intentioned, so honest in their aims, and so peaceable in their nature.

They were, of course, a strange and curious sect, well aware that if they persisted in their cardinal tenet, celibacy, they would someday be extinct. Today they practically are extinct, for the settlement at East Canterbury, New Hampshire, shelters the last remaining thirty members. Their utopia was an interlude, a reflective pause, destined to be shattered by the rush of life that surged around them. Nonetheless, they created their settlements in the belief that God wanted them to be, for a little while, a testimonial of His teaching.

Their golden era covered the period from 1775 to 1875, during which more than 5000 Americans joined their society and lived in 18 villages situated in New York, New Hampshire, Vermont, Massachusetts, Ohio, and Kentucky. The austerity, dignity, and grace of Shaker life were reflected in the architecture of their buildings as well as in the furniture and handicraft for which they were to become universally famous. They found their joy in creative expression, and it was admitted by even their most rabid critics that they sought to make life, in all possible ways, better for all mankind.

Who were these people? Quaintly dressed, the men wore homespun suits with flowing ties, long, formal cloaks and broad-brimmed hats of white or gray felt; the women, extremely modest and refined, introduced to the world long pleated skirts as part of their attire, wore spotlessly white wimples about their shoulders, and scarves or bonnets depending upon the seasons and the time of day. Their voices, ever soft and low, with the Quaker "thee" and "thou" and "thine," inspired a visitor to say, "You cannot walk among them without lowering your voice and being a bit more reverent with life." Their honesty and pride became proverbial; their generosity an example for their neighbors. It is regrettable that they are dying out.

Their leader, a woman with a simple name, Ann Lee, preached a simple gospel, "Put your hands to work and give your hearts to God." She was born in Manchester, England, on February 29, 1736, the third of eight children in the family of a blacksmith, John Lee. To help support the household, Ann worked, during her childhood, in a cotton factory and, later, as a cook in an infirmary.

More important is the fact that frequently during her youth she was given to psychical experiences and remained fixed and enchanted while spirit voices spoke to her. Because she had these visions and received inspiration during trancelike states, the Shaker faith was to be strongly spiritualistic. Throughout her life, Ann was to be sympathetic with those whose charismatic experiences were often misunderstood. She was never to ridicule anyone's claim of direct revelation or turn away from those who said they had seen a vision or heard a voice, for she remembered how patiently, and with what understanding, her mother had listened to her whenever she confided that, "Angels appeared and talked to me."

Early in her mystical experiencs, she had been told psychically that life's greatest evil is sex. She claimed that she saw "clearly in a vision," the "whole sinful act of self-indulgence engaged in by Adam and Eve." Disguised as a serpent, sexual lust had crept into the garden of God, accounting for the fall of the first parents. Solemnly convinced that it was never God's intention that children should be created through the intercourse of the flesh but rather through the rapture of spiritual love, the virgin birth became for her a demonstration of the divine intent. The Virgin Mother had conceived because the purity of Mary's soul was able to realize the ideal, and it was Ann's secret desire that she, too, might find this realization.

Her father and her friends however, insisted that she lead a "normal life" and rid herself of what they called hallucinations and witchcraft which had sent others like her to the gallows. Although the last execution of a sorceress in England had taken place some thirty years ago, in 1716, the hunt for those having "familiar spirits" still went on. Ann was reminded that more than two-hundred-thousand women had been put to death on the European continent because of spirit manifestations of the kind she claimed.

An elder brother of Ann's, a favorite of their father, became so enraged when he heard her singing a song she had received mediumistically that he took a stick and beat her over the head and face. Ann forgave him, saying that she had distinctly seen and felt bright rays from God pass between her face and the stick so that she had not felt the blows.

But because her father wanted her to be "normal," he prevailed upon her to marry his friend Abraham Stanley, a blacksmith like himself. Friends also coerced her into marriage by reminding her that the Bible spoke of honoring one's father and mother and that the Scriptures enjoined a woman to be fruitful and multiply. So she married, with the tragic aftermath that her four children died, two at birth and two during infancy. Ann felt that this was the hand of God writing admonitions upon her heart, warning her to be true to her voices and obedient to her visions.

So it was that Shakerism was to reflect her intensified distaste for the act of procreation. "Lust," she said, "hath destroyed pure, heaven-born love, and the whole creation groaneth and travaileth in sin, passion, and despair."

There was also her unsatisfied yearning for children which the Shaker experiment was one day to fulfill. The Shaker settlements were to become places for the ingathering of orphans and illegitimate children, children of "the world," born of physical passion, which Shakerism sought to renounce. All were to be accepted as children of God in the hope that perhaps through a new and sinless generation, children would one day be born of spiritual love.

Most of all, the Shaker settlements were to reflect the influence of the Society of Friends (Quakers) in their highest and most cultured form. Quakerism was the matrix from which Shakerism was born. The word "Shaker" was itself a nickname, attached to those Quakers who began to tremble when moved by the power of God. They became known as the "Shaking Quakers" or simply "Shakers."

Ann Lee was introduced to Quakerism in England at about the time of her marriage in 1747 when, in company with her mother, she attended a meeting in Manchester conducted by James and Jane Wardley. She immediately found spiritual kinship with these prominent Quakers and began to absorb the tenets of this tranquil faith: direct revelation by way of the "inner light," the spiritualization of the traditional sacraments instead of their outward observance, the emphasis on a lay ministry, and devotion to the "good life" which included nonresistance, a rigid discipline in conduct and attire, and an exceptionally high code of morals.

Like the Quakers, the Shakers were to suffer extreme persecution because of their uncompromising stand against the established church, their refusal to pay the required tithes, and their stubborn determination to defend and live by what they considered the "voice of God in the heart."

Unlike the Quakers, however, the followers of Ann Lee were never to modify or change either their customs or beliefs. There was to be no adjustment to the trends of the times. Ann herself, because she consistently preached against the distastefulness of sex, was the object of much ridicule. Because she condemned the scriptural injunction, "Be fruitful and multiply," and urged people to come out from among the sinful preaching of church religion, she was frequently thrown into English jails.

Once in Manchester she was imprisoned in a windowless cell which was so small that she was unable to stand upright. A young man, James Whittaker, who was to become one of her most devoted followers, smuggled milk and wine to her by means of a pipestem inserted through the keyhole of the door. Released after fourteen torturous days, she astonished her jailors by forgiving them for their cruelty.

Later a delegate from Manchester was dispatched to seek authority from George II to put Ann Lee to death for sorcery. It was reported that the delegate died suddenly along the way and the event was taken as a judgment of God. So impressed and awe-stricken were the officials that for two years Ann was unmolested and her following grew.

Shakerism became a cult, a sect, hated and feared, but honored by those who came under the influence of Ann Lee. James and Jane Wardley maintained that she was blessed with a "beatific vision," and that the Spirit of God moved in her soul. She was described as "somewhat below the common stature of woman, straight and well-proportioned in form and feature. Her complexion was fair and her eyes were blue, keen and penetrating; her countenance was mild and solemn, her manners plain, simple and easy. She possessed a dignity that inspired confidence and commanded respect."

To those who knew her well she was beautiful. To those who loved and followed her, she was Mother Ann, possessed of "a heavenliness which has never before been discovered among mortals." Then there were those who said she was a prophetess living in two worlds at once, or else she must be the bride of Christ. Some called her the incarnation of the Holy Virgin. Whatever she was, she was Shakerism and Shakerism was Mother Ann. There is no separating the story of her life from the utopia she inspired, and no way of explaining her wisdom and knowledge but to say they were imparted to her spiritually, for until the day of her death, Ann could neither read nor write.

The history of American Shakerism began on May 19, 1774, when a group of nine, obedient to Ann's revelation, set sail from Liverpool for New York. The contingent included Ann, her husband, one brother, her niece Nancy Lee, James Whittaker, Mary Parkington, John Hocknell, the sponsor of the trip, and his son, James Shepherd.

The account of the perilous seventy-two day voyage in an unseaworthy vessel has become part of Shaker lore, but it is more than legend. It is verifiable commentary on the indomitable faith of a woman who believed that God would fulfill the visions He had imparted. She claimed she had foreseen actual people and places in America which were to become part of Shakerism's utopia. She had been told psychically that there would be an "ingathering" of converts, and she had not the shadow of a doubt that this would come to pass.

Consequently, in the midst of a raging storm, it was Mother Ann who calmly reassured everyone on board that the danger was an illusion. Had she not already foreseen their safe arrival in New York? When water began flooding the ship, she informed the captain and the crew, "Have no fear. I just saw two bright angels of God standing on the mast." Setting an example of faith and resourcefulness, she and her companions courageously manned the pumps. "But for these people," the captain is reported to have said, "we would all have perished at sea."

But for Ann Lee, her small group of Shakers might also have perished in America, for it so happened that when they arrived in August, 1774, the prologue to the American Revolution had begun. English immigrants were under suspicion; English spiritualists were foreign witches; English colonists were being kept under close surveillance. The little party separated for the purpose of getting jobs and somehow earning a living. Ann supported herself and a suddenly ailing husband by taking in washing and working as a maid. Her husband Stanley, after his recovery, deserted her by running off with another woman. The extreme privation which Ann endured for two years was conquered only, she confessed, through the visions and the divine messages which persistently assured her that, "Great numbers will embrace the faith as the fullness of time draws nigh."

Meanwhile, John Hocknell had bought a small tract of land near Albany at Niskeyuna, New York. Moved by the faith exemplified in Ann Lee, he returned to London to bring his family and several other Shakers to America. He wanted them to be ready and working toward the "Lord's Day," when, according to Ann's prophecies, people would be "coming like doves." Fired by this confidence, the newcomers, together with the original group, and inspired by the presence of Mother Ann, "dug in" at Niskeyuna in September, 1776.

There were only thirty of them in the group that struggled to subdue the swampy wilderness and make things ready for the time when the world would discover the Shaker faith. They were caught in the midst of the war's activity with all its suspicions and fears. There were days of near-starvation and nights filled with despair, but a large, impressive home was rising over the land, and barns and granaries were being built, and the little band of Shakers lived possessed of a sense that "God encompassed them on every hand."

But as the months of waiting for the predicted fullness of time dragged on into years, it continually fell upon Mother Ann to hold the group together and to justify her claim that more crops should be planted, more buildings constructed, and an ever more dedicated life should be lived. She explained God's delay by saying that they were evidently not yet ready, for surely God was.

They did not stress prayer, these wilderness Shakers, because they never saw the need for telling God what He already knew or of petitioning Him for things He surely realized they needed. Instead they sang—hymns composed by spirit inspiration—and worked as though work was worship, and sat in the darkness of the groves listening for heavenly voices or waiting for signs from mentors in that other world.

In times of great disillusionment, as when the crops failed, or when mysteriously the great white, three-story frame house burned to the ground; or when the inevitable question of "Why?" and "How much longer, O Lord?" became cries of despair, this strange and curious Mother Ann led the little group into a forest clearing and commanded that they dance, the men and women apart, praising the Lord. Suddenly she would stand transfixed, her eyes uplifted by a blinding light, her body shaking, and exclaim, "I see the angels of God! They are all around us! I see great numbers of people coming to us and believing our gospel. I see men bow down and confess their sins."

And as they watched, they saw her as if enfolded in a cloud of light, and they believed.

They were living in log cabins while rebuilding the big house in the wilderness of Niskeyuna when the fullness of time came. It was the winter of 1779. They had not only heard, psychically, that America was in the grip of a post-war religious revival, but occasional travelers had told them about strange happenings in Lebanon, New York, where people, possessed by uncontrollable bodily manifestations, were being baptized by the Holy Ghost. There were reports that mysterious lights had been seen in the sky and that the end of the world was near. A wave of repentance was consequently sweeping the land.

Many people, whom the revivals had convicted of sin, were looking for a place where they could live life as it had been experienced by the early Christians: communally, compassionately, apart from "the world." They were searching for saints and, having heard about the Shakers, they came to Niskeyuna.

When they arrived they saw the food that had been stored in preparation for their coming. They found buildings which had been erected in the foreknowledge that pilgrims like themselves would one day come to this wilderness retreat. And they met a woman in whose eyes a light of faith was burning and whose words were unlike the words of other religious leaders. She spoke, they said, like Jesus.

The illusion grew. The word spread. The people came—like doves. Mother Ann was acclaimed as "the Christ revealed in woman." She accepted the title and quietly allowed the devout to deify her if they wished. It mattered little to her whether they called her the Maternal Spirit of God or the True Mother of Israel or the Promised One or, simply, Mother Ann. She told them to put their hands to work and to give their hearts to God; she heard their confessions, blessed them, and challenged them to live the celibate life.

Soon she began to travel about, preaching as Jesus had preached to the hungry multitudes wherever they would listen. She lived as she believed He had lived, "in purity." She gathered children into her arms as He had done. She prayed for the sick, and fed the hungry, and retreated into the quiet places to commune with her visions and voices. The fullness of time had come.

She did not live, however, to see the full flowering of the work she inspired. In fact, she was granted only four short years of something comparable to public acclaim, and even these were years of trouble. Rabid mobs, accusing her of witchcraft and sorcery, many times dragged her from public meetings and left her lying on a roadside, half dead. Religionists felt justified in persecuting her because she was heretical. Rarely was she safe or free from merciless fanatics, and her followers, pledged by her to non-resistance, were powerless to interfere. They quietly complained that it was "barbarous torture like that inflicted upon Jesus" and the records substantiate their claims. They also bear out her strange and curious practice of forgiving her oppressors.

When asked why she constantly returned good for evil, she said, "You can never enter the kingdom of God with hardness against any one, for God is love, and if you love God you will love one another."

She died in Niskeyuna, which had been renamed Watervliet, on September 8, 1784, at the age of forty-eight. Three years later to the day, her church was founded under the title: The Millennial Church or the United Society of Believers. It was formed upon the doctrines she had expounded and which her followers had extended to include:

1. God is male and female.
2. The distinction of sex is eternal and inheres as male and female in every soul.
3. Christ is a Spirit who appeared first in Jesus representing the male, and then in Ann Lee representing the female element in God. That neither should be worshiped, but that each should be emulated and adored.
4. There are four great dispensations. The first ended with Noah and the flood, the second with the coming of Jesus, the third with the advent of Ann Lee, and the fourth is now in progress.
5. The principles of the Millennial Church reestablish the five most important features of the early Christian church: celibacy, community of goods, non-resistance, a divine government, and power over disease.
6. Communication with discarnate spirits is a fact and is the true communion of saints.
7. The true servants of God ought to live a sinless life: chaste, honest, gentle, diligent, temperate, frugal, confessing their sins one to another, making restitution for past misdeeds, providing for the education of children, employment for themselves and others, and provision for themselves and the community members.
8. The Millennial Church is the Inner Order of life and is supported by the Outer Order, the world. That the mission of the Inner Order is to purify and refine the Outer Order through efforts in the present life and in the life to come.

Had Mother Ann lived she would have seen the ingathering which she so confidently predicted, and she would have been pleased by the thoroughness with which the administrators of the settlements worked out each detail for the Novitiate (those wishing admission) and the Church orders. Shakerism wanted to provide a "foretaste of heaven" through orderliness, cleanliness, discipline, and quiet joy. They called it utopia, the kind of place that Jesus or Mother Ann could return to at any time and say, "Well done."

For more than a hundred years the eighteen communes drew followers from every Christian denomination which ever engaged in a revival until, by the middle of the 19th century, approximately 3000 souls were living the communal, celibate life. The members lived together as families, ranging in number from thirty to ninety persons in each society. Their homes, built of wood or native granite, were symmetrically and impressively proportioned, and were usually three stories in height, although some were five and even six stories high. The first floor provided a spotless kitchen, a highly polished, immaculate refectory, and spacious store rooms. On the second floor were accommodations for the adopted children, and on the third was the dormitory area which consisted of sleeping quarters for the men and women separated by a hallway, across which trespassing was strictly forbidden.

A number of these houses, enclosed by a white board fence or a sturdy rock wall, comprised a Shaker village. Conveniently located around the homes, with spaciously landscaped areas in-between, were the shops. Flagstone paths led to the furniture factory or the printing establishment or a house of looms, to a broom factory, a shoemaker's shop or a tailory. Swept-out lanes, as clean as scrubbed pine boards, brought the seed houses and dairies and leather shops into the community pattern. Some of the communes had steam laundries and mangles and other ingenious machines for lightening the chores. Guest rooms were added to the homes for, as the villages grew, visitors and curiosity seekers came to investigate these peculiar people. Often they came as skeptics, amused by the posted rules:

> Married persons tarrying overnight are respectfully notified that each sex must occupy separate sleeping apartments while they remain.

> At the table we wish all to be as free as at home, but we dislike the wasteful habit of leaving food on the plate.

> Here we eat in silence.

> Pork we do not eat or serve.

> It is necessary that someone (an elder) should always know where everybody is at all times.

Or they laughed at the Shaker rhymes which said:

> From all intoxicating drink
> Ancient Believers did abstain:
> Then say, good brethren, do you think
> That such a cross was all in vain?

Or found it entertaining to read special notices in Shaker publications:

> OBITUARY: On Tuesday, February 20, 1873, died, by the power of truth and for the cause of Human Redemption, in the following much-beloved Brethren, the Tobacco-Chewing Habit; aged respectively in Brother D.S. it had lived for 51 years; in Brother C.M. for 57 years, in Brother A.G. for 15 years. No funeral ceremonies, no mourners, no graveyard, but an honorable record has been made thereof in the Court above.

As the hospitality of the Shakers was noised about, beggars and transients began thinking up ingenious schemes for living in the settlements. Many who came in late autumn professed heartfelt sorrow for their sins or enthusiastic interest in the Shaker life. Generously the communes took them in, quite aware that most of these worldlings were seeking an easy living for the winter months ahead. Nonetheless, the elders, remembering Mother Ann's reminder that since no one came without the

Father's will no one should be denied, gave them quarters in which to live and assigned them work. With the coming of spring, these "winter Shakers" usually traveled on, some to return again in the fall, although a few occasionally did become true converts. Whoever came, whether for a day or for a season, carried away with them the romance of Shakerism, the story of a people who seemed to prosper despite their seemingly impractical generosity.

The Shaker life was leisurely, orderly, spiritualized, with the rising-time in summer set at half-past-four and in winter at five, with the making of the beds and the tidying up of the rooms almost a ritual, with the kneeling prayer before each meal so impressive that no one was ever quite the same after having shared in it, and with the commune work so reverently pursued that the sound of a hammer was like a temple gong and the ponderous turning of the presses a holy chant.

Evenings were spent in singing and in lectures on scientific subjects or discussions of world news from which the morbid and sensational had been deleted. Sunday worship in the inspiringly plain meeting houses consisted of hymns and an address on the holiness of living. And always there seemed time for the dances which, in their simplicity, precision, and beauty, were so remarkable it was believed by Shakers and many onlookers that their source was the spiritual realm. An elder once said, "They are learned from the seraphs who dance around the throne of God."

The dancers, men and women who never so much as touched hands, were often jubilant as they symbolized with the movement of their hands and arms the intaking and outpouring of love, or the joy of being washed clean from sin, or the ecstacy of getting rid of sin by shaking it out of their bodies until it quivered only in the arms, then in the fingers, and was then eventually absorbed in space.

There was an alchemy in the dance that worked wonders in Shakerism. Whatever there may have been of physical passion was here sublimated in beauty and joy. In work and worship, too, the body was deliberately "spiritualized" and physical force and energies were sought to be made "pure and undefiled." It was not emotion that Shakerism sought to curb, it was *physical* emotion toward which its injunctions were directed. It was not marriage that the society disavowed; it was sex. It was not the love of a man for a maid that it objected to; it was the sexual act.

In the villages, therefore, husbands were separated from wives and no physical contact was permitted between men and women. They never shook hands with one another. They ate at separate tables. They worshiped standing or kneeling in divided groups, and in most of the buildings there were two doorways, one for the men and one for the women, as well as two staircases inside the dwellings. Yet each man had a woman assigned to him. She took care of his clothing, commented on his appearance, and kept watch over his habits and needs. Addressing each other as "brother" and "sister," and living as such, there was rarely any scandal or need for discipline in the settlements.

So effective was their training of orphan children that there was never any case of delinquency, and so impressive were their schools that many outsiders sent their children to receive the thorough Shaker training. Parents did this even at the risk of having their youngsters absorb some of the "queer" Shaker beliefs, like spiritualism. For it was a well-known fact that orphans, adopted and trained in the villages, participated in mediumistic sessions. These children, like Ann Lee in her girlhood, had their spirit guides who watched over them. "We are guarded," they would say, "in all we do by our invisibles and Mother Ann."

In the schools they were taught to sing:

I will walk in true obedience, I will be a child of love,
And in low humiliation I will praise my God above.
I will love my blessed Mother, and obey her holy word,
In submission to my elders, this will join me to the Lord.

'Tho beset by wicked spirits, men and devils all combined,
Yet my Mother's love will save me if in faithfulness I stand;
No infernal crooked creature can destroy or harm my soul,
If I keep the love of Mother and obey her holy call.

They called it utopia and critics obliquely admitted that it had its merits. The world soon coined new phrases: a Shaker child, a Shaker bench, a Shaker hat, a Shaker-type of person, and they all meant that qualities of artistry and truth were inherent in each. The Shakers also received credit for certain "firsts": the first patented washing machine, the first centrifugal drier, the first circular saw, the first flour sifter, the first nails with heads, the first packaged seeds. Some say they were the first masters of scientific soil conservation whose farms all looked like gardens, and whose gardens looked like bits of paradise.

Mother Ann died too soon. She never saw the wonder villages of Alfred and New Gloucester and Sabbathday Lake in Maine; or lovely Canterbury and Enfield in New Hampshire; or Harvard, Shirley, Hancock, and Tyringham in Massachusetts; or Mount Lebanon and Groveland in New York; Union Village, North Union, Whitewater, and Watervliet in Ohio; or South Union and Pleasant Hill in Kentucky.

Though she lived to see but one of these utopias: Watervliet in New York, where she is buried, there are Shakers who believe that she has visited them all in spirit, and that she watches over these settlements, though nearly all are now sold or being sold, one by one. To her do they still exist, these places of ingathering, where every day was a Sabbath and every home a church, where every member sought to live his best, and where every event and every life were watched over by a guardian angel?

It is regrettable that the Shakers are dying out. They were good for America and good for the world.

16 § THE AMANAS

In the Song of Solomon, chapter four, verse eight, the lovelorn poet passionately sings, "Come with me from Lebanon, my spouse, with me from Lebanon! Look from the top of Amana!"

The transition, both in time and spirit, from ancient Lebanese meadows to modern cornfields in Iowa, U.S.A., may seem incongruous to many people, but to a group of 19th century spiritual adventurers it was a logical step. The adventurers were 800 German Pietists. They founded their Amana colonies in Iowa in 1854, establishing seven villages upon a unique spiritual emphasis and dedicating them to a strict communal pattern. Then they took as their motto: *Bleib treu*—stay true. Written into their charter was the warning that if the original principles were ever abandoned, God would withdraw His blessing from them in "time and eternity."

Today the old Amana way of life is gone, but the colonies, thriving, industrialized, and catering to the tourist, are still very much in existence. The seven villages, situated in the midst of 25,000 lush acres in Iowa County, with their quaint old churches and colony shops may easily be visited. Within a radius of six miles from the intersection of highways #220 and #149 lie Main Amana, East Amana, Middle Amana, High Amana, West Amana, South Amana, and Homestead. Even a few of the early Amana settlers, aged now, still remain. These are the ones who lived in the Amana-that-was, a remnant of those who tasted deeply of utopia. They stroll thoughtfully in the yards of their espaliered homes or putter in seclusion in their immaculately kept gardens or sit in their rooms in antique rockers, slowly swaying back and forth like pendulums on the eternal clocks of time.

In memory, these half-forgotten utopianists relive the days of sixty, seventy years ago, when Amana was at its spiritual height, when they and their fathers, deep-rooted in tranquility, were isolated in a world within a world. Now they are encompassed by a new world not of their making. Wistfully they look out upon modern ranch type homes and small stereotyped dwellings cut to order, so strangely incongruous with their tradition. They walk past colorfully painted houses in villages where paint was never used; houses now studded with TV antenna and equipped with attached garages, so modern there is no room for the vegetable gardens, once so much a part of their life.

They close their eyes and conjure up the life of old, the life they believed in, and lived for, and finally lost. Only when they shut out the present can they see the past, the seven-villaged Amana, with its vine-covered, gable-roofed homes of red brick or unpainted boards or native sandstone. All had been built with thoughtful care and with the harmony of the community as a whole in mind. Restful in unpretentious dignity, many of these brick homes still stand, their thick walls unharmed by time, and even the houses of weather-worn, unpainted boards are things of beauty.

Beyond each truck-and-tourist-crowded street, the old Amanaite sees a well-remembered, quiet thoroughfare of the past, the long friendly Main Street of a German hamlet upon which the villages were patterned. In memory, the shaded, elm-lined streets reappear, bordered by wooden sidewalks of oak boards, along which families walked to church, men made their way to their work in the shops, and women to their duties in the community kitchen. Here no one ever loitered, except to breathe the air of quietude. Six days a week the Amana children, on their way to and from the colony schools, walked as they had been ordered: the boys on one side of the street, the girls on the other.

On Sundays when the young people walked in the fields, the boys went in one direction and the girls in another. If they met by pre-arrangement, as some undoubtedly did, they would do so with a sense of guilt which, in turn, would impress upon them the colonies' warning against the sinfulness of sex. "Fly from intercourse with women," warned an Amana proverb, "as a very highly dangerous magnet and a magical fire."

Women chose their clothes in a deliberate attempt to conceal or minimize their attractiveness. A long, full skirt, sewed to a loose-fitting, long-sleeved blouse, was, in effect, a uniform worn by young and old alike. In summer it was fashioned of gray or blue Amana calico; in winter it was an equally modest attire of Amana wool. A kind of cape was worn over the shoulders and pinned inconspicuously at the breast, for jewelry was considered a snare of Satan. In the summer small, close-fitting caps or sunbonnets were worn over neat, plainly-dressed hair. To wear the hair loose was unwomanly and to curl the hair was an offense to the Lord. On cold days a hood or heavy shawl was the conventional headcovering. No beauty aids were allowed nor were any available. With these regulations vigilantly enforced, it was hoped that physical attraction between the sexes would, at best, be minimized.

Marriage itself carried with it something of a fall from grace, though, by the age of twenty-four, a young man had usually decided upon a girl within the colony of whom his parents and the elders would approve. So great was the aversion to sex that a family of two children was considered more holy than a family of three, a family of one more holy than a family of two, and a childless marriage was commonly construed as a sign that chastity reigned supreme.

As if to justify their old morality, the veterans of utopia, lolling in their chairs, continue to weave their contrasts between the Amana-that-is and the Amana-that-was. The whirr of cars reminds them that in their day there was no desire or need to go out into the world, for each village had its general store, cabinet shop, bakery, shoemaker's shop, pharmacy, and tailory. Everything that was needed for modest living was close at hand.

Industries in those days were designed to provide honest labor for the members of the community and to supply the community needs. This was especially true of the large and productive woolen mill whose steady rumble at Main Amana was a testimony to the success of the cooperative enterprise.

For the most part, however, the work was farming. Around the villages lay the land with its grazing meadows and its rich black fields nourished by the Iowa River. Here, too, were the orchards, vineyards, granaries, village barns and sheds, dairies, saw mills, grist mills, and wine cellars. Amana was mutualistic living, as God intended community life to be. People had all things in common. The buildings were owned by all, the industries belonged to the people, and the farms were shared by everyone. A man did not work *for* someone. He worked *with* someone, and that someone shared in his experience. Each phase of business had its foreman, and these were the managers in each village who met together every evening to plan the labor for the following day. Thus if any department required extra help, the necessary adjustment could be made and the workers could be alerted. All of which made for efficiency and abundant prosperity.

There was ample opportunity for ingenuity, too. The water power for the woolen mill was supplied by a canal seven miles long. It was a mill race walled in by willows and pickerel weeds, by elderberry bushes and wild grape vines. The canal was spanned by quaint wooden bridges where families strolled together on Sunday afternoons, congregating finally at the lily pond into which the canal expanded. Amana was a garden, a spirit, an aspiration. Life was orderly living; life was discipline and reflection. A man could find his deepest aspirations in the homeward walk and see himself reflected in the lives of those who shared with him in this utopia.

Each family had a house of its own, although it belonged to the community, and when a young couple married they lived for a time at one or the other of their parental homes. Sometimes they remained indefinitely, and the colony carpenters skillfully added a room or two. The people of each village, summoned by the ringing of a bell, came together to eat in a common refectory and took their assigned places at the tidy, unpainted tables. Here the sexes were again segregated, to avoid, it was said, "silly conversation." Here the children ate under strict supervision so that every table might be an altar pleasing to the Lord. Before and after each meal, everyone stood while an elder intoned a prayer to which the brotherhood responded, "God bless and keep us safely every one."

The words still echo in the hearts of the disenfranchized utopianists as they sit in their plain, old-fashioned rooms. Self-possessed, endlessly rocking in chairs made by former Amana craftsmen, they are fortified by the past, surrounded by colony-made furniture and mementoes of other days. Through the small-paned windows in the thick, kalsomined walls, the last of the utopian colonists still see themselves happily going, day in and day out, to breakfast at an early hour according to the season, to dinner promptly at half-past eleven, and to supper at six. There was usually a mid-morning break for coffee or beer, if desired, and an afternoon lunch. Somehow, there was always time. The Amana-that-was, they insist, never knew the meaning of rush or tension or worry or concern. Visitors who found the *gemütlichkeit* of leisure contagious said there was no place in America where people were so convinced of the rightness of their beliefs or where the aged, the sick, and the orphan were as well cared for as here in utopia.

As for money, of what use was it to an individual? What could it buy when fellowship was a free gift and security for all was automatically assured? Each adult male received an annual allowance according to his need in amounts ranging from fifty to one hundred dollars. Each adult female received twenty-five dollars a year, and each child was given from five to ten dollars. Since all the basic needs of life were already provided, these amounts were more than ample in a community where everything was sold to the members at cost, where the calico was manufactured, and the shoes were made, and the cloth for men's suits was homespun.

When anyone required an article or an item in a store, he made his selection which was then charged to him and the amount entered in a book he carried with him. At the end of the year, the amount was deducted from his allowance and the balance, which represented his savings, was his "spending money" which he rarely spent, although he often gave it away to charitable causes outside of the community, such as to victims of war or other tragedies.

While books were discouraged, every home had its German Bible, Luther's translation, even though the Amana people were not Lutheran. What were they then when it came to religion? They were neither Protestants nor Catholics. They were not a sect, not a creed, not a denomination. They were Inspirationists. And what was this? They claimed it was a spiritual heritage that had come from the first man who had ever heard the voice of God. Abraham was an Inspirationist and so were Moses and Elijah and David. Jesus was admittedly the greatest of them all, and in the church He had established there were others to be found; men and women who spoke as the mouth-piece of God. Amana was The Community of True Inspiration built around such talented ones existing within their midst.

The Amana people had a descriptive German word for these divinely attuned individuals: *Werkzeuge*, those who show forth the works of the Lord. The *Werkzeuge* were the awakened people, vibrant to the whisperings of the Spirit. They fell into trance-like states, their countenances changed, their voices became thunderously prophetic, they cried out, "Thus saith the Lord!" and from their lips flowed admonitions, prophecies, and counsel which no one would dare say was self-induced. And what was so strange or curious about this? If it had happened to a boy like Samuel in Palestine, why could it not happen to a man in Amana? The seven thriving, prosperous colonies were there to prove that it had indeed happened. Here were people who had been led step by step to Utopia because of it.

Old Amana liked best to trace its history back to the German Pietists of the 16th century, to the mystic Jacob Boehme, to Philip Spener and his *Collegia Pietatis* in Halle, Germany, to the enlightened educator Paul Gieseberg Nagel. Most of all, the Amana colonists were indebted to Eberhard Ludwig Gruber and Johann Frederick Rock who, in the early 18th century, had gathered together a small group of believers in Himbach, Hesse. Gruber was a Lutheran pastor who had wearied of stereotyped theology and statistical religion; Rock was the son of a Lutheran clergyman whose questing soul had failed to find its answers in his father's faith.

On November 16, 1714, a date agreed upon as the birthday of the Community of True Inspiration, Rock, after much prayer in the company of four other seekers, hearing the voice of God in his heart, had begun to prophesy. He was the German *Werkzeug* whose people were destined to migrate someday from Europe to America. Wherever he went he was accompanied by a *Schreiber* (scribe) who faithfully recorded his utterances whenever he "fell under the spirit."

But how was it determined whether the spirit was true or false? The aging Amanaite can answer that question without pausing in his rocking. There is something within the soul of a man that knows, something that can discern whether the spirit is good or bad. There were other tests, however. The prophecy had to be constructive. It had to be selfless and, eventually, provable. It had to be in keeping with morality and truth. It had to feel true. But most conclusive of all, it had to be accompanied by physical manifestations recognizable by all Inspirationists.

Gruber described the testing of the spirit by saying, "If perchance a false spirit was among the congregation, or if an insincere member wished to distinguish himself at our meeting in prayer or in some other manner, then I was overcome by an extraordinary shaking of the head and shivering of the mouth; and it has been proven a hundred times that such was not without significance, but, indeed, a true warning."

Thus, the tried and tested *Werkzeug* was the presence of God in the community around whom the life and law of the people revolved. "What does the *Werkzeug* say?" was equivalent to, "What does the Lord require of us?" That, according to Inspirationists, was the secret of utopia. That was the secret of the old Amana.

Inspired with such a reason-defying faith, a group of German Inspirationists came to America from Ronneburg in 1842, led by the most famous *Werkzeug* of all, Christian Metz. Though none of the utopianists now living, not even the oldest among them, ever saw Christian Metz, they all know him intimately. Through the telling and re-telling of countless tales, it is as though they had walked and talked with him. They have been told how he often walked at night because the Spirit of God had summoned him from sleep, how he strolled along the peaceful slumbering streets or roamed the moonlit meadows, and how, with his eyes upraised and set upon by the Spirit of God, he proclaimed in poetic language the infallible orders of the Most High. And always these directives had been for the good of Amana and for the sake of brotherhood and peace.

The early Amana people were well informed in these details, for they had learned in colony schools that Christian Metz had been born into a German Pietistic home in the community of Neuwied on December 30, 1793. Here he had lived until, at the age of seven, he had gone with his parents to Ronneburg and grown up in the bracing climate of the Inspirationists. As a young man he had prophesied so unerringly that people had come from as far away as Switzerland to unite with the German Inspirationist communities. They purchased great tracts of land near the Castle of Ronneburg, converted an abandoned convent at Arnsburg, and developed a large farm at Engelthal into a village where rich and poor, educated and uneducated, laborers and farmers banded together; all committed unquestionably to the law of God as expounded by Christian Metz.

He was a diminutive man, this *Werkzeug* of the authoritarian word, an inch over five feet, a stocky, bearded man whose gentle eyes became glazed with fierce intensity when God invaded him. In 1842, when he was forty-nine, the spirit of the Lord possessed him with such exceptional force during a meeting at Engelthal that he cried out in a voice that could be heard a half-mile away,

> "Thus saith the Lord!
> Your goal and your way leads towards the west;
> To the land which is still open to you and your friends.
>
> Behold, I am with you to lead you over the sea!
> Lay hold on Me, call upon Me,
> When the storms of temptation arise.
> Go now, four of you,
> Endowed with full power to act for all the members,
> And to purchase land where you deem best."

The Inspirationists claimed that this directive was infallible guidance. "West to the land which is still open to you," meant America. Germany had already imprisoned many of the brethren for their failure to comply with the military draft, had accused them of fanaticism, and had legislated against them when they sought to buy more land. The communities had also been split by a questionable *Werkzeug*, Michael Krausert, an itinerant tailor of Strassburg whom Christian had finally been forced to deny. Now the voice was clear and the way lay charted before them.

And so four men, of whom Christian Metz was one, set out for the New World. After a stormy voyage of thirty-eight days, they docked at New York harbor. The bitter winter of 1842 in which the four men looked for a suitable tract of land, the machinations of unscrupulous real estate agents, the tedium of travel and waiting were, for the rugged fifty-year-old *Werkzeug*, simply the unfolding chapters in the book of God's plan for His people. His "Thus saith the Lord" inspired his companions to the point where there was never a question about the final outcome of their mission, never a doubt about its ultimate success, nor hardly a show of surprise when they were informed that a large and suitable tract, the Seneca Indian reservation, was up for sale. They bought it, five thousand acres near the city of Buffalo, at ten dollars an acre, and advised their brethren in Germany that God, as always, had kept His word. Metz lived by faith, worked by guidance, and counted no event outside the province of heaven.

Three hundred and fifty Inspirationists came over during the first year, 1843. Within four months after the arrival of the first contingent, they had built a village. Christian, during one of his *Bewegungen* (spirit manifestations), called the place Ebenezer, as Samuel had done when he set a stone between Mizpeh and Shen, and said, "Hitherto the Lord hath helped us." But the *Werkzeug* put his revelation into a song:

> "Ebenezer you shall call it,
> Hitherto our Lord hath helped us;
> He was with us on our journey,
> And from many perils saved us;
> His path and way are wonderful,
> And the end makes clear the start."

Three hundred and seventeen more Inspirationists came from Germany in 1844, and by 1850, under the infallible guidance of the *Werkzeug*, some 1200 people had turned the reservation into a garden, had purchased 4,000 additional acres of land, and had built two more villages called Upper and Lower Ebenezer.

The start in Ebenezer, however, was marred by trouble with the Indians who had been given the impression by the land company that the reservation had merely been leased and would be returned to them. Then there were troubles with the land agents who admitted they had been "careless" in their negotiations and were now being investigated by the government. And, finally, in the spring of 1859, an even greater trouble came upon them straight out of the unknown. A raging plague hit the Ebenezer colony, a form of "military fever," which struck its victims wherever they might be, whether they were in church or in the field or even at prayer within their homes. The fever struck and in several hours its victim was dead. People could not flee the village for fear of being accused of spreading the malady, since neither the city of Buffalo nor the surrounding communities were affected. It was like a divine judgment centered on Ebenezer alone. More than a hundred graves were plotted out and then the *Werkzeug* himself, the man who spoke for God, was stricken. Only he did not die. The hours passed, the days passed, until two weeks had gone by, and Christian lay like a sacrifice. His lips moved in prayer as he feebly whispered a prophecy that the Lord was preparing His people for another chapter in their quest. Recovered, after a month of dying, he was recognized as a greater leader than ever before.

Even though the colonists endured times of strenuous difficulties in these Erie County settlements, times beyond the *Werkzeug's* comprehension, the trials served always to strengthen their faith. What the old Amana utopianists say about Christian Metz is true, "He saw what ordinary men did not see, and always persuaded his followers that 'the end makes clear the start.' "

In retrospect, those who rock and reminisce in the Amana-that-is see the unfolding of God's plan as Christian saw it then in Ebenezer. They see how the city of Buffalo, to them a symbol of the world, moved toward Ebenezer to absorb and destroy it.

They hear the *Werkzeug*, Christian, as he spoke one day in old Ebenezer in a mighty *Bewegungen*:

> "Thus saith the Lord!
> Oh, my people, my people,
> Leave this place!
> Turn your eyes toward the West,
> There you will find
> An entrance and a settlement!"

In profound obedience to his word, the Inspirationists stoically prepared for their exodus, leaving behind all that they had built and beautified and improved, leaving it with the calm assurance of their faith. It was not long before city people came to live in the well-built homes of these strange collectivistic experimenters, and they must have wondered what insanity had driven men away from such a thriving environment, westward to the new frontier of Iowa, which only eight years previously, in 1846, had become a state. They did not know that Christian's God had spied out a better land and a more isolated one! They did not know that in utopia there can be no compromising with "the world" and that the growth of the city of Buffalo itself had become a threat. But the Inspirationists whom Christian had delegated to remain to dispose of the land knew all these things. Patiently they stayed on, selling section after section in thrifty, profitable fashion, and then journeyed westward with a song:

> "Come with me from Lebanon, my spouse,
> With me from Lebanon! Look from the top of Amana!"

Amana—*Bleib treu*—stay true!

But Amana did not stay true. It was utopia, but it did not last. It ended for the simple reason that the *Werkzeug* died. When the voice of God was no longer heard in the land, the decline of the life began. And this is what the aging utopianist recalls as his rocking chair counts out his remaining years and carries his dreams away. For him, Amana has followed the pattern of Spengler's *Decline of the West*: in the spring, philosophy and religion are one; in the summer, philosophy begins to examine religion; in the autumn, it dissects it; and in the winter, a culture dies.

The working out of this pattern can be seen if one visits the old Amana churches, especially the one in Main Amana, for the church was the heart of the community. There is a sense of peace which haunts this spacious, pale blue rectangular house of God, a sensation the visitor feels but cannot always explain. The symmetry of the room resembles the ordered and disciplined life of a people who no longer exist. The equally-spaced windows, deeply recessed in the thick sandstone walls, and the austerity and the plainness of the surroundings are of another era. The much-scrubbed pine benches, compelling a person to sit erect, still seem to be filled with those silent worshipers who once had gathered here, the men on one side, the women on the other. The church was the symbol, the visible sign of God in the community; the church was His house, where His presence was singularly localized. The communal living, which was introduced at Ebenezer, the simple life which was traditional, the remoteness from the world, were all merely the devices which were necessary to maintain the purity of worship and the faith in the *Werkzeug*.

It was unthinkable during the years when Amana was young to close a day without evensong, a church service at which the *Psalter-Spiel* (hymn book of psalms) was taken from its cardboard case and where the *a capella* singing reminded the worshiper that a spiritual victory would be gained only through the denial of self and the awareness of the soul's quest for quietude and peace. Each Wednesday and Saturday morning work was deferred long enough for the members to gather for a few moments of prayer, and on Sunday morning at the regular church service they worshiped with the *Werkzeug* who sat with his elders behind an unadorned table covered with green cloth upon which rested the open Bible.

The members also brought their own Bibles and, following the prayers and hymns, after the leader had intoned a verse of scripture, each man in the congregation would read a verse in turn. Then an elder recited a psalm and the women read whatever verses still remained in the prescribed text. It was at churchtime that the *Werkzeug* was most likely to go into a *Bewegungen*. Often Christian needed only the singing of a hymn to find that music was the spark that waked the slumbering Voice within his breast. When the Spirit forced him to his knees or caused him to stand before the congregation, trembling as if shaken by a mighty wind, the people knelt at their benches while their hearts were thrilled with the glory of what they heard and felt. Accepting his utterances as a second gospel, the segregated men and women meditated on them as they filed slowly out of the church, each worshiper pledged to silence until he reached his home.

Sometimes, when he was even more inspired, Christian proclaimed a message that heralded the greatest annual service of the Amana year, the *Unterredung* (confession) and the *Liebesmahl* (love-feast or communion). This special observance included all of the colonies. The summons, usually poetic, rang out authoritatively:

> "I am commanded to call you together
> For the observance of the Supper of Love!
> Make ready your heart,
> Cleanse out all sin,
> Prepare your spirits,
> For the Lord is again to reveal Himself!
> In all who are worthy
> He shall make His righteousness known!"

As the elders carried the message from house to house, they repeated these instructions so that the people could prepare themselves for this event, "The instrument of the Lord has commanded the day for the Lord's Supper for all and the ceremony of foot-washing for the highest spiritual order!"

Then on the appointed day, the noise of the mills was quieted, the sounds in the shops were hushed, the cattle and sheep were entrusted to nature, and the day was set aside as the day of the

Lord. They still relive this scene from their rocking chairs, these ones who can remember the Amana-that-was which their fathers shared. In a dimming vision they see the utopianists coming as families and as village groups, as they walked along the familiar trails across the treasured land. They can see the men, wearing broad-brimmed hats, black suspendered pants, and white tieless shirts; the women, dressed in their full gray garments with the white cowls tied under their chins; the girls wearing over their shoulders the dark-colored shawls pinned at the breast, and the little boys dressed much like their fathers. Closely tucked under their arms, the pilgrims carried their Bibles and hymnals and, as they walked, they sang songs which were often picked up by first one group and then another. As they made their way onward to the Main Amana church where the *Werkzeug* and the elders waited, they were truly united in their shared reverence and their love of one another.

And then, publicly, the "confession" took place: an examination before the elders, whose own confessions had already been heard by the highest authority, the *Werkzeug*. "Soul, what is thy purpose?" each person was asked. "For what art thou longing and seeking? How and in what manner hast thou found the work of true inspiration? Unlock the door of your heart! Amend your time! Repent ere you present yourself at the table of the Lord!"

For days the soul searching continued, and Christian was frequently overcome by the Spirit to exhort and chasten those who had erred and bless those who had a right to blessings. Finally on the lovefeast day when all had been examined and the men had reverently washed the feet of the men and the women the feet of the women, Christian blessed them all and welcomed them in the name of the Lord to partake of the memorial of Christ's death. Christian stood as straight and tall as he could, his bearded face a study in hypnotic strength. Around him were gathered the Great Council of Thirteen chosen elders and the scribes who were ordered to record his words as they always did when he was beset by the Spirit.

As a song swept through the eager worshipers, the *Werkzeug* trembled under its magical power. His body shook. He closed his eyes. He walked as in a trance back and forth before the elders' bench which stood against the wall. At his first word, the music stopped. As he stood before the people like Moses upon Sinai and in a thundering voice once more reminded the inheritors of the valley that they should *Bleib treu*, stay true.

> "Thus saith the Lord!
> 'I have chosen you for a purpose,
> A light unto the world
> And an example for the people!' "

Yet even after he had become calm and come to himself, it seemed as though the light of God still enfolded him as he conducted the communion service. He blessed the bread which was passed by twenty elders among the communicants; he blessed the wine which was sipped from the spotless glass chalices, one glass to every twelve participants. The people sang, the spirit of the Lord moved through the congregation, and, to those who believed, there was no greater evidence of His presence anywhere on earth.

It was surrounded by great glory, this Amana of utopian days, but it lives on now only in the solemn rooms where modern Amana children occasionally stop in to hear quaint stories from a great-grandfather or a great-grandmother, and where visitors find their way only if they are interested in a bit of Americana that has passed. For when the *Werkzeug* died, the voice of God died with him. His grave, nestled among the humble graves of many Amana dead, says simply, *Christian Metz, 24, Juli, 1867.*

True, there was another *Werkzeug* who took his place, a gifted woman, Barbara Heinemann Landmann, upon whom a great deal of his authority and some of his power were bestowed. Hers is another story, the story of the afterglow of faith, through which she moved, and to which, as a valid prophetess, she added lustre for more than twenty years. But the questioning among the people had begun: Is collectivistic living superior to private enterprise? How much of our faith is just romanticizing and a sentimental adherence to the past? If God wants this form of community life perpetuated, why does He not raise up another prophet? Is a "grade school" education sufficient or has the time come when our youth must "go on to school?" What is a luxury and what is a necessity and what is a convenience? Can it be that we are merely a strange people who thought we were specially chosen?

When Barbara Landmann died in 1883, the last authoritative source for answers disappeared. True, there were still the Scriptures and the recorded sayings of the *Werkzeuge*, but they suddenly seemed more possessed of shadow than substance. Even though the messages of the *Werkzeuge* were still read at church-time, the church was changing. The only sure and acceptable answer seemed to be lurking in the world, the world which had come ever nearer through highway systems, through the trade in Amana products, through communication media, and the thousand and one innovations all the way from beauty aids to automobiles, to say nothing of the liberation and the intermingling of the sexes.

Then began the final dissecting, caused by criticism from within. Some now said that the Amana of old had always been a man's utopia where masculinity had the upper hand, where the women, oppressed, were palliated with little things like music boxes when they complained of boredom or a bright red scarf when the drabness of their attire got them down. The self-examination continued as some contended that there were drones in this utopia who lived off the labor of others; it was time, too, some declared, for all the people to take an interest in community affairs and politics and good government and that they should compete with the world rather than fear it.

And so it went. So went utopia. It went by way of adjustments to the Amana constitution, and votes on reorganization and legal counseling until, finally, in 1932, the inevitable *Übergang*—the changeover—manifested itself and utopia was absorbed by its arch enemy, the world. But it was a triumph for those who said they had a right to live their lives and share in all the greatness and glory and trial that is the privilege of every man. Big business came in, and with it a new kind of prosperity and a modern kind of happiness with all its problems and complexities until today the Amanas are seven Iowa villages, no better and no worse than communities of their size anywhere in the American Midwest.

But there are those few who still sit surrounded by the sentimental past, a past made more romantic and tinged with more perfection by the rush and madness of the present age. They are the utopianists who cannot rid their minds of the incessant warning that was drilled into them, *"Bleib treu—stay true."* Nor will their dream end when the last patriarch is discovered in his rocking chair, silent and still, rocking no more.

For the seed has been sown. There will always be someone who will walk where Christian Metz walked and someone who will always sing the song of the dreamer who said, "Come with me from Lebanon, my spouse, with me from Lebanon! Look from the top of Amana!"

17 § THE HUTTERITES

How much longer can the Hutterites hold out against the world? Why have they not been assimilated long ago? Here they are, the last of the utopian experimenters, priding themselves on the fact that they have not succumbed to their arch enemy, the *Weltgeist* (spirit of the world), confident that they will outlast it, and convinced that the Lord is on their side.

They came to the United States from the Russian Ukraine in 1874, a corporal's guard of some twenty families. They were not Russian, however, but Swiss-German, remnants of a people who had migrated for centuries through Switzerland, Moravia, Germany, seeking freedom to worship and to live their simple life. Now they had come to the promised land, America. Because land was easily acquired in South Dakota, they settled on a thousand stubborn acres along the muddy Missouri River in Bon Homme County.

Little attention was paid to them when they came. In those days rugged, bearded men were no oddity, even when they wore, as did these newcomers, black homespun suits, tieless shirts, hook-and-eye jackets and broad-brimmed "preachers' hats." The stolid and obedient women, attired in drab, long-skirted dresses, their ruddy faces framed by polka-dot head-scarves, represented typical Old Country peasants. They had children, of course, as did most immigrants. The boys were dressed like their fathers and the girls like their mothers, but there was nothing unusual about that.

The only extraordinary feature about these people was that they began to live communally. No one owned anything; every-one owned everything. This, apparently, was why they had come to America, to live an insular, isolated life, a highly moral, deeply religious life. The bearded pastor in the group was the authority and acted as spokesman for the little settlement. He made it clear there was to be no traffic with the *Weltgeist;* no compromise in principles; no aping of the world's people; and no participation in politics, social activities, or church programs in the nearby towns. They had their own way of worship. Every night and every Sunday morning, the solemn pastor preached his extempore sermons out-of-doors or in the tiny building that was used as a colony school.

Although the neighbors were too far away to hear the sermon itself, occasionally they could hear the mournful sound of chant-ing as it drifted over the land. It was *a capella* because these colonists abhorred the use of musical instruments of any kind; they sang in high-pitched, nasal tones, intoning a line at a time after the minister had recited it in a singsong fashion. These long, ponderous hymns, dolefully chanted in German, were recitations of suffering and death, of judgment and salvation, and of the sorrow and the crucifixion of Christ for sinful man. Most of all, however, they were admonitions for an everlasting viligance against the *Weltgeist* which lurked just outside the commune grounds, waiting to pounce upon God's people.

To the citizens in the nearby towns of Tabor and Scotland, South Dakota, and to the businessmen of Yankton, these ex-clusive religionists were a thrifty, hard-working, conservative lot, engaged in a farming cooperative. To all appearances they looked like members of one family; all inter-related and repre-sented by only three family names: Waldner, Hofer, and Wipf.

The fact that they did not send their children to school was understandable, for schools were few and far between and, as everyone realized, many religious groups had an aversion to secular education. After all, these new settlers were teaching their children in the German language, and there was no doubt that the training was strict and severe. It was logical that they should be shy about enrolling their children in English rural schools, for in the daily life of the commune they spoke a Tyrolean dialect and discouraged the use of English among the children.

But for these few noticeable characteristics, the Hutterian advent into America was unpretentious and hardly newsworthy. Many South Dakotans were not even aware that these immigrants had arrived, and most citizens of the Coyote State never even knew who or what they were. Some who did notice them called them either bearded Mennonites or Amish or likened them to the Pennsylvania Dutch; others pointed them out as Russian colonists or German homesteaders, or simply referred to them as "those people," leaving no doubt that they considered them obviously curious and strange.

From this unheralded and obscure beginning in Bon Homme County, the Hutterites have exploded into a web of communes which today includes twenty-nine in the United States and thirty in Canada, with a total membership of nearly 10,000 dedicated souls. Present legislation in South Dakota, reflecting an aroused citizenry, has restricted them from buying more land within a radius of 40 miles from an already established colony. Other states have begun eyeing them suspiciously, sociologists have taken an academic interest in them, psychiatrists are impressed by their lack of nervous disorders, birth control experts are shocked by the discovery that they are the most prolific people on earth, and a statistician has estimated that if their population increase keeps on at the present rate there will be 438,000,000 Hutterites in North America in another hundred years! These actions and reactions to their mode of life, however, seem to leave the Hutterites relatively unimpressed, for they have found a scriptural basis for everything they do:

"Be fruitful and multiply," justifies their large families. They have an average of eleven children per couple and their population doubles every nine years.

"The early Christians had all things in common," gives them the authority for their communal system. They control some 140,000 acres of land in the United States, all of it colony owned.

"Be ye in the world and not of it," is the Biblical text that takes care of all their so-called peculiarities.

How peculiar are they? Their criticis answer, "Annoyingly peculiar!" Citing the fact that the Bible also enjoins chastity self-control, moderation, they point out that the Hutterites have deliberately selected the "Be fruitful" text in order to make marriage an excuse for sex gratification. They contend that although the Hutterians preach against materialism, they are actually highly materialistic, drive a shrewd bargain, and are as commercially-minded as any money-motivated farmer anywhere. Certain law-makers believe that the Hutterian religion is merely a pretext and a facade, behind which a successfully functioning farming cooperative is seeking to evade taxes on the grounds that Hutterianism is a religion. Most of all, however, the case against the Hutterites claims that their communal system is a dictatorship within which a favored few enjoy liberties and freedom, while many of the colony members, especially the youth, are hopelessly enslaved.

Are these claims justified? You can discover the answer, or try to, for yourself, for the Hutterites are quite willing to have you investigate their utopian experiment anywhere and at any time. You will find them living together in communities called *Bruderhofs* (places of the brothers). Each such community or commune numbers about 120 members who seem to have changed very little in appearance, dress, or attitude since they first came to America. Each *Bruderhof*, located off the beaten path, consists of a cluster of nondescript homes, barns, and sheds. Although the barren, swept-up yards around the houses suggest that these farmers are in sombre need, such an impression is far from the truth. Hutterians, although owning nothing individually, are highly prosperous collectively.

Each settlement has in its barnyard inevitable flocks of thousands of chickens, geese, and ducks, and in its adjoining pastures herds of cattle and sheep. Each has its dairy herds, apiaries, turkey flocks, and plenty of hogs. Vineyards as well as orchards and gardens leave no doubt that Hutterianism is nearly one hundred percent self-sustaining.

If the men are working in the fields, you will find the *Bruderhof* apparently deserted when you drive into the dusty yard, for the Hutterian women are reticent with strangers. Gradually they will appear, however, as they emerge shyly from the community kitchen, the community laundry, or the commune homes. Soon you will be surrounded by a bit of the Old World: serene-faced women, wearing the traditional blue-and-white polka-dot headscarves; teen-age girls carrying tiny brothers and sisters, and toddling children, wistfully blinking up at you from behind the folds of the long, full skirts of their mothers.

Showing no envy for your late model car or your freedom to come and go, these plainly dressed retreatants from the world, who have no private possessions and who rarely leave the commune grounds, will impress you with their obvious peace of mind. The faces of the women, untouched by make-up, reflect an inner contentment and serenity. As they gaze at you with confidence and a sort of wonder, you sense that they almost pity you because you have, apparently, not found the Hutterian way of truth; you are still misguidedly seeking happiness in the sinful rush of the impersonal world.

These women seem to share the same belief as do the Hutterian men. You will find them self-assertive, dominant in their views on Hutterianism, and avowedly suspicious of all worldlings. All of these bearded men seem to be convinced that the world's people are tainted by the *Weltgeist* and are spiritually lost. They feel that this is borne out by the fact that there has never been a true convert to Hutterianism from the "outside."

Yet both Hutterian men and women, and especially the Hutterian children, have an insatiable curiosity about visitors, for to them all non-Hutterians are a strange and curious people. For example, it is strange to them that the world's citizens have such a horror of growing old, that they falsify their ages, and try to act younger than they are. In the *Bruderhof,* age is a mark of dignity and a token for respect. Hutterian children enjoy being with their elders because it is from them that they learn the old truths and new wisdom. And as for beauty aids and beauty treatments, these are a source for much fun-making among Hutterian people. "Whom are you trying to fool?" they laughingly demand when they see a "made-up female." The unadorned woman, they contend, is more attractive and certainly more pleasing in the sight of God than those who have fallen prey to the practice of the whores who, in Biblical times, were the only women who painted their faces as a mark of their trade.

The world's people are also strange and curious to the Hutterites because they seem to be unhappy in the midst of their vaunted luxuries, restless though they claim they are free, sick despite the fact they spend large sums of money and expend great effort trying to stay well, and rushed to death while boasting about their speed and time-saving gadgets.

They will tell you all this in English, which is replacing more and more the Tyrolean dialect in this utopian experiment. But you will be assured that even a change in language will never mean a change in their way of life.

Following such an analytical briefing, the Hutterian will invite you into his home to show you how utopians live. It is a small, compact, and certainly unpretentious home; there is no kitchen because everyone eats in a common refectory. There is no bathroom either because such a luxury would represent an initial victory for the intrusion of the spirit of the world. Electric lights are a necessary concession, but radios and TV sets are taboo, as are telephones with the exception of a single one in each colony, which is usually placed in the home of the colony boss.

The rooms are colorless and unimaginative, strictly utilitarian with highly varnished floors and sombre walls punctuated with uncurtained windows. For the most part, the furniture is colony-made and consists of practical pieces: sturdily built chairs, tables, and cupboards. A coal stove or an oil burner provides heat and because there is no running water in the house, a wash basin standing close by on an improvised stand provides the washing facilities. Hot water can be transported easily in the tea kettle which, in the winter, sings continually on top of the stove. Most of the colonies have deep wells for drinking water, while rain water for washing is stored in huge barrels outside each home.

Nearly every room in the Hutterian abode is a bedroom, with the floors varnished and polished to a shining finish. The beds are equipped with feather beds, a continuation of an early tradition, and somewhere in every girl's room is a wedding chest made by the colony carpenter. Every Hutterian girl upon reaching the age of fifteen receives as a gift from the commune one of these large, highly polished "cedar chests." In it she tenderly hoards small personal treasures bought with her dollar-a-month allowance or given to her as gifts: headscarves, pieces of yard goods, towels, and embroidered linens to be used when she is eventually married. On the wall above the chest or elsewhere in the house may sometimes be found a calendar or a religious motto such as "The Lord is the Head of this House," a rather recent concession to adornment in a utopia where pictures have been sternly *verboten* down through the years.

No people anywhere are more averse to being photographed than the Hutterites. Visitors may take pictures of the commune, the buildings, the cattle and the poultry, and, on occasion, may succeed in persuading a youngster to shyly pose, but the adult members will have none of it. To them, pictures are explicitly forbidden by Scripture on the basis of the Second Commandment, "Thou shalt not make unto thee any graven image."

Consequently, attendance at moving picture theatres is also forbidden, although educational films have on occasion been shown in the colonies, and it is said that townspeople have sometimes seen some of the Hutterian youth slip into a town movie. Such "escape" is difficult, however, for Hutterian life is strictly regulated and highly disciplined. The only mode of transportation from colony to town is the commune truck or station wagon. Private cars are, of course, unthinkable.

Since there are no stores within the commune, frequent trips to town must be made, and the truck man does the shopping for the community, usually taking a few passengers along if they have received permission from the proper authority. Then there are the inevitable trips to the town dentist or doctor, for the Hutterians have never permitted any of their youth to leave the colony for such professional training. Although some of the communes do have self-styled naturopaths and "bone setters," pursuing a talent with which they are natively endowed, education beyond the colony school is frowned upon.

"We know what has happened to other communal systems," Hutterians will tell you, "when the young people go to college. The world spoils them. Education spoils them. Better to look to God for wisdom, as the Bible says, than to look to men."

In the olden days nearly every woman was trained as a midwife. This is still true to a large extent, but doctors from "the world" are called in ever more frequently, and more and more Hutterian women now go to hospitals to have their babies. There is nothing wrong with that, Hutterian authorities affirm, unless it might get to be "too comfortable!"

In a utopia such as this, idealistically based upon absolute equality, it is difficult to pin down just who the authorities actually are. In the household the husband rules unchallenged because Ephesians 5:23 clearly states that "the husband is the head of the wife, even as Christ is the head of the church." The women apparently do not object. They have developed a seeming affection for discipline, knowing what every woman knows, that there are subtler methods to get their way than by the bombastic authority so typical of Hutterian men. They have also been taught that in the realm of the spirit they are co-equal with their husband and indispensable to the heavenly fellowship of which colony life is but a foretaste. Women are excluded from voting in the affairs of commune life, however, and, in conformity with Scripture, "remain silent in church."

The actual head of the commune is the pastor, a man chosen because of his wisdom, character, and ability to interpret the Word of Truth. He is not only the spiritual counselor but a link between the Hutterites of the past and the present. His sermons, based for the most part on the threat and challenge of the *Weltgeist*, are hand-written in personal notebooks which become the prized possession of the commune and which are frequently publicly read after the pastor's demise. The pastor and his wife are the only ones among the colony members who enjoy the privilege of being served their meals in the quiet of their home. But even the pastor does not travel to other colonies or embark on an infrequent trip without the permission of the elders. The pastor and the elders, varying in number, form the governing council, and it is they who regulate the affairs of colony life.

Every elder and almost every adult male is a "boss" over something. There is a farm boss, a cattle boss, a carpenter boss, a bee boss, and many more. Even the women are bosses and serve on a rotating system. There is a kitchen boss, a laundry boss, a goose boss, a duck boss, and one for almost every phase of domestic chores.

"We never have any labor and management problems here!" boast the Hutterians. "Why should we? We are all bosses!"

Bosses are selected because of their special interest and capabilities in their respective areas. The farm boss says, "Tomorrow I need ten extra men in the fields," and he gets them. The sheep boss declares, "It is shearing time and we must all work together in my department," and it is so ordained. The cattle boss makes it known that men are needed to ride herd, and it will somehow be arranged.

Though Hutterians have ample time for rest and conversation, the basis of their lives is the sacredness of work. The Hutterite believes that unless a man works he shall not eat. There are few if any drones in their utopian scheme, for the work of all shames the indolent into activity.

That a man must earn his daily bread by the sweat of his brow is impressed upon the youth at an early age. The firstborn son, who customarily takes his father's name, also follows in his father's occupational footsteps. Boys are apprenticed to jobs at fifteen, at about the time they are accepted into the commune. At this time, too, members make their profession of faith in Hutterian life and are said to do so at their own free will. Very few renounce the commune life, not more than five percent, and, while a few "run away," they invariably return after having tasted the world. They are readmitted to community status after they make a proper penance and, if so ordered, a public confession before the entire congregation. In true theocratic fashion, the Hutterian society insists it is first and foremost a religious order which, according to its constitution and the Word of God, holds "the key to loose and to bind even as Christ has commanded. It is authorized to exclude the vicious and to receive the contrite. One who submits himself to obedience to God and His Church must not be obstinate, but must permit himself to be guided and used according to his need."

There are two things, however, that the Hutterites do require as their price for utopia: freedom and the abandonment of privacy. But in return they are offered security and fellowship. This security is evidenced whenever a Hutterian walks the commune grounds; he strides boldly and with pride. His gait is free, his manner confident, and his voice authoritative. Everything is his, and what is his belongs to everyone. He discusses his personal problems and concerns openly and freely with his brethren. If he is "overtaken in a sin" he may, in extreme cases, be ordered to make a public confession. He is then forgiven, warned to mend his ways, and his transgressions are then forgotten. A Hutterite never carries a grudge, never considers himself an outcast, never feels inferior, frustrated, or emotionally disturbed. He is a cog in the spiritual and social mechanism of his group and this, perhaps, is one reason for his phenomenal predisposition to a well-adjusted and integrated life.

Here in this utopia everyone rises at an appointed hour. Here one eats at the ringing of the refectory bell and works as ordered and lives as told. There must be no feeling of wanting "my way," or of "doing things the way I want them done." Here custom is king and tradition is the pattern of the empire. Here the individ-- ual must be subordinated to the group or all is lost. He is unbothered by such common annoyances as personal finances, unsatisfied desires, competitive struggle, or family conflicts. There are no divorces among Hutterians, no crimes of passion, and few cases of drunkenness. No Hutterian has ever been on relief and never has a commune member been in jail excepting in times of war when he takes up unyielding stand in favor of pacifism. How can he take up arms in any cause when the Scripture clearly warns that, "He who lives by the sword must perish by the sword?"

When the inevitable question arises as to whether any man has the right to enjoy the liberty and the advantage of a country and not assist in its defense, it is stubbornly answered by the staunch Hutterite who declares that his way of life is a leaven in the midst of a military-minded world. On the other hand, however, he is quite ready to support agencies which deal with rehabilitation or the relief of suffering among those whom war has harmed. Non-resistance as a cardinal principle among Hutterians reaches back to the historic root of their faith. Jacob Hutter, from whom they take their name and who instituted this Christian communal movement in the Tyrol in the 16th century, was an Anabaptist. This parent group of such denominations as the Mennonites and the Amish emphasized baptism of adults as over against infant baptism, refused to take oaths, stood in opposition to worldliness, and had a long list of martyrs in the cause of non-militarism. Jacob Hutter (a maker of hats) added to these principles the practice of a community of goods. He taught that individuals should surrender themselves and all they possess to a fellowship set apart and dedicated to seeking first the kingdom of God. Hutterites insist it is the only way to live; it is an adventure in utopia, carrying with it the guarantee of salvation.

You sense that this conviction stands like a wall against any allurement from outside the colony or any possible questioning from within. You feel it in every aspect of commune life. As you visit with the members you are aware of the close family ties. Parents seem to love all commune children as much as they do their own. Each event—a birth, a death, an accident, excessive rain, excessive drouth, sunshine and shadow are collectively shared. Wise sayings, a new interpretation of Scripture, an innovation in some type of work are cherished ideas which provide unusual diversion and an almost recreational thrill in a community where play and games are practically unknown. There is no encouragement in the fields of art or in educational advance. The goal of each one strives to become a better Hutterite, in faith, in fortune, and in family life.

Romance goes on in the communes under the ever watchful eyes of the elders, and marriage for a young man of twenty or twenty-one with a girl of eighteen or nineteen is a foregone conclusion. In all of the colonies there are not more than a dozen unmarried Hutterites. Because family names are few, not more than twenty in all the colonies combined, a genealogical chart called a *Stammbaum* (family tree) is kept by each pastor. This is consulted to guard against consanguineous marriages.

Marriages are always intra-communal and these relationships are jealously guarded from any "worldly contamination." This is why critics call the Hutterian utopia a "nepotic corporation," pointing out that because the Hutterians are not at all interested in gaining converts for their cause, they never send out missionaries into the world.

The Hutterites contend that one must grow up within the commune in order to fully understand and embrace their way of life. Why should they send out missionaries? "If anyone wants to join us," says an elder, "let him come. We are not hard to find." The Hutterian contention has always been that where men have thrived on freedom, as have the world's people, communism, even the Christian communistic system of the Hutterians, is bound to have a bitter taste for the uninitiated.

Change is the *Weltgeist*, and to keep the *Weltgeist* from threatening the communal life, any change is repulsed wherever possible. A man lets his beard grow as soon as he gets married because that is how the fathers ordained it, and there is also a Biblical injunction advising against touching a razor to the "corners of the face." Here hook-and-eyes are used instead of buttons on the men's jackets because long ago, during the Thirty Years' War, buttons reminded the fathers of the German militarists. Here a man does not smoke nor does he dress for vanity, nor shall he look upon a woman with lust. Here secular books and magazines are considered silly, comic strips are called stupid, and games and sports are regarded as a waste of time. Here in utopia, Hutterites will tell you that everything men work for in the world is willingly abrogated: personal success, freedom, comfort, luxuries, travel, amusement, personal possessions, privacy, and all the other "phantoms" of the *Weltgeist's* realm.

But as you walk the commune grounds you cannot help but wonder whether these claims are really true. Are the Hutterites really as dedicated to their quest for utopia as they claim? In sharp contrast with the historical past, many changes have crept across the closely-guarded commune "walls." You catch the children listening avidly to the visitor's car radio. You see a girl furtively primping before a mirror, changing her braided hair-do just to see how she would look if she were a "woman of the world." A close observer can see that the hooks-and-eyes on the men's jackets are giving way to zippers. There is more and more emphasis on "staying young." Even the beards are being trimmed ever shorter as the years go by. Secular books, romantic magazines, and comic books are eagerly accepted from visitors by the Hutterian teen-agers and adults alike. A "little wine for the stomach's sake" is permitted more and more, and it need not especially be colony wine. New farm machinery, new and better colony trucks, kitchen conveniences and gadgets, little luxuries are stealing in. And when travel is mentioned or the wonders of the world are cited, a wanderlust creeps into the eyes of Hutterian men and women alike. You have reason to wonder just how tightly the commune gates are locked against the encroaching world.

There is something else. In olden times, no Hutterite would ever have closed his day without attending evensong, but today the custom has relaxed. There is too much to do, they explain. The thousands of commune acres are too demanding, the pinch of competition with world cattle and grain markets is being felt, and it is sincerely trusted that the good Lord will understand.

The old pastors are passing and the newly appointed ones are well aware that the gap between Hutterian religion and Hutterian life is widening. Nor can they fully analyze the reason. There is something "in the air," the scent of secularism drifting in from the materialistic world. Each generation must be reindoctrinated with the ancient traditions, but with each generation that indoctrination grows more difficult. The new and conscientious pastors will tell you that though the Hutterites are growing and though they could conceivably number 438,000,-000 million (!) in another hundred years, the colonies are having no easy time of it. The pleasures of the outside world, the American way of life, and the call of freedom have crept into previously unassailable minds and it may be that the end of this utopia is near.

But occasionally at eveningtime, when the commune chores have been finished, and as the deepening shadows enfold the closely huddled homes, the bearded pastor makes his solitary way to the small school building. Two books, the German Bible and the Hutterian hymnal, are clasped affectionately under his arm. The sturdy, bearded men brush the dust from their drab garbs, the women adjust their polka-dot headscarves, and the children come running from their improvised play. Together they make their way to the schoolhouse. It is church time.

The pastor is seated up front behind the desk with the elders flanking him at left and right. At his right, facing him, sit the

men of the community, at his left the women. Children are
seated in the front benches. The curtainless windows, the barren walls, the black hats hanging on the wall pegs once more
affirm the Hutterian objection to whatever would tempt the
mind away from the simple, sheltered life. Now the pastor rises,
opens the hymnal and intones the first line of an age-old hymn,

"All the world is full of sorrow. . . ."

At his last word, the responding worshipers chant the line in
voices that are in reality the battle cries of conquest against the
Weltgeist,

"All the world is full of sorrow. . . ."

Shrill soprano tones mingle with the harsh and guttural voices
of the men. The wailing strains overpower the room. The
women's voices become more piercing; the men's weave their
doleful spell. Overlapping the final syllables, the pastor chants
another line,

"All the world is fear and fright. . . ."

Again comes the strident antiphon,

"All the world is fear and fright. . . ."

The pastor:

"Only God can bring contentment. . . ."

The people:

"Only God can bring contentment."

The pastor:

"Only God can give men light. . . ."

The people:

"Only God can give men light!"

One verse, five, ten; the entrancing pattern forces attention on the Hutterian defiance of change—there is a kind of fighting against the world in every line. Voices trample the night with their impassioned tones as the stolid figures, generating this inward intensity, fix their eyes on the slightly swaying figure of their leader.

The hymns, projected out across the commune grounds, out into the world which continues on in its relentless, steady way, are an assertion that of all utopian attempts in America only the Hutterites remain. But how much longer can they hold against the insidious forces of the *Weltgeist?* Or have they already been conquered by the enemy they had hoped to suppress? A little more time will tell.

18 § THE MORMONS

Mormonism has outlived its persecutors and out-lasted most of its critics. And with good reason. It is the most truly American of all America's religions. Its founders, its miracles, its holy books, its prophets, its martyrs, and its spirit grew out of American soil. Across America from coast to coast are the credentials of its faith, and it is in America that it has built its holy city and its sacred state. Its only loss amidst its many triumphs is utopia.

Some say it never really had utopia in mind, insisting it merely wanted the right to worship freely, but that is only because they do not know the story.

The Mormon utopia was a dream born in the heart of a farm boy in upstate New York one mid-summer's afternoon. He was an ordinary boy of his time, the early 19th century, given to work and play and having a yen for roaming through the woods and hills like any other lad of fourteen. He had a most ordinary name: Joseph Smith.

He had come with his parents from Sharon, Vermont, where he was born two days before Christmas in 1805, to a farm near

Palmyra. A grove not far from the modest farmhouse intrigued young Joseph and he often wandered there and knelt to pray. He was given to much praying and questioning about religion as were many sensitive youths and even more seemingly insensitive adults, for these were the days of the Great Revival which had swept full force into New England from the Cumberland country in Kentucky and Tennessee.

The camp meetings and evangelistic extravaganzas held in open fields often became orgies of emotion accompanied by strange "bodily exercises." Caught in the whirr of the irresistible seduction of songs and sermons, worshipers leaped and danced, babbled in unknown tongues, and often fell unconscious to the ground. Ministers debated about the rightness of these goings-on. Some insisted that inasmuch as people were "changed" and "converted" and "reborn" by these manifestations, it must be the work of the Lord. Others maintained that since the emotionalism often led to sexual infamy and unreasoning conduct fully as wild as that induced by drink, it was obviously the work of the devil.

Meantime there was a great deal of vying among denominations for members, competition among revivalists for prestige, and bitter feuds between theologians. Old denominations were splitting up because of the Great Revival and new faiths were rising, sparked by a high-powered gospel hymn or a sudden, catchy gospel phrase. It was time for some earnest soul-searching about sectarianism. It was time for prayer.

One afternoon as young Joseph knelt in the grove, his mind was filled with great confusion about churches and God. If religion was as important as people said it was, if it meant life or death, heaven or hell, then it was certainly necessary to know which denomination was right and which was wrong. And while everyone was glibly talking about God, no one seemed to know just who or what God really was.

The soft glow of late afternoon filtered through the grove and wove its magic patterns on the grass-covered ground. Above him the transparent clouds lined with the mystic blue of the sky might have been spirit forms brushing the topmost branches of the trees. Joseph prayed aloud, a boy's prayer, trying to break through a man's world into God's world. He prayed for what the wisest of seekers have always prayed: wisdom. He asked for wisdom not to do what was right, but to learn what was right to do. What he wanted to know was how to determine which denomination was true and which was false. What he longed to learn was which voice among the revivalistic babel of his time he should follow.

Suddenly a shaft of light flared through an opening in the grove. It was like a marble pillar, glistening white, blindingly bright, and in it appeared two glorious personages, heavenly beings with outstretched hands, looking down at him. Dazed and overcome with wonder, he heard a voice, "This is my beloved Son. Hear Him!"

The heavenly words continued, "They draw near to me with their lips, but their hearts are far from me. They teach false doctrines and the commandments of men. They have a form of godliness but deny the power thereof. Join none of them. Soon the fullness of the gospel will be revealed to you."

There are several versions as to what happened following this modern miracle. Some say that Joseph "kept all these things in his heart." Others contend that his countenance was changed, that his father and mother were soon advised of his experiences, and that friends began to realize that a chosen instrument of the Lord had been discovered in their midst. Skeptics said that during the days of the Great Revival "everybody was having visions," and Joseph's report was discounted as the hallucinations of an impressionable fourteen-year-old lad, or as the vivid fabrication of a highly imaginative mind. Several erudite critics explained that some boys see dragons or fiery serpents or ghosts, but that Joseph happened to see angels.

The truth is, he did. And whether the experience was, as some insist, neurological or "divine," the Palmyra lad continued entertaining these etheric visitors. One particular angel who, he claimed, came often to his room, was called Moroni. This celestial personage revealed to Joseph that he (Moroni) had once been an earthly prophet and historian for a people called the Nephites who, about 600 B.C., had migrated from Jerusalem to the American continent.

The history of this migration, Moroni advised, had been carefully recorded on plates of gold which were now hidden at a place he promised to reveal. And reveal it he did. He led Joseph to the Hill Cumorah, some eight miles south of Palmyra, and showed him the spot where the plates were concealed, instructing him not to unearth this great archeological treasure for three years at which time Joseph would have passed his twenty-first birthday. Moroni also informed him that the world was living in the "latter days," that Christ would soon return to establish His kingdom, and that Joseph was to play a significant part in these portentious events. Thus, while the old religions continued to preach their impassioned gospel and sought to build their denominational walls ever higher and more secure, a farm boy was being groomed for a prophetic role in American religious history.

Shortly before his twenty-first birthday Joseph married Emma Hale of Harmony, Pennsylvania. He shared the secret of Moroni's messages with her, but he went alone on that eventful morning, September 22, 1827, when he climbed the Hill Cumorah for the "great excavation." Kneeling for a moment in prayer on the sacred spot, he dug away the earth from the surface of a rock. Then he fixed a lever under the rock and pried it up. Before him in a stone repository lay the religious quarry: plates of gold about seven inches wide and eight inches long, paper-thin and fastened together by three rings near the edge. In thickness the book measured about six inches. Part of it was sealed, which meant that it contained a prophecy for a still later revelation. Near the book of gold lay a breastplate, together with two crystal stones in the form of spectacles, called the Urim and Thummim and resembling the phylacteries of ancient priests.

Endowed with superhuman strength to carry these precious apports and hiding them beneath his coat, Joseph hurried to the base of the hill where his wife was waiting. Excitedly, he concealed the treasure in the wagon, showing it to no one, not even to his wife, in keeping with the angel's instruction. Upon reaching home, he related the story to his father and mother, then to his two brothers and his sister. Carefully he concealed the plates, announcing that soon the work of translation would begin. "Truly," said the father, "this thing is of the Lord."

Today the imposing statue of Moroni, with right hand upraised and left hand covering a book of gold, stands high and proud on the Hill Cumorah. And in Fayette, New York, there is a shrine, a log cabin on an isolated farm, where the Mormon Church was founded on April 6, 1830, in circumstances as sensational as the discovery of Moroni's book. Here in the Whitmer cabin the plates were translated by Joseph Smith as he sat behind a curtain wearing the breastplate and peering through the crystal spectacles which magically interpreted for him the hieroglyphics—"reformed Egyptian characters"—etched upon the plates of gold.

Outside the curtain sat a rural schoolmaster, Oliver Cowdery, obediently writing down the rapidly translated words. With him were two farmers, Martin Harris and David Whitmer. When the book was published in 1830, the names of these three witnesses attested to its authenticity. Together, with eight other men respected in their communities, they went on record to say that they had been permitted to see and handle the plates and that, after the work of translation was completed, they beheld the plates, the breastplate, and the Urim and Thummim given back to the angel Moroni. The names of these witnesses have appeared in the published book through more than a hundred editions, and the controversy over the book's origin has continued for over a hundred years.

"Where did it come from, if not from God?" was the inevitable question. For here was a religious tome dealing with historical data that went back to 2200 B.C., tracing in Biblical language highly involved events, offering wisdom and knowledge, and making the profound claim that Christ after His resurrection visited America! It propounded the theory that the people called Nephites and Lamanites not only lived on this continent, but that the Lamanites were the ancestors of the American Indians. This book, called The Book of Mormon, in honor of the father of Moroni, was announced by Joseph Smith to be an auxiliary scripture to the Bible, and it became the cornerstone for a religious movement which was to be remembered long after the evangelists of the Great Revival were laid to rest in half-forgotten graves.

"Plagiarism!" was the cry which opponents and theologians leveled against The Book of Mormon. They said it contained material stolen from a manuscript written by a Presbyterian minister, Solomon Spaulding. The clergyman had written a historic novel, mostly fiction, which he had intended to title, "The Manuscript Found in the Wilds of Mormon." He gave the manuscript to a printer in Pittsburg and there, it is said, it was stolen by a young employee, Sidney Rigdon, who, in turn, worked out a hoax with Joseph Smith. The accusation was conclusively refuted by the Mormon Church and was also defeated by the very weight of testimony in the book itself, for no one man or group of men could have devised such an auxiliary scripture in their lifetime. As for the suggestion that the farm youth might have written the book himself, as some prejudiced critics have proposed, it had to be remembered that Joseph could barely read and write, and that his knowledge of history, Biblical or otherwise, was negligible.

So the Mormon Church began. It began with a farm boy, an angel, and a book of gold. The founders called it The Church of Jesus Christ of Latter Day Saints. They meant that the imminent second coming of the Lord was now setting the stage for a vast spiritual ingathering. The six charter members, including Joseph, who organized this church in the Whitmer cabin, grew to six hundred within a matter of months. Converts carried the gospel of the "latter days" and the story of modern miracles through New England and Pennsylvania. In Kirtland, Ohio, they built their first temple. To those who called this strange and curious sect heretical, Joseph replied that that was what the world called Christianity when it began. When they labeled him, "Fraud, Fake, and Anti-Christ!" he replied that he was quite prepared to be persecuted for righteousness sake. When he was told that all of Christendom was opposing him, his answer was, "We will build more temples." They organized against him and he said, "We will build a perfect city for the Lord!"

Utopia was in his heart. He foresaw a city four-square on earth as, he was sure, one existed in heaven. He had a vision of a city of God where men would live together, equal in opportunity, Christian in conduct, and God-like in jurisdiction; a city where there would be neither need nor waste, and where Christ would reign supreme—the kind of city desired by many hearts, ready for Jesus when He returned to earth.

In search of this utopia, a trek was started westward, Joseph claiming it had been revealed to him that the Promised Land lay somewhere in the heart of the nation. The call went out for men and women of vision, those who were weary of the way of the world, who looked for the millennium, who wanted to live religion and not merely talk about it. A modern prophet was talking about a modern Zion.

The converts grew to a thousand, two thousand, three thousand. They came from eastern states, from Canada, and from Great Britain where volunteer missionaries had zealously carried the story and the promises of The Book of Mormon. New members were also proselytized from midwestern farms and villages where revival fires were still smouldering. They were summond from the churches themselves and the gospel spread with the speed of scandal all the way to the Missouri River. Mormon camps grew into towns; Mormon songs were being sung; Mormom words of wisdom were being quoted.

The Prophet Joseph, as he was affectionately called by those who felt the power of his faith, was at this time a tall, broad-shouldered pioneer. Men said that his clear blue eyes still saw visions and that he continually communed with God. He was a modern Moses, a Joshua whose rallying cry ran through the divided Christian sects: "We go to build a city for our Lord!"

As his influence swept across the frontiers and outran the gospel of the circuit riders, his enemies also increased. Often, when people followed him, they left their farms and families and surrendered all their worldly goods to help his cause. Homes were divided. Villages were thrown into confusion. The temper of life was disrupted. It was a revivial of work and purpose, a series of camp meetings without the hollow cries of "Halleluiah" and the parroting of "Praise the Lord!" There was no rolling in the dust, no altar call, no fanatical exhibitionism, no talk of hell and lakes of fire; there was one indomitable cause: utopia, the city of God.

The "Saints" admitted they were a peculiar people, and they made a clear-cut distinction between themselves and the Gentiles, as they called the non-Mormons. Their challenge was "If a man is a Mormon, let him live the Mormon life." And what was that? Something strange and revolutionary, involving a commitment designed to capture the total life of man, dictating what he should believe and not believe, what he should eat and not eat, drink and not drink, what his personal habits should be, what he should tithe (one-tenth of his income), how he should care and provide for his fellowman, and what he should expect in this world and in the world to come. It was the gospel of restoration. It was Mormonism, a nickname that had come to stay.

In July, 1831, the Prophet Joseph designated Independence, Missouri, as the holy city and center of the faith. There is still today a small group of Mormons, some 500, who call themselves The Church of Christ (Temple Lot), who insist that it is here in Independence that the headquarters must one day be. It is here that Jesus will come because Joseph so ordained. A much larger and more important group, The Reorganized Church of Jesus Christ, numbering more than 150,000 also have their headquarters in Independence, and all Mormons have an affection for the historic Mormon aspect of the city, as well as for other Missouri towns named in remembrance of the Mormon pilgrimage: Smithville, Paradise, Far West, Bethany, Mt. Moriah.

But they never built utopia in Independence. In fact, the Saints were driven out of Missouri almost as soon as they came marching in. In the mid-1830's their homes were burned and their properties destroyed by non-Mormons of many religious persuasions. They accused Joseph's people of heresies, of putting the law of the Prophet above the law of the land, of superstition and sorcery, of living an almost communal life. Many non-Mormons held slaves; the Mormons did not, claiming that slavery was forbidden by the Prophet and The Book. Many "Gentiles" feared that their children would be "corrupted" by Joseph's people, feared their farms and businesses would be usurped, feared that their churches and their Masonic orders would be despoiled, accused the Mormons of stealing Masonic secrets, of building a hierarchy, and of defrauding the public out of money and land. Fanatical antagonists contended there would be no peace until the Saints were exterminated.

This was the beginning of bloodshed in the Mormon story. One of the first martyrs was a Mormon boy of nine, Sardius Smith. He was shot in the face as he gripped the muzzle of a "Gentile's" gun while his mother pleaded that his life be spared. With the cry, "Kill the young wolves and there will be no old ones," the assassin pulled the trigger. Sardius fell dead and his mother's clothing was splashed with blood.

At gunpoint the Mormons were forced out of the counties they had peacefully invaded. They fought back, but the Missourians retaliated by seizing Joseph and his brother Hyrum and locking them in a dungeon in the jail at Liberty in Clay County. Out of the whirlwind of hate came the clamor that they be put to death. Out of a hasty militia court-martial came the penalty: execution by hanging. But in his dungeon cell the Mormon Prophet said, "It will not come to pass. You cannot take my life until my ministry is fulfilled. That is not yet. But it is the will of God that I should not live to see my fortieth year." He was now thirty-two.

While hostile crowds kept their impatient vigil outside the Liberty jail, word spread that Mormon forces under a powerfully built follower of the Prophet, a man named Brigham Young, were being mobilized to rescue their leader. The Missouri militia had been alerted. Days passed. It was claimed that the executioner had refused to put a good man, the Prophet, to death. Some said that the judge, in the role of a modern Pilate, had repented of the sentence he had passed. Rumor had it that the Prophet's escape was being planned by a citizen's group in the town of Liberty itself.

Weeks went by. Then, when time had momentarily quieted the affair, the report of an escape from jail sent the enemies of Mormonism back to their guns. There was talk of a miracle. The Saints told it with rejoicing, comparing it to the release of the Apostle Peter from his cell at Philippi. Free under circumstances that no one seemed able to explain, Joseph and Hyrum returned to the Mormon camps strung out along the west bank of the Mississippi in southern Iowa and on the eastern shores in Illinois. Brigham Young went forth to meet the Prophet. Humbly and in willing submission, he gave the leadership back to Joseph Smith. Had he wished, he could have said, "Here are those whom thou hast entrusted to me. Not one has been lost."

Persecution had only increased the ranks of the Saints and strengthened their faith. Ten thousand ragged but dauntless heirs of the new Israel waited their Prohpet's word. They gave him a title, "Seer and Revelator." He led them to a marshy, abandoned village on the Illinois side of the Mississippi where six river shacks stood among the brushwood and muddy flats. The land was cheap. The houses were deserted. Here the Prophet climbed to the hard crust of a grassy knoll in the midst of a stagnant swamp and proclaimed to his people, "It is the will of God that we build our city here."

He spoke and a village began to rise out of Mormon resourcefulness and Mormon zeal. Once the place had been called Venus, then Commerce, but when the first impressive red-brick Mormon home was dedicated on June 11, 1839, Joseph declared, "It is the will of God that we name our city Nauvoo, that is, the Beautiful."

Never in the history of America was a city built by more consecrated hands. Never was a greater city built in less time. As home after home arose and as the magnificent temple grew stone by stone, the people, singing at their work, bound together by the Prophet's words, declared that surely here in this place the builder and maker was God.

Hancock County, where Nauvoo the Beautiful took form, became the center of interest in Illinois and a token of Zion in many parts of the world. Canadian, English, and European converts came to stay. Americans who cast their lot with the Saints felt that this would be a modern Jerusalem where miracles were bound to happen and where a returning Christ was pledged to come.

Frequently in early evening, when the sound of work was stilled and it was time for worship, and when the Prophet walked to the knoll where first he had stood, utopia never seemed more real. Linking together the well-built, red brick, New England type homes in a pattern that extended from the mighty Mississippi to distant rolling hills were tree-lined roads and flowered lanes. The swamp had been transformed into a fertile valley with gardens, grain fields, and meadows with dairy herds. Over it all stood the temple, inspiring in its stateliness and symmetry, built of hand-hewn limestone blocks and rising to a height of sixty feet. Thirty polished pilasters gave it the appearance of ancient greatness and its dome, gold-leafed, two hundred feet in height, made it look like a cathedral unsurpassed in the American midwest. Built at a cost of a million dollars, it was Joseph's answer to those who said the Mormons had not come to stay. It was surrounded by a garden, as was nearly every home. The Prophet's home, where he lived with his devoted Emma and their two sons, stood on the bank of the river not far from the dock where paddle-wheelers came almost daily with families for Zion.

In 1843, Nauvoo, with its more than 20,000 Saints, was the largest city in Illinois, larger than Chicago. It had its municipal university, its music hall, its thriving business district. It had its own militia and its own courts; it maintained an unusually high moral code and permitted freedom of worship for any creed or sect. It had no rich and no poor. Every true Saint was a tither. Every man had a job. Every day and every night was another dawning for the possible second coming of the Lord.

It was utopia.

But it was short-lived. From 1839 to 1844, a brief, elusive, almost fictionary five years cover its golden era. In 1844, Joseph was thirty-nine. He had prophesied he would not live to see his fortieth year. At the height of his career—he was even planning to run for president of the United States—the twin enemies of utopia, dissension from within and opposition from without, conspired to bring the experiment to a tragic end.

The Prophet's program had become too aggressive. His position as president of the church and the appointment of Hyrum, his brother, as patriarch were factors in the inner uprising. Though the Nauvoo charter provided freedom of religion, Joseph, his opponents claimed, was insisting on a union of "church and state." Within Nauvoo, an "enemy faction" began publishing what the Mormon leaders labeled as "libelous statements," and the militia was ordered to destroy the presses. This done, rioting broke out which assured Mormon antagonists outside Nauvoo that the Saints were vulnerable.

The world around Nauvoo had, from the start, looked upon Mormonism as a subversive and exclusive movement. It was ready to believe any scandalous story that filtered out of the city foursquare. It accused Joseph's people of amassing great fortunes and usurping political power. Furthermore, the strange and curious claims of "Israel restored" emanating out of Nauvoo and the shocking reports of clandestine temple services from which non-Mormons were barred had built up the case against the hated Smithites. Then there were the extravagant doctrinal claims, including such "superstitions" as baptism for the dead, the progressiveness of God, and the concept of a priesthood said to have been given Joseph in a vision.

This ecclestiastical structure, which had started long ago, was now openly ridiculed by Mormon enemies. Joseph Smith and Oliver Cowdery had stated that an angel, John the Baptist, had conferred upon them the "Priesthood of Aaron" and had instructed them to baptize each other by immersion. Later on, they declared, three other heavenly visitants, Peter, James, and John conferred on them the Melchizedek Priesthood and the Keys of the Apostleship. The Melchizedek or higher priesthood, so-called after Melchizedek, the King of Salem, held the power of the presidency and the right of authority over all the offices of the church. Its officers were designated as apostles, patriarchs, high priests, seventies, elders, and bishops. The Aaronic or lesser priesthood held authority in the temporal affairs of the church, and its officers were priests, teachers, and deacons.

But neither this web of organization nor a direct revelation from God through His holy angels was to save utopia. As the riots swept the City Beautiful, the city council of Nauvoo was ordered to appear in Carthage for a hearing. They refused to go, and Joseph, instead, invited the governor of Illinois to come to Nauvoo and arbitrate, assuring him that he would abide by the governor's decision. Instead, Governor Ford ordered Joseph and Hyrum to appear in Carthage, assuring them safe conduct along the way and during their stay.

The Prophet and his brother, together with two Nauvoo officials, John Taylor and Willard Richards, complied with the governor's order. The first night they stayed at a hotel. The second night, for safety's sake, they were lodged in the Carthage jail and the governor posted a guard. Whether it was a guard or a gang will never be known, but on that night, the evening of June 27, 1844, the guards were joined by a mob of anti-Mormons. Some had painted their faces to conceal their identity. All carried guns. They shot away the lock where the Prophet and his men were hopelessly entrapped and broke into the cell.

Some Mormons say a Calvary was made of Carthage jail that night, an American Golgotha where a true prophet was mercilessly slain. They have the word of John Taylor and Willard Richards, who escaped, that Hyrum was murdered in the cell and that the Prophet, wounded and bleeding, jumped through a window and died in the yard below, his last words being, "O Lord, my God!" There was a "centurion," too, they say, among the executioners on this bloody night. He was one of the mob, and threw away his empty gun with the cry, "We have killed a man of God!" There was also a "Peter" on hand that night, an old man, a Mormon, who had followed the Prophet from Nauvoo, followed him from afar and who, when word of the murder spread, cried out, "He told us clearly, 'I'm going like a lamb to the slaughter. I shall die innocent and it shall be said of me that I was murdered in cold blood!'" And there was a "Joseph of Arimathea," a farmer named Ebenezer Rand. He laid the bodies of Joseph and Hyrum gently into his ox cart, covered them with blankets, and took them to Nauvoo.

The Prophet was dead, and Nauvoo died with him. And utopia died.

There is another story, the story of a trek westward across the plains and mountains and into a desert under the leadership of the strong man, Brigham Young. He had no angel guides. He heard no heavenly voices and gave no scriptures to the world, but he carried in his heart the Prophet's dream. There is a story of a valiant people, quite unmatched in the history of American religion, of the winter flight from Nauvoo, of persecution and suffering, of hand carts and death; the chronicle of a courageous people who had a strange and curious feeling that only their undying faith could ever validate their Prophet's claims. They proved their loyalty to him through the posthumous scandal of polygamy, through revelations challenged in the courts and sensationalized in the press; they remained dedicated to him despite the infamy heaped on them by the churches and the world. They heard Brigham Young say, "This is the place!" as he drove a stake into the arid space beside a great salt lake, and, weary and homeless, they began building a city once more, 1400 miles from where the ravaged and dismantled temple of Nauvoo once had stood.

They built a city with a zeal that Joseph would have admired and of a kind that Jesus would, no doubt, have willingly approved. They built many cities with a vision uncommon among the builders of their day and with a passion that again aroused the envy of countless people of the world. They built a state, an empire, and, most of all, they built individual lives consecrated to a deeply personalized God. They built so stubbornly in faith that for nearly a hundred years it was impossible for any "Gentile" religions to gain more than a token following in the Mormon cities of Utah. Only now are any such conquests being made.

They have outlived their persecutors and outlasted most of their critics. Even their enemies now ascribe to the 1,000,000 present-day Saints an exceptionally high morality, a practical social consciousness, and a church program which puts religion at the very center of the personal life. Mormonism's missionaries are among the best trained and most consecrated of any creed or sect; its affection for its traditions is boundless, and its magnificent temples now form a chain of faith around the world. Its only loss among its many triumphs is utopia.

CONCLUSION

FAITH

IS A

FEELING

§ *FAITH IS A FEELING*

BY MARCHING in the cavalcade of faiths during the past two decades, I found my earlier impressions graphically confirmed: to the devout worshiper there is nothing strange or curious about his belief or practices; there are few heretics among those we often call heretical.

I learned something else, not about others, but about myself. I learned that there were many times when I felt that I could have become an equally ardent follower of the religions I was seeking to interpret and explore.

Gandhi once said he could identify himself with everyone that lives. When his critics remarked that this showed a monstrous inconsistency on his part, he replied that if a man reaches the heart of his own religion, he has reached the heart of others, too. Faith, he declared, is a kind of sixth sense which works beyond the purview of what we might call reason.

That is how it seemed to me as I walked the parquetry of religions on and off the beaten path. Rarely did I see anyone spiritually engaged in a devotional rite or ritual whose place I could not, under the same circumstances, have conscientiously as-

269

sumed. And this, to cite an extreme case, included the Penitentes as well as the equally extreme Voodooists. My sympathy and attraction for these people were often colored, I admit, by both their history and the fact that their religion placed demands upon them which went far beyond the easy disciplines to which I complacently conformed.

I often reflected on how painlessly my Protestant heritage was imparted to me. It was like slipping into my father's coat. I had accepted my religious moorings uncritically and apathetically, and what a startling contrast I now saw between my denomination and these groups which suffered ridicule and persecution in order to sustain their faith!

When I considered Voodoo, by way of example, and recalled how it was introduced into the Caribbean isle, the point became clear. I had been taught that my forebears had been free to come to America in their quest for God. The Voodooist, however, was brought, as we have seen, in chains as a chattel to be sold. I was in the tradition of a people whose first act was one of prayer and whose first service was one of thanksgiving. The black man from Dahomey was considered incapable of praying and his gods, he was told, were figments of his distorted mind. But even at that, the Voodooist and I had two things in common: the belief that religion, whatever else it might be, is a force that keeps our spirits free, and that God, who ever and whatever He is, will never leave us comfortless for long. Whether I was stirred by a solemn chant and a candle's light, and he by a jungle fire and a haunted drum, our quest was remarkably alike.

So was the quest of others within other groups. And even other contemporary "investigators" of religions have hinted that they, too, have felt the impulses and responses which I experienced. They would not, however, admit this publicly for the simple reason that it is considered highly unpopular to be all things to all men, or to try to comprehend the many faiths as actually being one.

Not that I wish to be an apologist for the "strange and curious" groups, but someone should explain how prone we are to pinpoint something in the historical genesis of a religious movement, as we have done with polygamy in Mormonism, or celibacy among the Shakers, or commercialism in Psychiana, and how we exaggerate and distort these views until we have robbed a group of its spiritual contribution to our life and time.

But they cannot actually be robbed just because they do not conform to our prescribed pattern. Nor will they be robbed. The wise old lawgiver, Gamaliel, assured us of this long ago when, referring to a so-called pernicious cult that was rising in his day, he said, "If this counsel or this work be of men it will come to nought. But if it be of God, you cannot overthrow it."

Incidentally, his reference was to a rapidly growing sect which had some amazingly strange and curious practices. They had all things in common, they were known for their meekness no less than for their dogged resistance to the world, they "turned the other cheek," they "walked the second mile," they believed in miracles and psychical demonstrations, and they followed a Man who, they insisted, had been crucified, dead, and buried, who had risen again on the third day, and who had ascended into heaven promising He would return again in the same manner in which he had departed.

Obviously, there were those who wanted these heretics destroyed, but Gamaliel advised differently. He knew that time would prove what his contemporaries could not even partially foresee. He also seemed to know that man is religious by nature, and that the sense of some unfinished business in every life can be fulfilled only by a Godward climb, even though some follow one guide, and others another.

That is how it seems to me. Since every religion is built upon this quest, each has discovered something, each has contributed something, and each has fulfilled something in man's urge to worship, no matter how strange and curious that worship may seem to you—or to me.

INDEX